loughton Mifflin Company

ne Beacon Street, Boston, Massachusetts 02108
17) 725-5000 Cable HOUGHTON

Dear Instructor:

In your hands you have the Instructor's Annotated Edition of BASIC READING SKILLS HANDBOOK, Second Edition. This ancillary provides answers to the exercises that support the instructional material in the text. For those exercises that require responses drawing on students' personal experiences or interpretations, examples of possible responses are often provided.

For this Second Edition of BASIC READING SKILLS HANDBOOK, we have added many new exercises and anthology selections. We have increased coverage of basic vocabulary skills and have expanded considerably instruction in inference. We have addressed in more detail than in the previous edition the very important skills of visual literacy by adding work on reading charts, graphs, and tables. We continue our focus on prereading exercises, finding the main idea, and SQ3R. And new to the Instructor's Annotated Edition is a "Correlations to Basic Reading Skills Tests" (pages xv–xvi).

BASIC READING SKILLS HANDBOOK is coordinated with its companion text for the next level of college reading instruction, READING SKILLS HANDBOOK, Fifth Edition. Together, the two books provide sequential development of skills; they can be used separately at the appropriate levels or together in a two-course reading sequence.

Available to adopters is a Test Package containing pre- and post-tests for most chapters in the Handbook. It includes complete information on the graded readability levels of the anthology readings. The Computerized Testing Program makes the tests available on disks that can be used with any word-processing software on IBM PC-compatible computers and Macintosh computers. New to this edition is a Computerized Vocabulary Program that gives students the opportunity to practice using key words from the text in yet another context.

Sincerely yours,

The Publisher

Basic Reading Skills Handbook

Second Edition

Harvey S. Wiener
The City University of New York

Charles Bazerman
Georgia Institute of Technology

INSTRUCTOR'S ANNOTATED EDITION

HOUGHTON MIFFLIN COMPANY ■ BOSTON

DALLAS GENEVA, ILLINOIS PALO ALTO PRINCETON, NEW JERSEY

To our children: Melissa, Joseph, Saul, Gershom

Cover illustration by Jim Baldwin.
Book design by Carol H. Rose.

Acknowledgments begin on page 435.

Printed in the U.S.A.

Library of Congress Catalog Card Number: 90-83017

Student's Edition ISBN: 0-395-53511-5

Instructor's Annotated Edition ISBN: 0-395-56962-1

ABCDEFGHIJ-RI-99876543210

Contents

Preface

Basic Reading Skills Handbook, Second Edition, is written specifically for the first-level college reading course. Following the successful approach and format of the next level companion text, *Reading Skills Handbook,* this text focuses on even more basic college reading, study, and literal comprehension skills. Important pedagogical features include:

- Special attention to using contextual clues and to learning multiple meanings of words.
- Chapters on prereading warm-ups, visual aids, and SQ3R.
- Extensive practice in comprehension skills such as finding the main idea, sorting out major and minor details, and inference skills.
- A "Writing to Read" unit that includes chapters on summarizing, underlining, and listing and on personalizing, where students learn to draw connections between their readings and their personal experiences, knowledge, and beliefs.
- Lively readings on a wide range of topics sure to interest today's student.

Organization

The text is divided into two main parts. The *Handbook* provides instruction in the essential reading skills, integrated with examples and extensive practice exercises. The *Reading Selections* include fourteen long reading passages accompanied by prereading, comprehension, interpreting, vocabulary, and writing exercises that are coordinated and cross-referenced with the skills taught in the *Handbook* part. Throughout the text, students will find questions that guide their understanding and interpretation of specific passages.

The organization of the book allows teachers to adapt it to specific courses in several ways. Instructors may teach the units in the *Handbook* in the early weeks of the term, postponing the study of the *Reading Selections* until students know the essential reading skills. The brief readings in the *Handbook* allow the reinforcement of newly learned concepts and students should be ready for the longer readings by the time they reach the *Reading Selections*. Or, instructors may choose to reinforce the skills taught in the *Handbook* by immediately assigning appropriate selections from the *Reading Selections*. As another alternative, instructors may begin with the *Reading Selections* and turn to key instructional units in the *Handbook* as specific needs arise in class.

Special Features

In this book, students read a careful explanation of a specific skill and an analysis of how that skill applies to a particular passage. Then they have a chance to test their mastery of that skill by means of the many exercises designed for practice and review. This step-by-step approach allows students to move from simple skills to more complex ones with confidence.

- Explanations of the basic skills appear in clear, easy-to-understand language.
- Each question in the *Reading Selections* is keyed to the appropriate section in the *Handbook;* if students have difficulty answering a question, they can easily find and review the material that covers that particular skill. Thus, a 6 after a question means that a review of Chapter 6, "Using Visual Aids," will help the student recall the techniques readers use to interpret visual material.
- The reading selections come from many sources, including material from magazines, how-to-books, advertisements, and newspapers, as well as from textbooks and other academic material.
- The functional design includes photographs, tables, charts, graphs, cartoons, and crossword puzzles to stimulate and maintain student interest in the use of visual aids.
- A vocabulary list with a pronunciation key at the back of the

book includes all highlighted vocabulary words in the *Reading Selections*.

- An expanded ancillary package is available with the text.

New to This Edition

For the Second Edition of *Basic Reading Skills Handbook,* we have changed some of the content and organization of the text and have added materials to strengthen even further an already strong book.

- About one-third of the reading passages in both the *Handbook* and *Reading Selections* are new; they include lively selections of fiction and nonfiction from books, newspapers, and magazines. We continue to emphasize materials from textbooks that students typically use — texts on career planning, sociology, business, health, psychology, computers, geography, and history.
- We have expanded considerably our efforts to teach students vocabulary through context clues.
- We have expanded our chapters on visual aids in order to give students more practice in reading charts, graphs, and tables and in understanding the powerful connections between words and pictures in our reading worlds.
- We have expanded our teaching of inference skills by concentrating on the broad techniques and strategies students need in order to infer vital elements from their reading.
- We have added a Computerized Vocabulary Program to an already rich ancillary package. With this program, students have yet another option for studying and learning key vocabulary highlighted in the text.

Acknowledgments

We have many people to thank for their ideas on the preparation of this text. Colleagues scattered around the country have made thoughtful suggestions and have guided us in writing this book. We are grateful to

Rose M. Cooper of Oakland University (MI)
Penne Devery of College of Lake County (IL)
Mary Dunn of College of Lake County (IL)

Ann R. Friedman of Borough of Manhattan Community College
Genetha Hollingsworth of Indiana Vocational Technical College
Harriet Johnson of Hunter College (NY)
Bette Kalash of Borough of Manhattan Community College
Doreen Kaller of Rio Hondo College (CA)
Miriam Kinard of Trident Technical College (SC)
Elizabeth S. Lindgren-Young of Skyline Community College (CA)
Patrick Pacheco of Santa Rosa Junior College (CA)
Jean Raulston of Imperial Valley College (CA)
Myrna Skidell of Nassau Community College (NJ)
Martha Stearns of Central Piedmont Community College (NC)
David A. Strong, Jr., of Dyersburg State Community College (TN)
Marge Thomy of Sumter Area Technical College (SC)
Hannalyn M. Wilkens of Fiorello H. LaGuardia Community College (NY)
Janice Buchner of Suffolk County Community College (NY)

We also wish to thank Dolores Shedd, Sheila Byers, Barbara Wiener, and Melissa Wiener for their help in bringing this project to fruition. To all these colleagues and friends and to our wives and families we owe much thanks and appreciation.

H. S. W.
C. B.

Correlations to Basic Reading Skills Tests

Many states require college students to demonstrate their competence in reading. In the tables below, the reading skills included in three representative state tests are correlated to the sections in *Basic Reading Skills Handbook* where the specific skills are covered.

Texas Academic Skills Program (TASP)	
Determining the Meaning of Words and Phrases	
Familiar words	1a, 1c, 1d, 1e
Words with multiple meanings	1e
Figurative language	1e, 11
Understanding the Main Idea and Supporting Details in Written Material	
Main ideas in narrative and expository writing	8a, 8d
Stated vs. implied main idea	8c(1), 8c(2)
Supporting details	9c
Identifying a Writer's Purpose, Point of View, and Intended Meaning	
Recognizing writer's intent	10, 11
Analyzing the Relationship Among Ideas in Written Material	
Organizational patterns and relationships in written materials	9b, 9c
Drawing conclusions from written materials	10, 11
Using Critical Reasoning Skills to Evaluate Written Material	
Steps in critically evaluating written material	10, 11
Applying Study Skills to Reading Assignments	
Notetaking, outlining, and mapping	12a, 12b, 12c
Interpretation of information in graphic form	6

Georgia Collegiate Placement Examination	
Vocabulary	
Determining the meaning of a word through context	1c
Determining meaning through word analysis (prefixes, suffixes, and roots)	1d(1), 1d(2)
Referring	
Literal comprehension	1a, 8a, 8c, 8d
Determining facts and details	9a, 9c, 10
Recognizing expressed relationships (such as cause and effect)	9b

Reasoning	
Making inferences from the text	11
Structural analysis:	
Identifying organizational patterns	9b
Recognizing point of view	10
Identifying mood and tone	11
Recognizing logical fallacies	10
Recognizing irrelevant data	9c

Florida College Level Academic Skills Test (CLAST)

Reading with Literal Comprehension	
Recognize main ideas	8a, 8b, 8c, 8d
Identify supporting details	9c
Determine meaning of words on the basis of context	1c

Reading with Critical Comprehension	
Recognize the author's purpose	10, 11
Identify the author's overall organizational pattern	9b
Distinguish between statements of fact and statements of opinion	10
Detect bias	10, 11
Recognize the author's tone	10, 11
Recognize explicit and implicit relationships within sentences	8a
Recognize implicit as well as explicit relationships between sentences	8b, 8c
Recognize valid arguments	10, 11
Draw logical inferences and conclusions	10, 11

Handbook

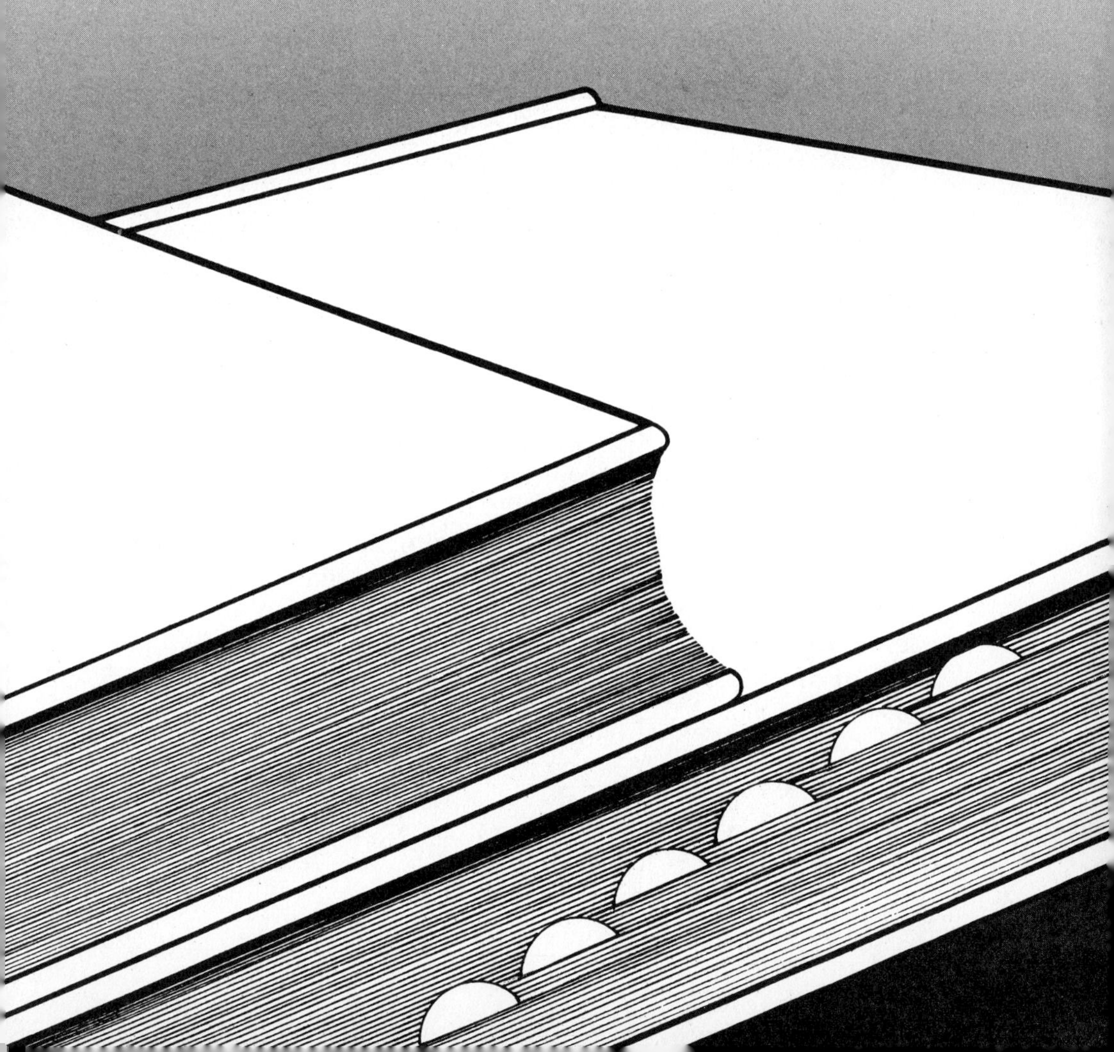

Introduction

Learning to read is not learning just a single skill. It is learning many skills that work together and build on each other. Each time you improve any one skill, it strengthens all the others. As your vocabulary improves, you will be able to understand and interpret your reading. And as you learn to comprehend and interpret better, you will gain more clues about the meaning of unfamiliar words.

The first half of this book teaches the basic skills of reading. Each skill is explained clearly in its own section. Exercises follow each section so that you can practice each skill as you learn about it. Teachers may assign sections for the whole class to study or may assign you sections to work on individually, depending on your needs. Also, as you find areas that you want to work on personally, you can go over sections on your own.

To help you find skills that you need to study, the skills are separated into five different units: Building Vocabulary, Using Aids to Reading, Understanding What You Read, Interpreting What You Read, and Writing to Read. The detailed table of contents and index will help you locate the exact page of any skill that you wish to work on.

Each skill is also given a number, based on the chapter and section it is discussed in. For example, finding main ideas in paragraphs is discussed in section *c* of Chapter 8, "Reading for the Main Idea." The number **8c** refers, then, to the section that you need to look at to gain help in finding main ideas in paragraphs. When you are reading one section, the book may cross-refer to another section by using the number of the other section. Your teacher may also write the number on a piece of your work to suggest that you go over a particular section. Finally, the second half of this book has reading selections with questions. Each question has a reference number that lets you know which skill is needed to answer the question. If you have problems with the question, you can look at that section in the first half of the book for help.

Unit One

Building Vocabulary

1

Recognizing Word Meanings

1a Finding Out What Words Mean

Most of us know enough vocabulary to read from many sources of information around us. We can read newspapers, magazines, signs, posters, advertisements, credit card and job applications, instructions, and recipes, to name a few examples. The richer our vocabulary the more sources of information available to us. The more we read the more our vocabulary grows. You may not be as confident about reading a textbook or a set of directions on how to work your stereo as you are about reading newspaper ads or signs in the supermarket. Still, adding to your usual readings with a wide variety of materials can help you expand your knowledge of words. It also can improve your reading skills.

First, you should realize that you cannot know the meaning of every word you see. Sometimes you may say to yourself, "I sort of know what this means" or "I can get by without figuring this one out." But often you really need to find out exactly what an unfamiliar word means. In the short run, not paying attention to words that you don't know may save you some work. But in the long run, not paying attention to words means that you just won't know as much as you should.

Here are some ways to find the meanings of difficult words:

- Learn to use the context — that is, the clues that surrounding sentences give about the meanings of new words.
- Learn to use visual clues, such as pictures, drawings, signs, and symbols, that can help you figure out meanings. Often a picture starts you thinking about an unfamiliar word on the page, and you can work out a usable definition.

- Look for familiar parts within a word you don't know. You might know what the parts mean. For example, if you know what the meaning of *art* is, you might be able to guess at the meaning of *artistic* or *artful*.
- Learn the difference between what a word means and what a word suggests or makes you feel. Even words that have the same meaning can suggest different things to different people. Although *happy* and *joyous* both suggest good feelings, *joyous* is a much stronger word and creates a feeling of very powerful happiness.
- Be aware that one word can mean many different things. The word *check*, for example, has more than thirty separate meanings! We check our facts, write a check to pay bills, get a checkup at the doctor's, and put a check next to a correct answer, just to name a few.
- Learn to use a dictionary so that you can find meanings easily. Dictionaries help you in many ways, not only for finding the meanings of words but also for finding how to pronounce the words, how to use them correctly, how to spell them, and how to change their forms, among many other uses.
- Keep a list of words that you want to add to your vocabulary. By writing down new words and trying to learn them, you can improve your vocabulary.

1b Remembering New Words

Once you've learned a new word and you think you understand it, try to make sure that you don't forget it. To remember new words, do the following:

- Write the word and its definition often, just for practice.
- Say the word. Learn to pronounce it correctly by using the pronunciation clues in your dictionary.
- Use the word when you talk — in class, on the job, and at home. Make sure that you pronounce the word correctly.
- Try to learn the word and its meaning the first time that you see it.
- Use index cards to study vocabulary. Write the word on one side of the card and its definition on the other side.
- Make up a sentence that you can understand using the word.

- Change the ending of the word: Try to make it plural; try to change the tense; try to add *ly*.
- Use the word whenever you can in your writing assignments.
- Say the word and its meaning over and over again in your mind.
- Don't try to learn long lists of new words. Study just a few words each day for several days so that you can learn by repeating.

1c Using Context Clues

An important part of building your reading skills is learning how to guess what unfamiliar words mean. Very often a word that you have never seen before will appear in a sentence. Perhaps it is a word that you *have* seen before, but you do not remember its meaning. Maybe it is a word whose meaning you thought you knew, but the meaning does not make sense in the sentence that you're reading.

All readers, even the best and the most experienced, come across such words from time to time. You see a word, and it stumps you. You don't know its meaning quickly. But don't reach for a dictionary right away! (Use your dictionary when nothing else works.) Often you can figure out what a word means from clues in the sentence that it appears in or in surrounding sentences. Such clues are *context clues; context* here means surrounding words, phrases, sentences, and paragraphs that help you find out meanings.

Sentences give clues that help a reader guess at definitions of unfamiliar words. Try to use clues to figure out the meaning of the word *pillory* from the sentences below.

> (1) An early form of punishment in America was the pillory. (2) A wooden framework with holes for the hands and head, the pillory stood in a central place for everyone to see. (3) A person who committed a crime was locked in the structure so that people could make fun of the criminal. (4) Even now, when we say that a person is *pilloried* we are saying that the person is exposed to scorn or ridicule.
>
> What is a pillory?

Student responses will vary.

You probably wrote something such as this: *A pillory is a wooden structure used for punishing criminals in America many years ago. The criminal's head and hands were locked in the pillory, and he or she was put in a public place for everyone to make fun of.*

How did you figure out the meaning? You didn't stop reading when you saw the word *pillory* even though you might not have known its meaning right away. You knew from the sentence in which *pillory* appeared that it was a form of punishment in early times in our country. Later sentences gave you other clues. You saw from sentence 2 that a pillory is a structure made of wood and that it had holes for people's hands and heads. You saw, too, that criminals were placed in these wooden traps so that others could make fun of them for their bad deeds. Sentence 4 explained how we use the word *pillory* even today.

Words that you think you don't know may be words you can figure out. Use the words and the sentences around the unfamiliar word to guess at the meaning. Of course, not every unfamiliar word is made clear by surrounding sentences. Sometimes you can read a word and the context gives you no help at all. But, in many cases, you can come up with definitions from sentence clues.

The chart that starts on this page names kinds of context clues, gives some examples, and explains how to use the clues for meanings.

Using Sentence Hints to Find Word Meanings

Hint	Example	Explanation
Some sentences set off the definition for a difficult word by means of punctuation.	The *principal* — money he put in his savings account to earn interest — was safe even though the bank	The pair of dashes sets off the definition of *principal*, here used to mean "sum of money." Other

Hint	Example	Explanation
	was closed by the police.	punctuation that may set off meanings includes commas , parentheses ( ), and brackets [ ].
Sometimes helping words, along with punctuation, introduce important clues to meaning.	Carlos looked *dazed,* that is, stunned, as if someone had shocked him with bad news or with a heavy blow to the head.	Helping words: *that is, meaning, such as, or, is called.*
Some sentences tell the opposite of what a new word means. From its opposite, you can figure out the meaning of the word.	During office hours, he looked very *tense* and anxious, but on weekends he was quite relaxed.	The word *but* helps you understand that *relaxed* is the opposite of *tense.* If you know that *relaxed* means "at ease," you can figure out that *tense* means "tight" or "at attention."
Sometimes you can use your own experiences to figure out the definition of a word.	Martha's husband and mother died within a month of each other, and she cried often at her terrible *sorrows.*	You know that family tragedy would fill a person with "great sadness," the meaning of *sorrows.*
Sentences before or after a sentence containing a difficult word sometimes explain the meaning of the word.	The lovely wooden tray had grown *brittle.* It was dry and hard, and it cracked easily.	Anything dry, hard, and easily cracked may be called *brittle.*

Hint	Example	Explanation
Some sentences provide exact definitions of difficult words — words that readers will need to know in order to understand what they are reading.	She wanted baked clams for her *appetizer*. An appetizer is the first course of a meal.	The second sentence defines the word *appetizer* exactly.
Because some sentences give examples for a new word, you can build a definition.	*Legumes*, such as string beans, lima beans, and green peas, are important in your diet.	The sentence doesn't say that *legume* is a name for a group of vegetables with pods, but you can figure out some of that meaning from the examples.
Some sentences use a word that you do know to help explain a word that you do not know.	The mayor wanted *privacy* because he knew that being alone would help him solve his problems.	You can tell from the sentence clues that *privacy* means "being alone."

EXERCISES

1. Sentence Clues

The words in italics (slanted type) may be unfamiliar to you. Try to use the hints in each sentence to make up a definition for the italic word. Then select the letter of the word that you feel is closest to the meaning. Write the letter in the blank space.

c ______ 1. Police work now often includes the use of the *polygraph*. A polygraph is an instrument used to detect lies.
Polygraph means
a. police work
b. guns and other police instruments

c. lie detector
d. liar

b ______ 2. The speaker used colorful *illustrations* — drawings and photographs — to help us understand her points about how to raise cactus plants indoors.
Illustration means
a. growing indoor cactus plants
b. a drawing or photograph
c. a speaker before an audience
d. gardening

a ______ 3. If you stand in the doorway and don't let anyone pass, you will *obstruct* the exit.
Obstruct means
a. block
b. doorway
c. pass
d. stand without doing anything

a ______ 4. When you trade one object or service that you do not need or want for another one that you do need or want, you are part of a *barter* system.
Barter means
a. trade
b. system
c. unneeded goods and services
d. dividing line between two states or countries

d ______ 5. She expected to lose the race; instead she was *victorious*.
Victorious means
a. being the loser
b. being wrong
c. being embarrassed
d. being the winner

b ______ 6. *Data* (information collected in research) are accurate only if they are checked carefully.
Data means
a. researchers
b. collected information
c. accurate details
d. month, day, and year

b ______ 7. Automobile, bicycle, and truck use has increased sharply over the last decade. However, local governments have not kept up the pace in developing roads for personal *vehicles*.
Vehicles means
a. local governments
b. means of transportation
c. road use
d. personal politics

d ______ 8. Eight-year-old Darryl always stayed out of trouble in school. He annoyed no one and caused no harm. However, his younger brother, Herman, was known for his *impish* behavior.
Impish means
a. well-behaved
b. cute
c. friendly
d. causing mischief

c ______ 9. The new parking rules were *imposed,* that is, forced on us by town leaders, and we felt that the rules were not fair.
Imposed means
a. voted on
b. unfair
c. forced
d. rules made by government leaders

a ______ 10. We were making excellent progress up the mountain until we saw a gigantic rock blocking the roadway. This was the one *barrier* that we could not overcome.
Barrier means
a. something that stops progress
b. mountain road
c. large-size animal
d. fear

d ______ 11. In order to frighten her younger brother, she decided to *concoct,* or make up, an imaginative story about monsters and ghosts.
Concoct means
a. frighten

b. write
c. read about
d. imaginatively make up

c ______ 12. The visitors wandered around the *gallery,* where people came to see and perhaps buy the artists' paintings hanging on the walls.
Gallery means
a. museum
b. store
c. place where artwork hangs
d. building that needs to be painted

a ______ 13. The lawyer had no time for *leisure;* she worked hard all day so that she would win her case.
Leisure means
a. freedom from work
b. losing a case
c. exercise
d. conversation

c ______ 14. I knew that I was *exhausted* when I felt that I could fall asleep standing up!
Exhausted means
a. sleeping
b. sitting down
c. very tired
d. falling

b ______ 15. In the barn, Sara Blake stored her farm *implements,* such as hoes, rakes, and shovels.
Implements means
a. machinery
b. tools
c. cooking equipment
d. animals

2. Meanings in Your Own Words

Use whatever context clues you can to find the meaning for each word in italics. Write the definition in your own words. Do not use a dictionary.

1. Use the silver *chalice* for the wine at Sunday's religious service.

   Chalice means **cup**.

2. Carlotta tried to *retrieve* her pet canary, but it flew quickly away as soon as it got out the window.

   Retrieve means **get back**.

3. Captain Herrara questioned the thief's *motives*. "What were your reasons for stealing a pound of tomatoes?" he asked.

   Motives means **reasons**.

4. The company displayed a bright red ten-*carat* ruby. A carat is a unit of weight used to measure the size of valuable gems such as diamonds, rubies, and emeralds.

   Carat means **weight unit for measuring gems**.

5. The mayor is honest and of good character. She has very high moral standards. No wonder people say that she's a woman of *integrity*.

   Integrity means **high moral standards**.

6. Seeds often can develop in moist soil; *arid* soil, on the other hand, needs moisture before anything can grow in it.

   Arid means **dry**.

7. The poodles, the spaniels, and even the mutts danced across the circus floor when the *canine* acts began.

   Canine means **dog**.

8. A fawn *bereft* of its mother will never survive this frozen winter. The mother's food supply, her warmth, and her support are all needed for the baby deer to exist in these surroundings.

   Bereft means **deserted; left without**.

9. *Dispose* of that garbage at once! If you do not get rid of it, it will start to smell.

   Dispose means **get rid of**.

10. The cashier realized that this was a *genuine* $100 bill, not a fake one as she had thought before.

    Genuine means **real; not fake**.

11. If you do not like to eat such large leaves of lettuce, I will *shred* them for you.

    Shred means **tear into small pieces**.

12. "Don't *scowl* at me," Karen's mother warned. "There is no reason for you to have such an angry look on your face."

    Scowl means **frown angrily**.

13. The mayor *proposed* a plan that would cut down on traffic, but the citizens did not like what he suggested.

    Proposed means **suggested; offered for consideration**.

14. To work the sewing machine, step gently on the *treadle.*

    Treadle means **foot pedal**.

15. He knew tiny, unimportant details about American history, but he did not understand major trends or patterns. Of what use was such *trivial* information, we wondered.

    Trivial means **small; unimportant; insignificant**.

3. Sentences from Textbooks

Using context clues, determine the meaning of the italicized word in the textbook sentences. Select the correct definition from the choices given and write the letter of the correct answer in the blank space.

b 1. If the animals eat up all the grasses, there is nothing to hold the soil in place. Then wind or water will carry it away, a process called *erosion.*

— Geography

Erosion means
a. feeding animals
b. the wearing away of soil
c. harsh, blowing winds
d. the need to keep soil in place

a ______ 2. The problem of limited resources in the world results in a *scarcity* of available resources to meet all the wants of a group of people. Scarcity is a lack of something that can be used to satisfy all the wants of a group of people.

— Economics

Scarcity means
a. lack of something
b. available resources
c. satisfying people's wants
d. problems of resources

c ______ 3. *Regression* means to act in an immature way. People are regressing when they sulk or throw tantrums instead of expressing disappointment maturely.

— Health

Regression means
a. mature behavior
b. disappointment
c. immature behavior
d. depression

d ______ 4. Some computer systems use *cryptography* (secret writing) to protect information. Such systems store information in the computer in coded or scrambled form.

— Computer Science

Cryptography means
a. protected information
b. computer systems
c. stored information
d. secret writing

a ______ 5. The source of the sun's energy is a process known as *fusion*. In this process hydrogen atoms combine to form helium atoms. The sun contains plenty of hydrogen fuel.

— Chemistry

Fusion means
a. the process by which hydrogen atoms join to become atoms of helium
b. confusion among atoms of the sun
c. the process by which the sun develops new hydrogen fuel
d. sunrise

4. More Sentences from Textbooks

Each example contains one or more words in italics. Clues in the sentences will help you figure out the meaning of the words in italics. Write their definitions in the space provided. Do *not* use a dictionary.

1. When you make a reasonable guess that explains how or why something happened, you are making a hypothesis. A *hypothesis* is a possible explanation that can be tested. It is based on what you already know. You are not sure that your hypothesis is correct. You can often make more than one hypothesis for a situation.

— Spaceship Earth: Life Science

Hypothesis means **possible explanation that can be tested**.

2. History books usually present events in *chronological* order; that is, they start with the earliest events and end with the most recent ones. Chronological order is order based on time.

— This Is America's Story

Chronological means **time order**.

3. He could not *log on* — that is, reach his file in the computer — because he had used a capital letter to spell his last name. The computer recognized his name only when the initial letter was in lowercase.

— The McGraw-Hill College Handbook

Log on means **reach a desired computer file**.

4. Corporations usually issue bonds that mature in 10 to 30 years with face values that are multiples of $1000. Bonds may sell at a *discount,* for less than the face value, or at a *premium,* for more than the face value. The cost of a bond is usually a percent of the face value, and is referred to as the *quoted price.* A price of 90 on a $1000 bond means that the bond sells for 90% of $1000, or $900. The interest that you receive from a bond is calculated on its face value.

— Consumer Mathematics

Discount means **less than face value**.

Premium means **more than face value**.

Quoted price means **cost of a bond, usually a percent of face value**.

5. The most important crop in South China is rice. If you could fly over South China during certain times of the year, you might think you were looking down into a giant mirror. What you saw would not be glass, however. Instead, it would be thousands of water-covered fields called *paddies.* Those are the fields where rice is grown. Fields are *flooded* with about fifteen centimeters (six inches) of water, and rice seedlings are planted. While the rice grows, farmers work hard to keep the fields free of weeds. Just before the harvest, the water is *drained* from the fields. The rice is then *harvested,* tied into bundles, and dried in the sun for about a week. Finally, farmers *thresh* the rice, separating the grains from the stalks.

— Geography

Paddies means **water-covered fields**.

Flooded means **overrun with water**.

Drained means **water removed**.

Harvested means **gathered, as a crop**.

Thresh means **separate into parts**.

6. The brain is the first organ affected by alcohol. This makes people more relaxed and more talkative for a while. However, alcohol is really a depressant. A *depressant* slows down important nerve activity. Alcohol slows down nerve activity in the brain and spinal cord. This affects the area of the brain that controls inhibitions, attention, and memory. *Inhibitions* are checks on the emotions. With inhibitions *weakened* by alcohol, people have less *self-control.* Buried feelings may come out, sometimes in sudden *bursts* of anger. While drinking, people may not be able to judge what is a dangerous act.

Alcohol slows the body's reflexes by *interfering* with nerve signals. *Reflexes* are automatic muscle responses to pain or danger. You depend on them to pull your hand away from a hot stove or to *jam* on the brakes of your bike or car. Thus alcohol affects muscle *coordination.* The drinker becomes clumsy and may have difficulty walking. Beverage glasses somehow get broken and things get knocked over.

— Houghton Mifflin Health

Depressant means **a substance that slows down nerve activity**.

Inhibitions means **checks on the emotions**.

Weakened means **made less strong**.

Self-control means **ability to make choices about what you do**.

Bursts means **sudden outbreaks; explosions**.

Interfering means **blocking; standing in the way of**.

Reflexes means **automatic muscle responses**.

Jam means **press hard**.

Coordination means **working together**.

5. A Magazine Advertisement

Use clues in the advertisement on page 21 to figure out the meanings for the words that appear beneath it. Choose the letter of the correct word and write it in the blank space provided.

d ______ 1. *Residence* means
- a. hotel
- b. motel
- c. lodge
- d. home

c ______ 2. *Perfect* means
- a. useful
- b. cheerful
- c. exactly right
- d. useless

b ______ 3. *Extended* means
- a. tired
- b. long
- c. overworked
- d. comfortable

b ______ 4. *Fully-equipped* means
- a. unnecessary
- b. complete with everything needed
- c. at an extra cost
- d. separate and private

d ______ 5. *Complimentary* means
- a. pleasant
- b. thoughtful
- c. hidden
- d. free

a ______ 6. *Sliding rate scale* means
- a. changing room prices
- b. expensive room prices
- c. new machines for height and weight measures
- d. unsure

After a few nights, you need more than a room. You need a home.

Admit it. After a few nights, a hotel room gets old. Hotel food gets old. The whole hotel experience gets old.

Which is why you should know about The Residence Inn. More pleasant, more private, more comfortable. More home than hotel.

Perfect for extended stays, we offer separate living room areas, fully-equipped kitchens, and private entrances. As well as a long list of complimentary extras. All for the cost of that ordinary hotel room. Less when you consider our sliding rate scale.

So call 1-800-331-3131. You'll find the longer you stay the more comfortable we get.

As close to home as we can make it.

1d Using Word Part Clues

1d(1) Compound Words

Occasionally, two words may be put together to form a new word called a *compound word.* If you look at each word unit, you sometimes can recognize the new word. Then you can try to understand the meaning. For example, look at these words:

bookmark (book + mark)
landlocked (land + locked)
openminded (open + minded)
undercut (under + cut)
broomstick (broom + stick)
paperwork (paper + work)
upstart (up + start)

EXERCISES

1. Two Words in One

Each word contains two or more words joined together to form a new word. Try to figure out the meaning of the new word by looking at the words that make it up. In the space provided, write a definition in your own words. Check your answer in a dictionary.

1. breadwinner **a person in a family who earns the money**
2. dayflower **a flower that blooms for only one day**
3. backpack **a satchel worn on the back**
4. guidebook **a book that tells you about a place**
5. waterproof **does not let water in**
6. fairground **a place where fairs and carnivals are held**
7. dateline **a line in a newspaper article that tells the place and day a story was written**

8. outfield **a distant part of a playing field**

9. kickstand **a support to hold up a bicycle**

10. threadbare **so worn down that the threads show**

2. New Words

Choose a word from column *A* and combine it with a word in column *B* to form a new word that makes sense. Write the new word and a definition of the word. Use a dictionary if you need help.

A	*B*
fall	guard
pay	point
door	boat
lap	person
sales	tire
flat	gap
main	out
near	board
life	frame
far	sick
floor	master
needle	sighted
stop	yard

Examples:

doorframe	the structure around a door
lifeguard	a person at a beach who saves people from drowning
stopgap	a temporary solution

	Word	*Your Definition*
1.	**Student responses will vary.**	
2.		
3.		

4. ______________________ ______________________

5. ______________________ ______________________

6. ______________________ ______________________

7. ______________________ ______________________

8. ______________________ ______________________

9. ______________________ ______________________

10. ______________________ ______________________

1d(2) *Prefixes, Suffixes, and Roots*

Words new to you may contain certain groups of letters that have meanings you can learn. If you don't know what the word itself means, these groups of letters may help you reach a definition.

When a group of letters with a special meaning appears in front of a word, it is called a *prefix.*

When a group of letters with a special meaning appears at the end of a word, it is called a *suffix.*

You've seen the word *emotion,* haven't you? It means *feeling*. Now look at the word *unemotional.*

The prefix *un* means "not" or "lack of."
The suffix *al* means "relating to."

When you break down the meaning of the parts of the word *unemotional,* you get "relating to a lack of feelings." Knowing the prefix and the suffix helps you figure out what the word means. You might not have to use a dictionary.

The *root* (or stem) is the basic part of the word. We add prefixes and suffixes to some roots and create new words. In the example above, *emotion* is the stem. You knew that word and could build meanings for words made by adding prefixes and suffixes.

Now look at a word whose root you might not know offhand:

transcription
The prefix *trans* means "across."
The suffix *tion* means "state of."
The root *scrip* means "to write."

The word *transcription* means "the state of writing across." When you transcribe something, you change it from one form to a written form — that is, you "write across." Secretaries use transcription to change shorthand symbols into written language that anyone can understand.

It's not always easy to figure out the exact meanings for words from prefixes, suffixes, and roots. But knowing these word parts can help you gain at least some idea of the meanings of many words without having to look them up in a dictionary.

Important Prefixes

Prefixes meaning "no" or "not":

Prefix	**Meaning**	**Example**
a	not, without	amoral
in	not	inexact
im	not	immobile
non	not	nonreturnable
mis	wrongly	mislead
mal	badly	malformed
anti	against	antisocial
ir	not	irresponsible
dis	not	disfavor
un	not	unknown
il	not	illegal

Prefixes dealing with time:

Prefix	**Meaning**	**Example**
pre	before	predate
post	after	postwar

Prefixes dealing with numbers, one or more than one:

Prefix	Meaning	Example
uni	one	unicycle
mono	one	monologue
auto	self	autograph
bi	two	bicycle
tri	three	tripod
poly	many	polygon
multi	many	multicolored

Prefixes dealing with placement:

Prefix	Meaning	Example
ab	away from	abnormal
circum	around	circumscribe
com, con	with, together	committee
de	down from	deceit
dis	away	discharge

Prefix	Meaning	Example
ex	out of	exconvict
in	into, within	inborn
inter	among	intermix
pro	forward, in favor of	pro-American
re	again	recall
sub	under	submarine
super	above	superior
trans	across	transition

Important Suffixes

Suffix	Meaning	Example
able, ible	able to be	manageable, defensible
al, ance, ence	relating to	regal, resistance, independence
ic, ion, ism, hood, ity, ment	state of, quality of	patriotic, union, Catholicism, brotherhood, legality, puzzlement

er, or, ite	one who	writer, advisor, Mennonite
y, ful	full of	soapy, wishful

Important Roots

Root	Meaning	Example
cred	believe	credence
duc, duct	lead, make, fashion, shape	deduct
equ	equal	equate
fac, fact, fic	do, make	factory
graph	written	monograph
log	speech	monologue
mis, mit	send	missile
mor, mort	die	mortify
nom, nomen	name	nominal
port	carry	portable
pos	place	position
scrip, scrib	to write	describe
spic, spec	look	spectator
tang	touch	tangible
ten, tin, tain	have, hold	detain
tend, tens, tent	stretch	extend
vid, vis	see	vision
voc	call	evoke

EXERCISES

1. Prefixes, Suffixes, and Roots

For each word, draw one line under the prefix, two lines under the suffix, and a circle around the root. Leave the spaces beside the words blank until you do Exercise 8 on page 34.

Example: misnomer

1. prescription ________ something ________

________ written ________

________ beforehand ________

2. conductor ______ **a person in charge of a railroad train**

3. disposal ______ **relating to getting rid of something**

4. nonextension ______ **cannot be extended**

5. incredible ______ **not able to be believed**

2. Word Parts in Words That You Know

Think of the many words that you know and use regularly. Do you recognize prefixes and suffixes in those words? Follow the instructions and make a list of the words that you know that have prefixes and suffixes. Write the definitions of those words. **Student responses will vary.**

1. Three words that begin with the prefix *a*

Word	*Meaning*
______	______
______	______
______	______

2. Three words that begin with the prefix *ex*

Word	*Meaning*
______	______
______	______
______	______

3. Three words that begin with the prefix *pre*

   Word *Meaning*

   ______________________ ____________________________

   ______________________ ____________________________

   ______________________ ____________________________

4. Three words that begin with the prefix *re*

   Word *Meaning*

   ______________________ ____________________________

   ______________________ ____________________________

   ______________________ ____________________________

5. Three words that end with the suffix *able* or *ible*

   Word *Meaning*

   ______________________ ____________________________

   ______________________ ____________________________

   ______________________ ____________________________

6. Three words that end with the suffix *ism*

   Word *Meaning*

   ______________________ ____________________________

   ______________________ ____________________________

   ______________________ ____________________________

7. Three words that end with the suffix *ful*

   Word *Meaning*

   ______________________ ____________________________

8. Three words that end with the suffix *er* or *or*

Word *Meaning*

3. Meanings and Prefixes

Define each word using what you know about prefixes. In the blank space write the meaning for each word.

1. *re*examine **look over again**
2. *post*date **put down a later date**
3. *pre*dawn **before the sun rises**
4. *anti*slavery **against slavery**
5. *un*settled **not relaxed; anxious**
6. *im*proper **not proper**
7. *non*binding **not binding**
8. *in*bound **coming in**
9. *in*active **not active**
10. *super*man **a person with more than human powers**
11. *bi*weekly **every two weeks**
12. *multi*talented **having several talents**
13. *dis*robe **undress**

14. *sub*heading a second-level title

15. *dis*please make unhappy

4. Meanings and Suffixes

In each word, the suffix is in italics. In the second column, write what each suffix means. In the third column, write the meaning of the complete word.

Word	*Meaning of Suffix*	*Meaning of Word*
1. boy*hood*	state of	state of being a boy
2. grain*y*	full of	full of grains
3. leg*al*	relating to	relating to law
4. real*ism*	quality of	quality of reality
5. laugh*able*	able to be	able to be laughed at
6. creat*or*	one who	one who makes or creates
7. flavor*ful*	full of	full of flavor
8. encourage*ment*	state of	state of confidence
9. blam*able*	able to be	able to be blamed
10. insur*ance*	relating to	relating to a guarantee; protection

5. Making Words with Prefixes

Combine a prefix in column *A* with a word in column *B* to create six correct new words. Write the new word in the first column. Write the meaning of the word in the second column. Use a dictionary to check yourself.

A	*B*
tri	exact
in	American
non	perfect
pre	cycle
im	honest
dis	equal
un	condition
anti	issue
re	set
mis	fat
	place

Possible answers:

	Word	*Meaning*
1.	**unequal**	**not of same value**
2.	**inexact**	**not precise**
3.	**nonfat**	**containing no fat**
4.	**reissue**	**make available again**
5.	**preset**	**to adjust or fix ahead of time**
6.	**displace**	**move away from where it should be**

6. Prefixes and Suffixes Together

Use what you know about prefixes and suffixes to figure out the meaning for each word. Do *not* use a dictionary.

1. irreplaceable **not able to be replaced**
2. unheroic **not like a hero**
3. inability **quality of not being capable**
4. nonjudgmental **not relating to judgment**
5. defogger **something that removes fog**
6. intangible **not capable of being touched**
7. discontentment **unhappiness**
8. maladjustment **state of not fitting in**
9. disagreement **conflict**
10. unknowable **not able to be determined**

7. Meanings and Roots

The words in each group have the same root. Circle the root in each case. Then try to figure out the meaning of each word and write the definition in the blank space. Use a dictionary only to check yourself.

1. description **a statement describing something**

   mistranscribe **to transcribe wrongly**

2. transportation **state of being carried from one place to another**

   report **an account presented in detail**

   deported **expelled from a country**

3. invisible **unable to be seen**

revision **a looking over; a correction**

supervisor **person who looks over someone else**

4. tension **the process of stretching**

extensive **large in range or amount**

retentive **having the ability to retain**

5. spectacle **a public performance or display**

spectator **an observer of an event**

introspection **self-examination**

8. Prefixes, Suffixes, and Roots

Go back to Exercise 1 on page 27. On the first blank line beside each word, write your own definition of the word. Use what you know about prefixes, roots, and suffixes. Then look up the word in a dictionary. On the second blank line, write a definition based on your dictionary's explanation.

9. Matching Definitions

Match each definition with one of the words listed below. The words contain prefixes, suffixes, and roots that you have studied. Write the letter of the best meaning in the blank space beside each word.

a. not able to be run away from
b. state of letting out air
c. able to be filled again
d. not judging
e. cannot be denied
f. someone who looks at something again in a new way
g. material that offers no resistance to electricity
h. related to the army
i. related to two cultures in one country
j. removed from ownership

1. militarism **h**

2. undeniable e

3. bicultural i

4. exhalation b

5. inescapable a

6. dispossessed j

7. refillable c

8. superconductor g

9. nonjudgmental d

10. revisionist f

10. Related Words in Groups

The words in each group are related. Write a definition for each of the words in italics. Use a dictionary if you need one. Then, from what you know of prefixes and suffixes, write definitions for all the words beneath the word in italics. Check a dictionary only after you try to figure out the meaning on your own.

1. *knowledge* **fact of knowing**

   knowledgeable **having knowledge**

   unknowledgeable **not having any knowledge**

   knowing **possessing knowledge**

   unknown **not known**

   know-nothing **someone who doesn't know anything**

   know-it-all **someone who thinks he or she knows everything**

2. *nation* **a people who share common customs**

national **of a nation as an organized whole**

nationalize **to convert from private to government control**

nationhood **the state of being a nation**

nationalism **devotion to the interests of a particular nation**

internationalism **mutual interests or culture of nations**

nationality **belonging to a nation by origin**

nationalist **one who believes in national independence**

3. *announce* **to bring to public notice**

unannounced **not announced**

announcement **a formal statement**

reannounce **to announce again**

announcer **a person who announces**

ex-announcer **a person who was once an announcer**

4. *estimate* **to calculate approximately**

reestimate **to calculate approximately again**

estimation **an opinion**

unestimated **not estimated**

estimator **one who gives an estimate**

underestimate **to calculate below**

5. *repeat* **to state again**

repetition **the act of repeating**

repeated **occurring again and again**

repeatedly **over and over again**

unrepeated **not repeated**

repeater **one who repeats**

11. Review

Return to the columns under *Important Prefixes, Important Suffixes,* and *Important Roots* on pages 25–27. Try to determine the meanings of the words in the column labeled *Example.* Write the word and your definition on a separate sheet of paper. Use a dictionary to check your work.

1e Considering Multiple Meanings

Some words have many different meanings. Did you know, for example, that the word *light* has more than thirty definitions? Among the meanings are: that which makes things visible, daytime, not heavy, pale in color, a gleam or sparkle in the eyes, and to set burning. Look at the uses of the word in the sentences below. What does *light* mean in each case?

1. Please *light* the fire in the fireplace.
2. Esteban wore a *light* jacket despite the cold.
3. I painted my room a *light* blue.
4. We didn't know about his criminal record; only today has it come to *light.*
5. The wall cuts off our *light.*

If you had just one definition of the word *light* in mind when you read, you would not get the meanings in every case above. You have to consider the multiple definitions — *multiple* means "many" — of a word before making a decision about its meaning in a sentence.

How can you decide? Of course you want to start with what you believe the word means, based on your own experience and knowledge. Then, and this is very important, *test the meaning in the sentence.*

Let's look at sentence 2 above. Suppose you knew that the word *light* often meant "not dark." Suppose, too, that you did not consider other possible meanings. You would think that *light* referred to the color of the jacket. But you'd be incorrect. If you looked at the surrounding words, however, you'd soon figure out what *light* meant.

Do you see the words *despite the cold* in sentence 2? They tell you that the jacket Esteban wore was not one that the writer thought he should wear that day. The sentence tells you that the weather was cold. In cold weather, you expect people to wear heavy jackets. But the word *despite* here says that this jacket is one opposite to what you might expect. *Despite the cold* is a context clue that tells you that the jacket was not heavy. The weather was cold, the sentence says, but Esteban wore an unexpected kind of jacket. You could pretty much guess at the meaning of the word *light,* then, as opposite to *heavy*. You can see how far off base the meaning "not dark" would be.

Here again, context clues **(1c)** are very important. Don't decide on a meaning until you see how nearby words and sentences affect it.

EXERCISES

1. One Word, Many Meanings

Three familiar words — *note, title,* and *dash* — appear below with many of their meanings. Next to each meaning is a letter. For each sentence that uses the word defined, select the letter of the definition that works best.

1. *note*
   a. a brief written record to help the memory
   b. a piece of paper money
   c. great merit or special quality
   d. a musical sound or tone
   e. a formal piece of writing between governments

e ______ 1. The diplomatic *note* to the prime minister asked his help in fighting drugs in his country.

c ______ 2. Her book was a novel of *note;* it won three major prizes last year.

d ______ 3. I knew that I would like the song from the very first *note.*

a ______ 4. She jotted down a *note* to herself so that she wouldn't forget the address and telephone number.

b ______ 5. The agent tried to bribe her lawyer with a fifty-dollar *note.*

2. *title*
   a. the name of a book or other work of art
   b. to give something a distinguishing name
   c. a championship
   d. a descriptive name used for someone with rank or office
   e. legal right to the possession of property

b ______ 1. She *titled* her watercolor painting "Evening with Two Swans."

e ______ 2. Mrs. Wilson took *title* to her father's old house in Missouri.

c ______ 3. The Houston Astros won their division *title* with excellent fielding and pitching.

d ______ 4. His full *title* is Lord Herbert, Earl of Gretham.

a ______ 5. The correct *title* of the film is *The Bored,* not *The Board.*

3. *dash*
   a. strike or break with violence
   b. apply roughly, as if splashing
   c. a short line used as punctuation
   d. a small amount of something mixed in with other things
   e. ruin something
   f. a short race
   g. write something quickly

f ______ 1. Miranda won the fifty-yard *dash* for the second year.

e ______ 2. The low score I got on my final exam *dashed* my hopes for an A in history.

a _____ 3. He *dashed* the picture to the ground in a fit of anger.

b _____ 4. The heat and the dust so weakened him that even the cold water he *dashed* across his face did not make him feel better.

d _____ 5. Use a *dash* of hot pepper sauce to spice up the gravy.

c _____ 6. Use a *dash* to show a sudden pause or break in a written sentence.

2. Many Meanings for Words That You Know

You should know several meanings for each word below. On separate paper, copy the words and then write at least two different definitions for each. If you need help, use a dictionary. **(2)**

1. bed
2. fall
3. part
4. sell
5. draw

3. Sentence Clues for Correct Meanings

For each word in italics, choose the letter of the correct meaning. Be careful! All the choices offer correct definitions for the word. However, only one definition works right in the sentence. Read carefully and use the context clues before choosing.

b _____ 1. With a sharp *plane,* he smoothed the surface of the table.
a. airplane
b. tool for finishing wood
c. glide
d. a level of morals or character, for example

c _____ 2. She wore the same *habit* that her mother wore as she rode across the mountain trails.
a. an act or behavior repeated often
b. custom or usual practice
c. a woman's riding dress
d. bodily or physical condition

d _____ 3. He dried the *lip* carefully after he poured acid from the jar.
a. the fleshy, outer part of the mouth
b. words that are insincere
c. the rim at the end of a pipe
d. the edge of a container

d _____ 4. When day *breaks*, you can see rays of brilliant sunlight over the Blue Ridge Mountains.
a. divides into parts
b. fractures
c. discontinues
d. dawns

a _____ 5. He *engaged* her attention with tales of travel through Africa's national parks.
a. occupied
b. planned to marry
c. entered into conflict
d. pledged

4. Review

Select the best meaning of each word in italics and write the letter of the correct answer in the blank space provided.

b _____ 1. "Pablo calls out all the time," his teacher said to the child's mother. "He hits the other children and will not stay in his seat. Such behavior is highly *undesirable* for a student in a third-grade classroom."
a. wild
b. not wanted
c. lively
d. evil

c _____ 2. Western farmers learned to grow crops on dry land. They *irrigated* the soil, using pipes or canals to carry water to the fields.
a. fertilized
b. harvested
c. brought water to
d. took water from

d ______ 3. Her effort was *tireless.* She woke up early, worked hard all day, took little time to rest, and was ready to start again at five the next morning.
a. lazy
b. weak
c. done without much thought
d. done without growing weary or bored

a ______ 4. For his hard work on her campaign, the mayor kissed her manager and gave him her *heartfelt* thanks.
a. deeply felt
b. hardly felt
c. politically active
d. election year

c ______ 5. In 1960, Jane Goodall *pioneered* a study of chimpanzees. She was one of the first people to observe the animals close up in the wild.
a. traveled across the country
b. carried out
c. was one of the first to do
d. photographed

c ______ 6. The smallest blood vessels branch into tiny *capillaries,* which can be seen only with a microscope. Capillaries are blood vessels with very thin walls.
a. small hatlike structures
b. veins
c. thin-walled blood vessels
d. large branches

b ______ 7. A few types of tall trees spread a thick cover, or *canopy,* of leaves over the forest.
a. darkness
b. thick covering
c. undergrowth
d. rain

b ______ 8. When she starts her diet for losing weight, hot-fudge sundaes and french fries are *unmentionable* in her presence.
a. fattening

b. not to be spoken of
c. not to be eaten
d. desirable

b
____ 9. To everyone's surprise, the monkey had *treed* the lion cub, who howled noisily from the topmost branches.
a. frightened
b. forced to climb a tree
c. made tired by running
d. bitten

b
____ 10. In the fifteenth century, Da Vinci's careful drawings and illustrations *prefigured* our modern airplanes.
a. looked nothing like
b. suggested with an early model
c. designed fully and completely
d. painted simply

c
____ 11. Although he could afford much more, he put only ten cents in the contribution plate. What a *paltry* amount!
a. generous
b. religious
c. small and not important
d. for charity

b
____ 12. In 1869, America had its first *transcontinental* (cross-country) railroad line.
a. successful
b. across the land
c. early
d. changing

a
____ 13. The people who wanted America to stretch from the Atlantic to the Pacific were called *expansionists* because they tried to expand U.S. territory.
a. people who wanted to expand land holdings
b. politicians
c. people who wanted to sail from the Atlantic to the Pacific
d. landowners in the West

d ______ 14. The children enjoyed colorful beads, bits of glass, cheap rings and necklaces, mirrors, and other such *trinkets.*
a. Indians
b. valuable items
c. money
d. small, fancy items of little worth

b ______ 15. Every time her mother spoke, Karen Loo said the same words her mother did. She copied every action of her mother's, too, coughing and clearing her throat each time just after her mother did. Finally, Mrs. Loo said angrily, "I wish you wouldn't *parrot* me like that. It's very annoying!"
a. squawk like a bird
b. copy
c. annoy
d. attach

a ______ 16. Her aides wanted to keep the discussion on the new law going; the mayor, on the other hand, insisted on *closure.* "We've talked enough," she said.
a. ending
b. continuing
c. eating
d. going out

c ______ 17. Mr. Gomez gave many tests and papers in his chemistry course, and everyone worked very hard for this *taskmaster.*
a. smart man
b. mean teacher
c. someone who makes people work hard
d. someone who makes people dislike him

a ______ 18. *Torrential* rains swept across the roadways, burying the cars in water.
a. wild
b. cool
c. warm
d. delayed

a ______ 19. A *sullen* child is always gloomy and resists cheering up.
a. sad and moody
b. bad and lively

c. tired and quiet
d. strange and helpful

d ______ 20. Maria has arrived late seven times in the last eight days at work on a new job. Her boyfriend knows that she is always at least a half hour late for their dates. Even as a child, she rarely arrived at school on time. This is a case of *chronic tardiness.*
a. bad behavior
b. poor planning
c. creative planning
d. constant lateness

5. Working with Words

Write in blank space *a* the definition of each word in italics. Then write in blank space *b* the definition of the related word in italics.

1. We could *pass* through the narrow hallway if we moved sideways.

   a. *Pass* means **move through**.

   b. *Impassable* means **not able to be moved through**.

2. That lively, cheerful blue tie *suits* your personality.

   a. *Suits* means **is right for**.

   b. *Unsuited* means **not right for**.

3. Our *annual* report comes out each year on June 15.

   a. *Annual* means **once a year**.

   b. *Biannually* means **twice a year**.

4. He saved twelve men in his platoon by risking his life under serious fire; they declared him a *hero* and gave him a gold medal.

   a. *Hero* means **brave person**.

   b. *Unheroic* means **not relating to bravery**.

5. The old ambulance stayed in *active* service at Community Hospital for over ten years without any problems.

   a. *Active* means **in service**.

   b. *Reactivate* means **put back into service**.

6. Review

Use whatever information you can — context clues, word-part clues, or multiple meanings — to figure out the meaning of each word in italics. Write your own definition on each blank line. **Student responses will vary.**

1. She made a *notation* in the margin to check the unfamiliar word in a dictionary.

   Notation means **note; written comment**.

2. We thought that we could *predict* the team's success this year from its last year's record of wins and losses, but we were mistaken.

   Predict means **tell the future about**.

3. When he tightened the small screw at the top, the *clipboard* once again held the papers in place.

   Clipboard means **board that holds papers together**.

4. Ricardo kept *embroidering* the story with unbelievable details so that it sounded like fiction instead of fact.

   Embroidering means **adding details to**.

5. At *intervals,* the lost climbers lit candles, but the periods of time that they had light grew shorter and shorter as their supplies ran low.

   Intervals means **periods of time**.

6. We knew that we could count on support from the *clergy;* all the local priests, nuns, and rabbis joined in the effort to raise money for the needy after the earthquake in Mexico.

   Clergy means **people who work for organized religion**.

7. With a sudden *jerk,* the truck door flew open, and cases of peanut oil smashed on the highway.

   Jerk means **abrupt pull**.

8. Consuelo's excellent selling skills *induced* him to buy a shirt he really didn't need.

   Induced means **convinced; caused**.

9. The senator's illness kept him from the Columbus Day parade, but he sent an *emissary* in his place.

   Emissary means **representative**.

10. It's a mistake to *rehash* that idea because you wrote about it twice before, and your teacher will see that it's just an old point in a new form.

    Rehash means **go over again**.

11. No wonder she refused to sell you her car; you offered such a *paltry* sum in payment.

    Paltry means **insignificant**.

12. The wind was *intense* — that is, strong and extreme — and we clung to the walls along the alleys so that we wouldn't be blown away.

    Intense means **strong and extreme**.

13. *Nomads* — people who wander in tribes from place to place according to the food supply — often travel in the deserts of Asia and Africa.

    Nomads means **wandering people**.

14. From the *hangdog* expression on his face, we knew that he had stolen the purse from the old woman.

    Hangdog means **unhappy; droopy**.

15. Charlene was an active, busy, and lively child. Maureen, on the other hand, was quite *passive.*

    Passive means **not given to action**.

16. In the heat of July, the family sat on the *veranda* out front every evening to enjoy the fresh air. Looking at the stars, I sat close to the screen and rocked back and forth on my chair.

Veranda means **front porch**.

17. Bats make *nocturnal* (nightly) searches for food and can travel long distances.

Nocturnal means **nightly**.

18. The *groom,* a thin, brown-haired girl from the next town, swept the stables and brushed the horses every night before she returned home.

Groom means **person who cares for horses**.

19. It was a horrible sight — with one powerful paw, the cat had *mauled* the sparrow, which lay bruised on the ground.

Mauled means **beaten up; injured badly**.

20. Kim Lee's mother gave in to her every demand, but her teacher refused to be so *overindulgent.*

Overindulgent means **too often giving in to a person's desires**.

21. He didn't want anyone to know that he wrote the letter; therefore, he used a *pseudonym.*

Pseudonym means **false name; alias**.

22. The hotel manager called his name many times over the microphone, but he never answered the *page.*

Page means **announced call**.

23. Bill didn't need his wool coat any longer, so he *donated* it to charity.

Donated means **gave**.

24. They started their law careers together. Kwan Lee's rise to success was *meteoric,* but her brother David's was slow and not particularly brilliant.

    Meteoric means **quick and brilliant** .

25. In the *infirmary,* Salvatore was treated for a serious stomach virus.

    Infirmary means **small hospital** .

7. Review

The selections below from textbooks include many words that you may not know. Look carefully at the words in italics and use what you learned in this chapter to figure out the meanings of whatever words you can. At the end of each selection, write definitions in your own words on the blank lines. Use a dictionary only when you cannot make an educated guess about the meaning.

1. *Life Science Text*

The Kidneys Get Rid of Urea

Respiration of sugar in your cells produces waste products. They are carbon dioxide and water. Water can be used by cells and is not really waste. Carbon dioxide, on the other hand, is useless to animals and must be removed from the body, or *excreted.* In Chapter 6 you will see that one function of your lungs is the excretion of carbon dioxide.

Cells can use nutrients other than sugar in respiration. When other nutrients are used, different waste products are formed. One of these waste products is *urea.* It results from use of protein in respiration. Urea is made in your liver cells, and from there enters the blood. If too much urea builds up in the blood, body cells will be poisoned.

To prevent this, urea must be removed by the body. The organs that do this make up the *excretory system.* . . .

Urea must get from where it is made to the excretory system. Blood carries urea from the liver to the kidneys. The *kidneys* are blood filters. They are located in the back above the waist. Blood enters and leaves the kidneys through blood vessels. The kidneys remove urea and some water from the blood and form *urine.* Urine passes through tubes called *ureters* to the *bladder.* Urine stored in the bladder eventually is excreted from the body through the *urethra.*

Each kidney is made up of about one million tiny filters. When blood coming into the kidney reaches the filters, many small molecules, including waste, water, and some food molecules, *diffuse* through the walls of the tiny blood vessels and enter the filters. Food molecules and much of the water in the filters later *re-enter* small blood vessels. If all these molecules entered the bladder, many important substances would be lost from the body. By the time the *fluid* reaches the ends of the filters and enters the ureter, water and urea are about all that remain and leave the body.

— Spaceship Earth: Life Science

1. respiration **a process by which a living thing combines nutrients with oxygen**

2. excreted **eliminated waste matter from the body**

3. urea **a powdery compound found in mammalian urine and other body fluids**

4. excretory system **organs that remove poisons from the body**

5. kidneys **body organs that filter blood**

6. urine **a substance secreted by the kidneys, stored in the bladder, and excreted from the ureters**

7. ureters **tubes that allow urine to pass to the bladder**

8. bladder **where urine is stored**

9. urethra **tube through which urine is excreted from the body**

10. diffuse **to pour out and cause to spread freely**

11. re-enter **to enter again**

12. fluid **a substance that flows easily**

2. *Earth Science Text*

A window pane *transmits* sunlight. It is nearly *transparent,* and much of the short-wave energy passes through. Only a little energy is *absorbed* to heat up the glass. However, the walls and furniture inside a room absorb a large part of the *solar* radiation coming through the window. The energy radiated from the furniture, unlike the original solar energy, is all long-wave *radiation*. Much of it is unable to pass out through the window pane. This is why the car seats get so hot on a hot, sunny day when all the windows are closed. Try putting a piece of glass in front of a hot object to see how the heat waves are cut off. A *greenhouse* traps energy in this way (when the sun shines) and so does the atmosphere.

— Investigating the Earth

1. transmits **lets through**
2. transparent **clear**
3. absorbed **soaked up**
4. solar **from the sun**
5. radiation **transmitted energy**
6. greenhouse **a building for growing plants**

2

Using a Dictionary

A dictionary is an important tool to help you build your reading skills. Here is what you can find in most dictionaries:

- the different meanings of a word
- how to spell a word
- whether or not a word is capitalized
- how to break down a word into syllables
- how to pronounce a word
- how a word fits into the English system of grammar (what part of speech it is: verb, noun, adjective, and so forth)
- how to spell a special plural or verb form of a word, or how to abbreviate a word
- a sentence or expression that uses a word correctly
- the meaning of important prefixes and suffixes
- the special usage of a word
- a word that means the same as a word that you look up (*synonym*)
- a word that means the opposite of a word that you look up (*antonym*)
- the history of a word
- words made from a main word

Look at a part of *The American Heritage Dictionary of the English Language* on the opposite page. The important features are labeled and explained for you.

2a The Guide Words

All the words in a dictionary are arranged in alphabetical order. Two words appear on top of each dictionary page. These guide words tell you what words to expect on that page. The guide word on the left tells you the first word on the page; the guide word on the right tells you the last word on the page.

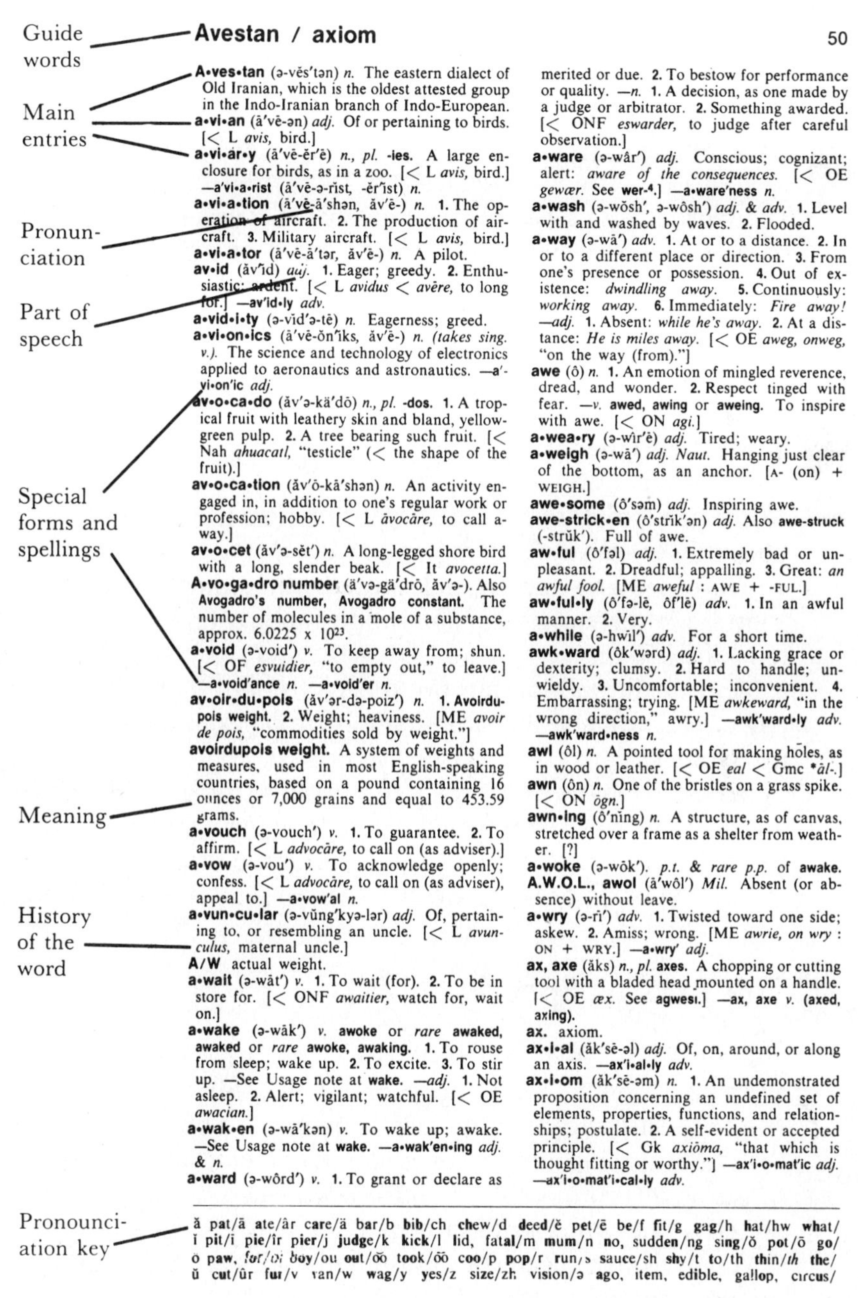

Avestan / axiom 50

A•ves•tan (ə-vĕs′tən) *n.* The eastern dialect of Old Iranian, which is the oldest attested group in the Indo-Iranian branch of Indo-European.
a•vi•an (ā′vē-ən) *adj.* Of or pertaining to birds. [< L *avis,* bird.]
a•vi•ar•y (ā′vē-ĕr′ē) *n., pl.* **-ies.** A large enclosure for birds, as in a zoo. [< L *avis,* bird.] —**a′vi•a•rist** (ā′vē-ə-rĭst, -ĕr′ĭst) *n.*
a•vi•a•tion (ā′vē-ā′shən, ăv′ē-) *n.* **1.** The operation of aircraft. **2.** The production of aircraft. **3.** Military aircraft. [< L *avis,* bird.]
a•vi•a•tor (ā′vē-ā′tər, ăv′ē-) *n.* A pilot.
av•id (ăv′ĭd) *adj.* **1.** Eager; greedy. **2.** Enthusiastic; ardent. [< L *avidus* < *avēre,* to long for.] —**av′id•ly** *adv.*
a•vid•i•ty (ə-vĭd′ə-tē) *n.* Eagerness; greed.
a•vi•on•ics (ā′vē-ŏn′ĭks, ăv′ē-) *n.* *(takes sing. v.).* The science and technology of electronics applied to aeronautics and astronautics. —**a′vi•on′ic** *adj.*
av•o•ca•do (ăv′ə-kä′dō) *n., pl.* **-dos.** **1.** A tropical fruit with leathery skin and bland, yellow-green pulp. **2.** A tree bearing such fruit. [< Nah *ahuacatl,* "testicle" (< the shape of the fruit).]
av•o•ca•tion (ăv′ō-kā′shən) *n.* An activity engaged in, in addition to one's regular work or profession; hobby. [< L *āvocāre,* to call away.]
av•o•cet (ăv′ə-sĕt′) *n.* A long-legged shore bird with a long, slender beak. [< It *avocetta.*]
A•vo•ga•dro number (ä′və-gä′drō, ăv′ə-). Also **Avogadro's number, Avogadro constant.** The number of molecules in a mole of a substance, approx. 6.0225 x 10^{23}.
a•void (ə-void′) *v.* To keep away from; shun. [< OF *esvuidier,* "to empty out," to leave.] —**a•void′ance** *n.* —**a•void′er** *n.*
av•oir•du•pois (ăv′ər-də-poiz′) *n.* **1. Avoirdupois weight. 2.** Weight; heaviness. [ME *avoir de pois,* "commodities sold by weight."]
avoirdupois weight. A system of weights and measures, used in most English-speaking countries, based on a pound containing 16 ounces or 7,000 grains and equal to 453.59 grams.
a•vouch (ə-vouch′) *v.* **1.** To guarantee. **2.** To affirm. [< L *advocāre,* to call on (as adviser).]
a•vow (ə-vou′) *v.* To acknowledge openly; confess. [< L *advocāre,* to call on (as adviser), appeal to.] —**a•vow′al** *n.*
a•vun•cu•lar (ə-vŭng′kyə-lər) *adj.* Of, pertaining to, or resembling an uncle. [< L *avunculus,* maternal uncle.]
A/W actual weight.
a•wait (ə-wāt′) *v.* **1.** To wait (for). **2.** To be in store for. [< ONF *awaitier,* watch for, wait on.]
a•wake (ə-wāk′) *v.* **awoke** or *rare* **awaked, awaked** or *rare* **awoke, awaking. 1.** To rouse from sleep; wake up. **2.** To excite. **3.** To stir up. —See Usage note at **wake.** —*adj.* **1.** Not asleep. **2.** Alert; vigilant; watchful. [< OE *awacian.*]
a•wak•en (ə-wā′kən) *v.* To wake up; awake. —See Usage note at **wake.** —**a•wak′en•ing** *adj.* & *n.*
a•ward (ə-wôrd′) *v.* **1.** To grant or declare as merited or due. **2.** To bestow for performance or quality. —*n.* **1.** A decision, as one made by a judge or arbitrator. **2.** Something awarded. [< ONF *eswarder,* to judge after careful observation.]
a•ware (ə-wâr′) *adj.* Conscious; cognizant; alert: *aware of the consequences.* [< OE *gewær.* See **wer-⁴.**] —**a•ware′ness** *n.*
a•wash (ə-wŏsh′, ə-wôsh′) *adj.* & *adv.* **1.** Level with and washed by waves. **2.** Flooded.
a•way (ə-wā′) *adv.* **1.** At or to a distance. **2.** In or to a different place or direction. **3.** From one's presence or possession. **4.** Out of existence: *dwindling away.* **5.** Continuously: *working away.* **6.** Immediately: *Fire away!* —*adj.* **1.** Absent: *while he's away.* **2.** At a distance: *He is miles away.* [< OE *aweg, onweg,* "on the way (from)."]
awe (ô) *n.* **1.** An emotion of mingled reverence, dread, and wonder. **2.** Respect tinged with fear. —*v.* **awed, awing** or **aweing.** To inspire with awe. [< ON *agi.*]
a•wea•ry (ə-wîr′ē) *adj.* Tired; weary.
a•weigh (ə-wā′) *adj. Naut.* Hanging just clear of the bottom, as an anchor. [A- (on) + WEIGH.]
awe•some (ô′səm) *adj.* Inspiring awe.
awe-strick•en (ô′strĭk′ən) *adj.* Also **awe-struck** (-strŭk′). Full of awe.
aw•ful (ô′fəl) *adj.* **1.** Extremely bad or unpleasant. **2.** Dreadful; appalling. **3.** Great: *an awful fool.* [ME *aweful* : AWE + -FUL.]
aw•ful•ly (ô′fə-lē, ôf′lē) *adv.* **1.** In an awful manner. **2.** Very.
a•while (ə-hwīl′) *adv.* For a short time.
awk•ward (ôk′wərd) *adj.* **1.** Lacking grace or dexterity; clumsy. **2.** Hard to handle; unwieldy. **3.** Uncomfortable; inconvenient. **4.** Embarrassing; trying. [ME *awkeward,* "in the wrong direction," awry.] —**awk′ward•ly** *adv.* —**awk′ward•ness** *n.*
awl (ôl) *n.* A pointed tool for making holes, as in wood or leather. [< OE *eal* < Gmc **ǣl-.*]
awn (ôn) *n.* One of the bristles on a grass spike. [< ON *ǫgn.*]
awn•ing (ô′nĭng) *n.* A structure, as of canvas, stretched over a frame as a shelter from weather. [?]
a•woke (ə-wōk′). *p.t.* & *rare p.p.* of **awake.**
A.W.O.L., awol (ā′wôl′) *Mil.* Absent (or absence) without leave.
a•wry (ə-rī′) *adv.* **1.** Twisted toward one side; askew. **2.** Amiss; wrong. [ME *awrie, on wry* : ON + WRY.] —**a•wry′** *adj.*
ax, axe (ăks) *n., pl.* **axes.** A chopping or cutting tool with a bladed head mounted on a handle. [< OE *æx.* See **agwesı.**] —**ax, axe** *v.* **(axed, axing).**
ax. axiom.
ax•i•al (ăk′sē-əl) *adj.* Of, on, around, or along an axis. —**ax′i•al•ly** *adv.*
ax•i•om (ăk′sē-əm) *n.* **1.** An undemonstrated proposition concerning an undefined set of elements, properties, functions, and relationships; postulate. **2.** A self-evident or accepted principle. [< Gk *axiōma,* "that which is thought fitting or worthy."] —**ax′i•o•mat′ic** *adj.* —**ax′i•o•mat′i•cal•ly** *adv.*

ă pat/ā ate/âr care/ä bar/b bib/ch chew/d deed/ĕ pet/ē be/f fit/g gag/h hat/hw what/ ĭ pit/ī pie/îr pier/j judge/k kick/l lid, fatal/m mum/n no, sudden/ng sing/ŏ pot/ō go/ ô paw, for/oi boy/ou out/ŏŏ took/ōō coo/p pop/r run/s sauce/sh shy/t to/th thin/*th* the/ ŭ cut/ûr fur/v van/w wag/y yes/z size/zh vision/ə ago, item, edible, gallop, circus/

If you wanted to look up *ax*, for example, on the sample dictionary page, the left guide word *Avestan* is a hint that your word is here, since *ax* comes after *av*. The right guide word is *axiom*: since *ax* comes before *axi*, you know that your word must appear between these two guide words.

2b The Main Entry

The word itself first appears in heavy black letters. (This kind of type is called *boldface type*.) In the main entry, periods show where to put a hyphen in case you have to break the word at the end of a line of writing. The main entry gives the correct spelling.

2c The Pronunciation Key

These groups of letters (coming right after the main entry) tell you how to say the word.

Letters stand for special sounds. In order to know what sound a letter makes, check the pronunciation key at the bottom of the page.

Check the key at the bottom of the entry on the sample page. You will see that the first *a* in *aviary* sounds like the *a* in the word *ate*.

You also learn from the accent marks that go with the pronouncing letters just which syllable to stress when you say the word. In *a've-er'e*, the heavy mark ' after the first *a* tells you that the first syllable gets the most stress when you say the word.

2d The Parts of Speech

This tells you how the word works in the system of English grammar. The *n.* after the pronouncing letters of *ax* means "noun." *Adj.* after *axial* means "adjective." Sometimes a word has different meanings based on what part of speech it is. *Awake* as a verb means "to rouse from sleep; wake up." As an adjective the word *awake* means "not asleep." (See **1e**.)

You're not expected to know what all the abbreviations or symbols mean (*n., adv., adj.*). Just check the special section in the front or the back of your dictionary whenever you need help.

2e Special Forms and Special Spellings

The word *axiomatic* is made from the word *axiom*. Therefore, *axiomatic* is included as part of the entry for *axiom* instead of as a main entry itself. Because not everyone knows that the plural of *aviary* is *aviaries*, a dictionary will show that word, too. Only specially formed plurals appear.

2f The Meanings of the Word

Meanings of words are numbered in boldface print. Because words often have more than one meaning, many meanings can appear. Numbers help separate them. Usually the most important definitions come first. If you see *syn.*, that is an abbreviation for *synonym*; the words that follow *syn.* are words that mean the same as the main word. Sometimes you will find *antonyms* (words opposite in meaning) for the word. The abbreviation *ant.* will tell you which words are antonyms. An example sometimes appears to show how the word is used.

2g The History of the Word

The information that appears in brackets tells the way that a word has developed in our language. Many words have origins in foreign languages such as Latin (*L*) or Greek (*G*).

Before you do the exercises below, review the chart "Some Dictionary Pointers" on page 56.

EXERCISES

1. Order of the Alphabet

Put the words in this list in correct alphabetical order. Rewrite them on the blank lines.

1. cauliflower caucus
2. cave caught

3. caught **cauliflower**

4. caucus **caution**

5. cavern **cave**

6. caution **cavern**

Some Dictionary Pointers

- Review your skill with alphabetical order. Can you arrange words correctly?
- Use the guide words. They save you time.
- Check all abbreviations and symbols in the special section.
- If you look up a word and it's not where you expect it to be, don't think it's not in your dictionary! Check under several possible spellings. If you couldn't spell the word *crime*, for example, the sound of the word might suggest these spellings:

  cryme krime
  kryme krhyme
  criem crhyme

  If you couldn't spell the word, you might have to check all the spellings before you found *crime*!
- Test the *meaning* that you find for the word in the sentence in which the word appears. You may not have picked a definition that works for the word as you want to use it.
- Try to say the word aloud after you look at the pronunciation key.

2. Guide Words

If the guide words on top of a dictionary page are *single* and *skeleton*, circle the words you would expect to find on that page. Put an X before any words that would not appear on the page.

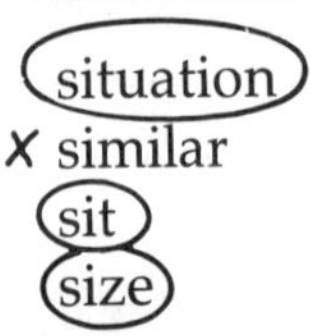

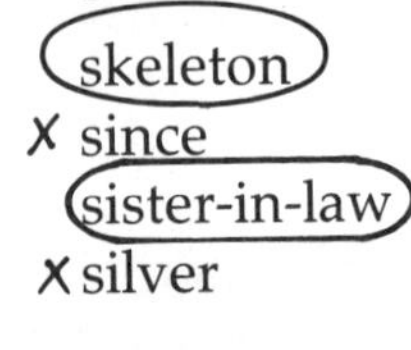

3. Guide Words

Under each numbered pair of guide words appear several other words. Circle each word that you would expect to find on a page that shows the guide words.

1. **discomfit / discredit**

discourage (circled) — discrete — discover (circled)
disclose — discount (circled)

2. **shirring / shoot**

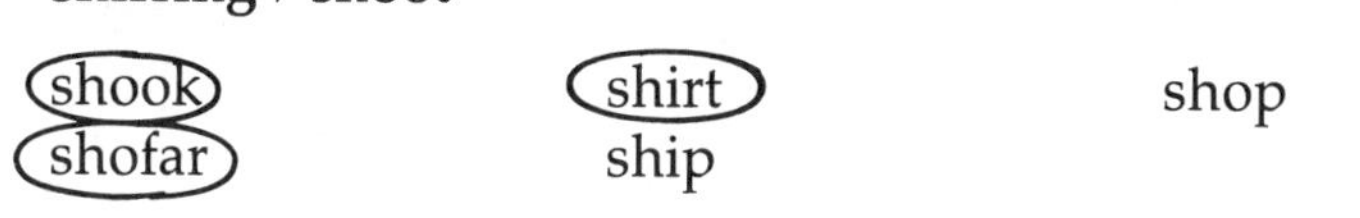

shook (circled) — shirt (circled) — shop
shofar (circled) — ship

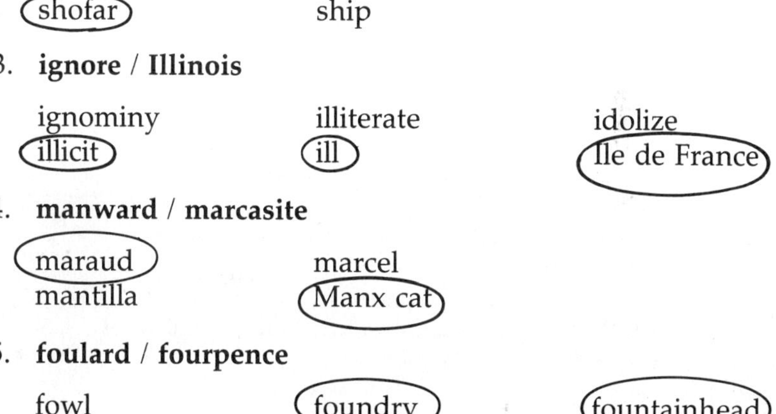

3. **ignore / Illinois**

ignominy — illiterate — idolize
illicit (circled) — ill (circled) — Île de France (circled)

4. **manward / marcasite**

maraud (circled) — marcel
mantilla — Manx cat (circled)

5. **foulard / fourpence**

fowl — foundry (circled) — fountainhead (circled)
fraction — fourpenny

4. One Word, Several Meanings

Each word that follows has several different meanings. Look up each word in a dictionary and write at least two different definitions. After each definition, write a sentence that uses the word correctly. **Student responses will vary.**

Example: **book**

a. *Definition*: a written work for reading
Sentence: I read the *book* titled *Sissy* by John Williams.

b. *Definition*: to engage a performer for a show
Sentence: David Merrick *booked* a Russian dance group for a U.S. tour.

1. bead **a. a small ball-shaped piece of material pierced for stringing or threading**

b. a small drop of moisture

2. lead **a. to show the way**

b. material used in containers and pipes

3. break **a. to crack or split**

b. a special chance or opportunity

4. baby **a. an infant**

b. to treat like an infant

5. flip **a. to turn over quickly**

b. insolent; rude

5. Pronunciation

Use your dictionary to check the correct way to pronounce each word.

1. February **Fĕb-roo-er′-ē**
2. ask **ăsk**

3. nuclear **no͞o-klē-ər (or nyo͞o′-)**

4. indict **ĭn-dīt′**

5. athlete **ăth′-lēt′**

6. Practice in Dictionary Skills

Using the sample from a dictionary on page 53, answer each question.

1. What is the plural of *aviary*? **aviaries**

2. What is the origin of the word *avouch*? **from the Latin *advocare***

3. Which three words or abbreviations are written with a capital letter? **Avestan, Avogadro number, A/W**

4. Circle the words whose *a* sound is the same as the *a* sound in *pat*: *avid, avoid, axiom, avocado, avow*

5. What is an aviary? **an enclosure for birds**

6. What part of the world does the dialect *Avestan* come from? **Iran**

7. Where would you find more information about using the word *awaken* correctly? **at *wake***

8. Write the plural of *avocado*. **avocados**

9. What do you think *aviarist* means? It appears under the word *aviary*. However, *aviarist* is not defined. Why not? **one who works in an aviary; knowing suffix *ist* helps us determine meaning on our own**

10. The symbol ə is a *schwa*. A schwa stands for a vowel sound in a syllable that is not accented. Find three words in which schwas are used to show pronunciation.

avocation, awake, avow, avouch, avuncular, and

others

7. Review

Using a good dictionary, find the answer to each question.

1. What is the plural of *elf*? **elves**

2. What parts of speech may the word *toy* be? **noun, verb,**

   adjective

3. What language does the word *burro* come from? **Spanish**

4. What do the following words mean?

   a. framework **a structure for supporting or enclosing**

      something

   b. timed **regulated**

   c. crucial **of supreme importance**

   d. berth **a built-in bed or bunk on a ship or train**

   e. irrational **without reason**

5. Write a synonym (a word that has the same meaning) and an antonym (a word *opposite* in meaning) for each of the following:

	Synonym	*Antonym*
a. gentle	**kind**	**harsh**
b. thrive	**prosper**	**decline**
c. expose	**show**	**hide**
d. mistrust	**doubt**	**trust**
e. encode	**put into symbols**	**decode**

Unit Two

Using Aids to Reading

3

Previewing the Parts of a Book

Even before you begin reading a book, you can learn about its subject by previewing. *Previewing* — viewing in advance — means looking ahead and checking for information. Thus, you can get a general idea of a work before you actually read it. Knowing about a book in advance helps you understand a little about its content and about its special features. Before reading your textbooks in biology, math, and business courses, for example, look them over carefully.

Here are some useful steps to help you preview a book:

- *Look at the title of the book.* A history book called *America: The Glorious Republic* will be much different from a history book called *Urban America: A History*. A title can tell you a great deal about a book. Before you read, take time to think about what the book title means.
- *Look at the table of contents.* The table of contents appears at the front of the book. The table of contents is a list of the names of the chapters and the pages on which they begin. Sometimes you also find subheadings listed under the chapter. If the book is divided into parts, that information also appears in the table of contents. Study the names of the chapters and subheadings. You can get an idea of what each section of the book deals with and how the topics relate to each other.
- *Look at the preface.* Coming before the table of contents, the preface is a brief essay in which an author gives reasons for writing the book. Not every book has a preface. Authors who write them are giving a personal message to the reader. In the preface you get an idea of:

1. the kind of reader the author is writing for
2. the aims of the book

3. what the author expects you to learn as a result of reading it
4. the topics in the book and the best approaches to those topics

- *Look briefly at the index.* An index appears at the end of the book. An index is an alphabetical listing of the topics, subjects, ideas, and names mentioned in the book. A quick look at the index will tell you the main points in the book.
- *Look at these special features that sometimes appear in books:*

1. After the chapters in a book a writer sometimes provides a *glossary*. A glossary is a list of difficult words or terms that appear in the book. The words are listed in alphabetical order with their definitions.
2. An *appendix* (plural is *appendixes* or *appendices*) at the end of the book adds information to the book. However, the book is complete without the appendix, and the information that you find there is extra. An appendix may include charts and graphs, special letters or documents, or facts about the lives of the people mentioned in the book. It may give information to explain something that the author felt needed more attention. A look at the appendix, if the book has one, will indicate how a writer deals with special issues.

- *Read the introduction.* Often the first chapter of the book is the introduction. The introduction states the basic idea, issue, or problem that the author will deal with. It gives background information about or discusses the history of the topic. It may summarize what others have said about the subject. It may even explain research that the author did. Sometimes someone other than the author writes the introduction. Such an introduction often explains the book to the readers, pointing out key ideas worth noting.
- *Look at the bibliography.* At the back of the book, an author sometimes gives a bibliography or a list of works cited. A bibliography is a list, in alphabetical order, of some or all of the sources (such as books and magazine articles) that the author used to write his or her book. The list of works cited gives full publishing information about all sources referred to directly in the book.

EXERCISES

1. A Table of Contents

Look at the brief table of contents that appears on page 66 from a book called *Business*. Figure out as much information as you can about the book. Then answer each question.

1. Which chapters would give you information about human relations in business? **Chapters 7, 8, 9**

2. In which part of the book would you expect to find information about how to promote a product? **Part 4**

3. In which chapter would you look for information about the different kinds of business ownerships? **Chapter 3**

4. Which chapter would give you information about how to do business in another country? **Chapter 23**

5. What specific information would you expect to find in Chapter 22? **how government controls and helps businesses**

2. A Table of Contents

The table of contents from a book called *Spaceship Earth: Earth Science* appears on pages 69–72. From this table of contents figure out as much information as you can about the book. Then answer each question.

TABLE OF CONTENTS

1. What would you expect to learn from Chapter 2?
how we find out about galaxies and what we know about them

2. What are the five main units of the book? **Earth in the Universe; Earth's Air and Water; Earth's Crust; The Changing Crust; Earth's History**

3. From which unit would you learn about the history of the earth's development? **Unit 5**

4. In which chapter would you learn about weather?
Chapter 9

5. Which chapter explains about the motion of air and water?
Chapter 8

6. Where in the book could you find some of the qualities of the different planets in our solar system? **Chapter 4**

7. Which chapter would you have to read to find out about the relation between humans and their environment?
Chapter 20

8. Where would you find information about the metric system of measurement? about the planets' features? about volcanos that are extinct, that is, no longer active?
Appendix A; Appendix K; Appendix Q

9. On which page would you learn about Florence van Straten? **page 203**

10. What do you think you would learn from the chapter called "Deposition" (Chapter 15)? **how the earth's elements affect the sea; sediments**

3. An Index

Look at the excerpt (short piece from a longer work) from an index on page 73. Then answer each question.

b 1. This is probably a book about
   a. astronomy.
   b. American history.
   c. Russian history.
   d. the state of Alabama.

c 2. If you see the letter *c* before a page number, it means
   a. caves.
   b. canyons.
   c. charts.
   d. Confederacy.

3. On what pages would you find
   a. information about the Alien Acts? **191–192, 193**
   b. information about Susan B. Anthony? **533**
   c. facts about Vietnam War airplanes? **742, 743, 744, 749, 756, 757**
   d. maps of the city of Albany? **86, 106, 139, 293, 297**
   e. a picture of Abigail Adams? **189**

CONTENTS

Unit Four The Changing Crust

Unit Five Earth's History

Index

This index includes references not only to the text but to pictures (p), charts (c), graphs (g) and maps (m) as well. Page numbers that are marked n. refer to footnotes.

— *Henry F. Graff*

4. A Preface

Read the preface from a book edited by Ruth Graves about a program for encouraging young readers at home (page 75). Think about what makes the book special. Then answer each question.

1. What is RIF? What is its purpose? **RIF is an organization that encourages children to read.**

2. How many people volunteer their time to RIF? How many of these people are parents? **100,000 people volunteer; about 40,000 of them are parents.**

3. What are some of the settings in which RIF works? **RIF works in schools, libraries, parks, community centers, and homes.**

4. How was the *RIF Guide* developed? **The *RIF Guide* was developed through the help of parents and others.**

5. About how long has RIF been in use? **RIF has been in existence since 1966.**

5. The Parts of a Book

Select one of your textbooks or a book from the library. Locate the parts of the book in the following list. In your own words,

Preface

For more than twenty years, Reading Is Fundamental (RIF) has brought books and children together all across the country, in all kinds of settings. Whether in schools, libraries, parks, or community centers, children are reading because RIF has shown them how much fun reading can be. With this guide, RIF can now encourage young readers *in the home* — where their love for reading is first nurtured, and where parents can have such lasting influence.

Since 1966, when the organization was founded by Margaret McNamara, RIF and its board of directors have had a strong commitment to parents and their role in encouraging their children to read. Parents have responded many times over with their own commitment to RIF and children's reading. Today, of the nearly 100,000 people volunteering their time to RIF, some 40 percent are parents. In all fifty states, the District of Columbia, and the offshore territories, parents are working with RIF to encourage young people to read and to aspire through reading.

The RIF Guide was made possible by the creative contributions of parents and the many others who work with us. We are delighted that their ideas, which have worked so well for them, can now be shared with a wider audience. We invite you to use the guide in the same spirit in which it was created — a spirit of fun.

Mrs. Elliot Richardson
Chairman of the Board

write what you can find out about the book from each part. If the book does not have one of the parts, put an *X* on the blank line.

1. title and author **Student responses will vary.**

2. table of contents

3. preface

4. introduction or first chapter

5. glossary

6. bibliography

7. index ______________________________

____

____

8. appendix ______________________________

____

____

4

Previewing Individual Selections

Previewing a reading selection, such as a chapter or an essay, before you read it can give you important advance information. Like previewing longer works **(3)**, previewing a reading selection prepares you for the material and helps you get your mind ready to receive new facts, ideas, and opinions.

Here is how to preview a reading selection:

- *Look at the title.* Titles often give the main idea of the selection. Does the title tell what you will be reading about? If so, you can then set a purpose for your reading.
- *Look for subtitles or headings.* Essays, newspaper articles, and other longer readings sometimes print subtitles or headings. Appearing below titles in boldface print or in italics, subtitles suggest the kind of information that you will find in a portion of the reading.
- *Look at lists of goals or objectives.* Sometimes a selection gives a list of goals for a chapter. Here, the writer tells you what you should get out of the chapter. Check the goals before you read so that you'll know what to read for.
- *Look at the pictures, charts, or drawings.* Often an illustration helps you figure out in advance what your reading will deal with.
- *Look at the first sentence of each paragraph.* This gives you a quick idea of what the reading involves before you begin to read carefully.
- *Look at the first paragraph.* The first paragraph usually tells just what the reading will be about. Read it, and then try to say in your own words what you think that you will be reading about.
- *Look at any questions that appear after the reading.* If you look at the questions *before* you read anything, you will then have an

idea of what's important. Questions tell you what to expect from a passage. When you know the questions in advance, you know what kind of information to look for.

- *Look for key words in different print.* Sometimes boldface letters, italics, or even colored ink will call your attention to important words or ideas. Titles of books, for example, appear in italics. Noting these in advance can give you important information.
- *Look for a summary.* At the end of a piece, a writer sometimes summarizes the main points. Look at the summary before you read a selection. The summary can help you see more clearly what the selection deals with.

EXERCISES

1. A Magazine Selection

The selection on pages 80–83 appeared as an advertisement in many national magazines. Before you read the selection, preview it by answering each question.

1. Read the title. What does it tell you about the selection's contents?

   The title explains that the selection will give advice on increasing your reading speed.

2. Read the main headings. How do the headings help you understand main points from the selection?

   The headings give the main methods for improving reading speed.

3. Look at the words in circles. How do they help you understand both *skimming* and *clustering?*

   The circles illustrate the method visually.

4. Look at the words in italics. What are two of the ways italics are used in this selection?

   Italics are used to show book titles (such as *War and Peace*) and to emphasize important information.

5. Look at the last paragraph. What does it tell you the selection will deal with?

   The last paragraph tells you the selection deals with ways to read more in less time, whether comic books or difficult novels.

How to Read Faster

When I was a kid in Philadelphia, I must have read every comic book ever published. (There were fewer of them then than there are now.)

I zipped through all of them in a couple of days, then reread the good ones until the next issues arrived.

Yes indeed, when I was a kid, the reading game was a snap.

But as I got older, my eyeballs must have slowed down or something! I mean, comic books started to pile up faster than my brother Russell and I could read them!

It wasn't until much later, when I was getting my doctorate, I realized it wasn't my eyeballs that were to blame. Thank goodness. They're still moving as well as ever.

The problem is, there's too much to read these days, and too little time to read every word of it.

Now, mind you, I still read comic books. In addition to contracts, novels, and newspapers. Screenplays, tax returns and correspondence. Even textbooks about how people read. And which techniques help people read more in less time.

I'll let you in on a little secret. There are hundreds of techniques you could learn to help you read faster. But I know of 3 that are especially good.

And if I can learn them, so can you — and you can put them to use *immediately.*

They are commonsense, practical ways to get the meaning

from printed words quickly and efficiently. So you'll have time to enjoy your comic books, have a good laugh with Mark Twain or a good cry with *War and Peace.* Ready?

Okay. The first two ways can help you get through tons of reading material — fast — *without reading every word.*

They'll give you the *overall meaning* of what you're reading. And let you cut out an awful lot of *unnecessary* reading.

1. Preview — If It's Long and Hard

Previewing is especially useful for getting a general idea of heavy reading like long magazine or newspaper articles, business reports, and nonfiction books.

It can give you as much as half the comprehension in as little as one tenth the time. For example, you should be able to preview eight or ten 100-page reports in an hour. After previewing, you'll be able to decide which reports (or which *parts* of which reports) are worth a closer look.

Here's how to preview: Read the entire first two paragraphs of whatever you've chosen. Next read only the *first sentence* of each successive paragraph. Then read the entire last two paragraphs.

Previewing doesn't give you all the details. But it does keep you from spending time on things you don't really want — or need — to read.

Notice that previewing gives you a quick, overall view of *long, unfamiliar* material. For short, light reading, there's a better technique.

2. Skim — If It's Short and Simple

Skimming is a good way to get a general idea of light reading — like popular magazines or the sports and entertainment sections of the paper.

You should be able to skim a weekly popular magazine or the second section of your daily paper in less than *half* the time it takes you to read it now.

Skimming is also a great way to review material you've read before.

Here's how to skim: Think of your eyes as magnets. Force them to move fast. Sweep them across each and every line of type. Pick up *only a few key words in each line.*

Everybody skims differently.

You and I may not pick up exactly the same words when we skim the same piece, but we'll both get a pretty similar idea of what it's all about.

To show you how it works, I circled the words I picked out

when I skimmed the following story. Try it. It shouldn't take you more than 10 seconds.

My brother Russell thinks monsters live in our bedroom closet at night. But I told him he is crazy.

"Go and check then," he said.

I didn't want to. Russell said I was chicken.

"Am not," I said.

"Are so," he said.

So I told him the monsters were going to eat him at midnight. He started to cry. My Dad came in and told the monsters to beat it. Then he told us to go to sleep.

"If I hear any more about monsters," he said, "I'll spank you."

We went to sleep fast. And you know something? They never did come back.

Skimming can give you a very good *idea* of this story in about half the words — and in *less* than half the time it'd take to read every word.

So far, you've seen that previewing and skimming can give you a *general idea* about content — fast. But neither technique can promise more than 50 percent comprehension, because you aren't reading all the words. (Nobody gets something for nothing in the reading game.)

To *read faster and understand most* — if not all — of what you read, you need to know a third technique.

3. Cluster — To Increase Speed and Comprehension

Most of us learned to read by looking at each word in a sentence — *one at a time.*

Like this:

My — brother — Russell — thinks — monsters . . .

You probably still read this way sometimes, especially when the words are difficult. Or when the words have an extra-special meaning — as in a poem, a Shakespearean play, or a contract. And that's O.K.

But word-by-word reading is a rotten way to read faster. It actually *cuts down* on your speed.

Clustering trains you to look at *groups* of words instead of one at a time — to increase your speed enormously. For most of us, clustering is a *totally different way of seeing what we read.*

Here's how to cluster: Train your eyes to see *all* the words in clusters of up to 3 or 4 words at a glance.

Here's how I'd cluster the story we just skimmed:

My brother Russell thinks monsters live in our bedroom closet at night. But I told him he is crazy.

"Go and check then," he said.

I didn't want to. Russell said I was chicken.

"Am not," I said.

"Are so," he said.

So I told him the monsters were going to eat him at midnight. He started to cry. My Dad came in and told the monsters to beat it. Then he told us to go to sleep.

"If I hear any more about monsters," he said, "I'll spank you."

We went to sleep fast. And you know something? They never did come back.

Learning to read clusters is not something your eyes do naturally. It takes constant practice.

Here's how to go about it: Pick something light to read. Read it as fast as you can. Concentrate on seeing 3 to 4 words at once rather than one word at a time. Then reread the piece at your normal speed to see what you missed the first time.

Try a second piece. First cluster, then reread to see what you missed in this one.

When you can read in clusters without missing much the first time, your speed has increased. Practice 15 minutes every day and you might pick up the technique in a week or so. (But don't be disappointed if it takes longer. Clustering *everything* takes time and practice.)

So now you have 3 ways to help you read faster. Preview to cut down on unnecessary heavy reading. Skim to get a quick, general idea of light reading. And cluster to increase your speed and comprehension.

With enough practice, you'll be able to handle *more* reading at school or work — and at home — *in less time.* You should even have enough time to read your favorite comic books — and *War and Peace!*

— *Bill Cosby*

2. A Chapter Excerpt

Use previewing to learn about this chapter excerpt from a college textbook called *Marketing* (Sixth Edition). Follow the directions and answer each question *before* you read.

1. Read the title of Chapter 1. What will the article be about?

strategic marketing

2. What are the chapter objectives? Why have the authors given them on the first page? **to learn the definition of marketing; to understand why you should study it; to begin to understand the marketing concept and marketing strategy; to gain an overview of marketing issues; the objectives are presented so the reader will know what to get from reading the chapter**

3. Look at the illustration. How does it relate to the chapter? **It shows how products are advertised as part of the marketing.**

4. Read the main heading on page 85 and the various boldface subheadings. What do they tell you about the chapter? **They single out the main points of the chapter.**

5. Look at Figure 1.2 and the label in the left margin. What does the figure explain? **The figure illustrates how buyers give the seller goods, services, or ideas in return for money, credit, labor, or goods.**

1. An Overview of Strategic Marketing

Objectives

- To learn representative definitions of marketing, and to understand the definition of marketing used in this text.
- To understand why a person should study marketing.
- To gain insight into the basic elements of the marketing concept and its implementation.
- To understand the major components of a marketing strategy.
- To acquire an overview of general strategic marketing issues such as market opportunity analysis, target market selection, and marketing mix development.

Stouffer Food Corp., a producer of prepared frozen foods, several years ago conducted research that showed that purchases by larger families (those with two or more children) made up a significant portion of company sales. In response to these findings, Stouffer developed the Family Casserole line and marketed it in packages containing servings for four or more people. The line flopped because Stouffer's research failed to detect "split-menu dining" — a growing trend among larger, more active families. Such families are not always able to eat together, and even when they do, family members do not necessarily eat the same thing. Thus consumers buying Stouffer products tend to purchase smaller packages, suitable for one- or two-person servings. The failure of the Family Casserole line alerted Stouffer to the split-menu trend. "The fragmentation of eating has become much more normal than random," says Linda Smithson, director of Pillsbury Co.'s consumer center. All food manufacturers are concerned about the decline and projected ultimate death of the family meal. New products are being continually developed to appeal to diverse eating habits.

In contrast, Stouffer's Lean Cuisine line has been a success (see Figure 1.1). Stouffer's research indicated that women, smaller families, and single-person households would purchase the dinners. Stouffer found that working women wanted to watch their weight and to serve their families nourishing meals with minimal preparation. Stouffer's failure and success illustrate the necessity of both research into and accurate assessment of buyers' needs.

Although Stouffer's Family Casserole line failed, two Brenham, Texas, women have taken advantage of the same

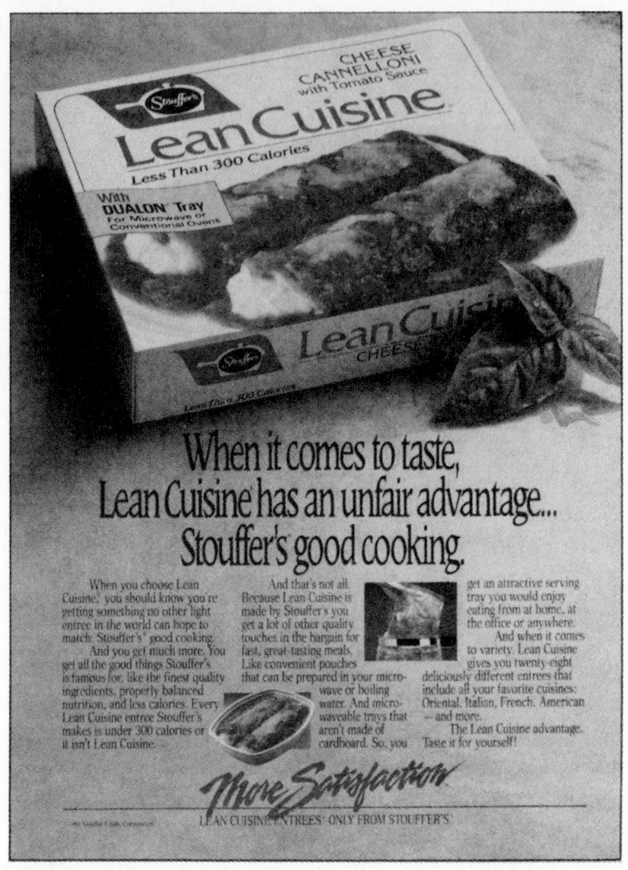

FIGURE 1.1 Stouffer's successful Lean Cuisine line targets the single-family household (SOURCE: Stouffer Food Corporation)

market niche to sell their family sized frozen casseroles. As Stouffer did, Virginia and Barbara Gaskamp recognized that more women are working outside the home and do not have the time to prepare nutritious meals. These working women, as well as couples who both work but have no children (known as dinks — double income, no kids), are willing to purchase large-sized, easy-to-prepare nutritious meals. The Gaskamps' Market Place Casseroles come in one- or two-pound sizes packaged in an aluminum tray, and they are priced competitively. The company recently changed its packaging so consumers are able to microwave the casseroles, making them more convenient.

In 1986, Market Place Casseroles sold $90,000 worth of the frozen casseroles. In 1987, sales were $185,000, and 1988 sales were expected to be double those of 1987. The casseroles have been so successful thus far because they are home-cooked with high-quality ingredients, and they are promoted on that basis. These dinners specifically meet the needs of the target market: working women in both large and small active families who simply do not have time to prepare nutritious meals. The company is small enough that it can take advantage of small niches in the market that are not profitable for a larger company such as Stouffer. The company also profits from the Gaskamps' local reputation for good, home-cooked food.

We can thus see that significant changes in the overall population can have a decisive impact on the success of a product. Marketers engage in research both to analyze and anticipate such changes, but important trends in consumer behavior may be overlooked, causing product failure, as is what happened with Stouffer's Family Casseroles. Also, a smaller company can sometimes more efficiently use its resources and knowledge of a market than a larger company to meet the needs of a specific group within a large target market.[1]

This first chapter is an overview of the marketing concepts and decisions covered in the text. Initially, we develop a definition of marketing and explain each element of the definition. Then we look at several reasons why people should study marketing and point out that marketing activities pervade our everyday lives. We introduce the marketing concept and consider several issues associated with implementing it. Next we discuss the major tasks of strategic marketing management: market opportunity analysis, target market selection, marketing mix development, and management of marketing activities. We conclude our overview by discussing the organization of this text.

Marketing Defined

If you ask several people what *marketing* is, they will respond with a variety of descriptions. Marketing encompasses many more activities than most people think. Remember, though,

[1]Based on information from Betsy Morris, "Are Square Meals Headed for Extinction?" *Wall Street Journal,* March 15, 1988, Section 2, p. 1; Ann Lloyd, "The Lean Cuisine Story," *American Demographics,* December 1984, p. 16; a marketing study on Stouffer's Lean Cuisine prepared by Jimmy Ashley, Jewel Hervey, Jim Paquin, Mike Quinnelly, Karen Reyes, and Lance Scott, Texas A&M, 1987; a marketing study on Market Place Casseroles prepared by Gerhard Baumann, Jill Hubred, Alan Blankley, and Chris Smith, Texas A&M, 1987.

that any definition is merely an abstract description of a broad concept. No definition perfectly describes the concept to which it refers. Marketing is practiced and studied for many different purposes and so has been, and continues to be, defined in many ways, whether for academic, research, or applied business purposes. Following are three such definitions:

1. Marketing is the process of planning and executing the conception, pricing, promotion, and distribution of ideas, goods, and services to create exchanges that satisfy individual and organizational objectives.[2]
2. Micro-marketing is the performance of activities that seek to accomplish an organization's objectives by anticipating customer or client needs and directing a flow of need satisfying goods and services from producer to customer or client.[3]
3. Marketing is the set of individual and social activities concerned with the initiation, resolution, and/or acceptance of exchange relationships.[4]

All these definitions contribute something to our development of a definition of marketing. One study found that the first definition, which was developed by the American Marketing Association, has been widely accepted by academics and marketing managers. This same study found that academics view exchange as the most important concept in a marketing definition, whereas managers view customer satisfaction as the most important concept in a definition.[5]

The second definition emphasizes that marketing focuses on activities to satisfy customers. The third definition focuses on marketing as activities that initiate or resolve exchange relationships. Although earlier definitions restricted marketing as a business activity, these definitions are broad enough to indicate that marketing also occurs in nonbusiness situations as practiced by nonbusiness organizations.

We agree with many aspects of these three definitions, but we believe that our slightly broader definition encompasses

[2] "AMA Board Approves New Marketing Definition," *Marketing News*, Mar. 1, 1985, p. 1.
[3] Jerome McCarthy and William Perreault, Jr., *Basic Marketing: A Managerial Approach* (Homewood, IL: Irwin, 1987), p. 8.
[4] Richard P. Bagozzi, *Principles of Marketing Management* (Chicago: Science Research Associates, 1986), p. 5.
[5] O. C. Ferrell and George Lucas, "An Evaluation of Progress in the Development of a Definition of Marketing," *Journal of the Academy of Marketing Science*, Fall 1987, p. 17.

the best features of these definitions plus one additional dimension: marketing activities occur in a dynamic environment. That environment determines what types of activities will develop effective exchanges. We will describe in detail our definition of marketing:

Marketing consists of individual and organizational activities that facilitate and expedite satisfying exchange relationships in a dynamic environment through the creation, distribution, promotion, and pricing of goods, services, and ideas.

In this definition, marketing is viewed as a diverse group of activities directed at various products and performed within many types of organizations. In marketing exchanges, any product may be involved. We assume only that individuals and organizations expect to gain a reward in excess of the costs incurred. So that our definition will be fully understood, we now examine each component more closely.

Marketing Consists of Activities Numerous activities are required to market products effectively. Some activities can be performed by producers. Some can be accomplished by intermediaries, who buy from producers or other intermediaries so that they can resell the products. And some activities may even be performed by purchasers. Marketing does not include all human and organizational activities; it encompasses only those activities aimed at facilitating and expediting exchanges. Table 1.1 lists several major categories and examples of marketing activities. Note that this list is not all-inclusive; each activity could be subdivided into numerous, more specific activities.

Marketing Is Performed by Individuals and Organizations Marketing pervades many relationships among individuals, groups, and organizations. All types of organizations perform marketing activities to facilitate exchanges. Businesses as well as nonbusiness organizations such as colleges and universities, charitable organizations, and community theaters and hospitals perform marketing activities. For example, colleges and universities and their students engage in exchanges. To receive knowledge, entertainment, room, board, and a degree, students give up time, money, effort, perhaps services in the form of labor, and opportunities to do other things. In return, the institutions provide instruction, food, medical services, entertainment, recreation, and the

TABLE 1.1 Possible Decisions and Activities Associated with Marketing Mix Variables

MARKETING MIX VARIABLES	POSSIBLE DECISIONS AND ACTIVITIES
PRODUCT	Develop and test-market new products; modify existing products; eliminate products that do not satisfy customers' desires; formulate brand names and branding policies; create product warranties and establish procedures for fulfilling warranties; plan packages, including materials, sizes, shapes, colors, and designs
DISTRIBUTION	Analyze various types of distribution channels; design appropriate distribution channels; design an effective program for dealer relations; establish distribution centers; formulate and implement procedures for efficient product handling; set up inventory controls; analyze transportation methods; minimize total distribution costs; analyze possible locations for plants and wholesale or retail outlets
PROMOTION	Set promotional objectives; determine major types of promotion to be used; select and schedule advertising media; develop advertising messages; measure the effectiveness of advertisements; recruit and train salespersons; formulate compensation programs for sales personnel; establish sales territories; plan and implement sales promotion efforts such as free samples, coupons, displays, sweepstakes, sales contests, and cooperative advertising programs; prepare and disseminate publicity releases
PRICE	Analyze competitors' prices; formulate pricing policies; determine method or methods used to set prices; set prices; determine discounts for various types of buyers; establish conditions and terms of sales

use of land and facilities. Even the sole owner and operator of a small neighborhood store decides which products will satisfy customers, arranges deliveries to the store, prices inventory, displays products, advertises, and assists customers.

Marketing Facilitates Satisfying Exchange Relationships For an exchange to take place, four conditions must exist. First, two or more individuals, groups, or organizations must participate. Second, each party must possess something of

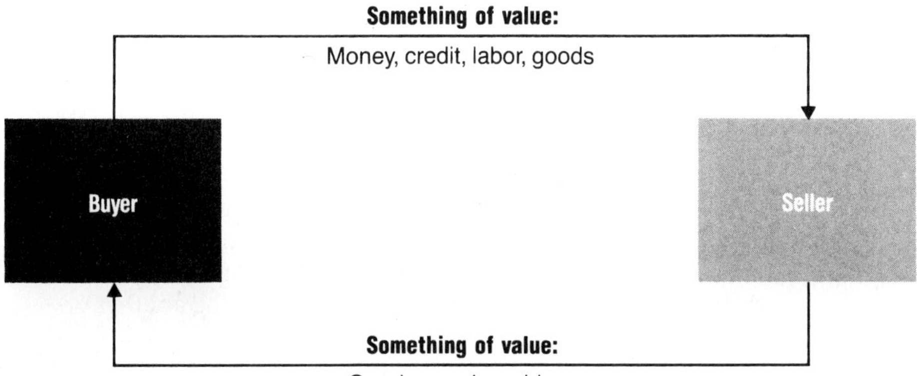

FIGURE 1.2 Exchange between buyer and seller

value that the other party desires. Third, each party must be willing to give up its "something of value" to receive the "something of value" the other party holds. The objective of a marketing exchange is to receive something that is desired more than what is given up to get it, that is, a reward in excess of costs. Fourth, the parties to the exchange must be able to communicate with each other to make their somethings of value available.[6] Figure 1.2 illustrates the process of exchange. As the arrows indicate, the two parties communicate to make their somethings of value available to each other. Note, though, that an exchange will not necessarily take place just because these four conditions exist. However, even if there is no exchange, marketing activities still have occurred. The somethings of value held by the two parties are most often products and/or financial resources such as money or credit. When an exchange occurs, products are traded for either other products or financial resources.

The exchange should be *satisfying* to both the buyer and the seller. In a study of marketing managers, 32 percent indicated that creating customer satisfaction was the most important concept in a definition of marketing.[7] Expediting exchange to facilitate satisfaction is the core concept of marketing. All marketing activities should be oriented toward creating and sustaining satisfying exchanges. To maintain an exchange

[6]Philip Kotler, *Marketing Management: Analysis, Planning, Implementation, and Control*, 6th ed. (Englewood Cliffs, N.J.: Prentice-Hall, 1988), p. 6.
[7]O. C. Ferrell and George Lucas, "An Evaluation of Progress in the Development of a Definition of Marketing," *Journal of the Academy of Marketing Science*, Fall 1987, p. 20.

relationship, both the buyer and the seller must be satisfied. The buyer must be satisfied with the good, service, or idea obtained in the exchange. The seller must receive something of value that permits satisfaction; this is often financial reward(s).

The most significant strategic choice any firm makes is deciding what customers are to be served.[8] A seller's satisfaction may derive from doing business with a particular customer or customer group, from making a profit through a particular exchange relationship, or perhaps from achieving another organizational objective.

Maintaining a positive relationship with buyers is an important goal for a seller, regardless of whether the seller is marketing cereal, laundry equipment, financial services, or an electric generating plant. Through buyer-seller interaction, the buyer develops expectations about the seller's future behavior. To fulfill these expectations, the seller must deliver on promises made. Over time, a healthy buyer-seller relationship results in interdependencies between the two parties. The buyer depends on the seller to provide information, parts, and service; to be available; and to provide satisfying products in the future. For example, in Figure 1.3, Ford surveys report that they are designing and building the highest quality cars and trucks of the past seven years. The seller depends on the buyer to continue to make purchases from the seller and to seek information. The 60,000- and 70,000-mile limited warranties on many new American automobiles illustrate an attempt to create long-term buyer-seller relationships.

There is a growing trend among consumer goods companies to establish communication channels with buyers to maintain long-term relationships. For example, many such companies now have toll-free numbers consumers can call to make inquiries, make complaints, ask for information, or the like. In a number of industries — large appliances, computers, telecommunications hardware, office automation, farm equipment, and industrial machinery — service support is emerging as the major area in which firms will soon be striving for competitive advantage.[9] Large projects or products, such as a weapons system, require considerable interac-

[8]Frederick E. Webster, Jr., "Marketing Strategy in a Slow Growth Economy," *California Management Review*, Spring 1986, p. 101.
[9]Midland M. Lele, "How Service Needs Influence Product Strategy," *Sloan Management Review*, Fall 1986, p. 63.

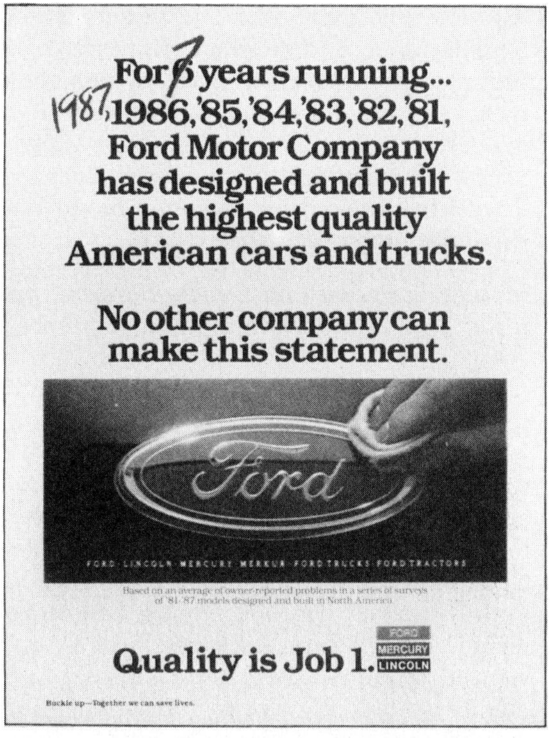

FIGURE 1.3 Ford promotes ongoing development of quality cars and trucks (SOURCE: Courtesy of the Ford Motor Company)

tion between the buyer and the seller after the sale and before and after delivery. Sellers of such products must be prepared to maintain favorable relationships with the buyer for a long period. The sale, in this case, is just the beginning of the relationship.

Marketing Occurs in a Dynamic Environment The marketing environment consists of many changing forces: laws, regulations, actions of political officials, societal pressures, changes in economic conditions, and technological advances. Each of these dynamic forces has an impact on how effectively marketing activities can facilitate and expedite exchanges. We explore such environmental forces later in this chapter and in Chapter 2.

Marketing Involves Product Development, Distribution, Promotion, and Pricing Marketing is more than just advertising or selling the product. Marketing people get involved with designing and developing a product. Marketing focuses on making the product available at the right place, at the right time, at a price that is acceptable to customers and on informing customers in a way that helps them determine if the product is consistent with their needs. Later in this chapter we discuss in more detail the areas of product development, distribution, promotion, and pricing.

Marketing Focuses on Goods, Services, and Ideas We already have used the word *product* a number of times in this chapter. For purposes of analysis in this text, a product is viewed as being a good, a service, or an idea. A good is a physical entity one can touch. A service is the application of human and mechanical efforts to people or objects. Services such as bank services and long-distance telephone services are just as real as goods, but an individual cannot actually touch them. Examples of marketers that deal in services include airlines, dry cleaners, beauty shops, financial institutions, hospitals, day care centers, and carpet cleaners. Ideas include concepts, philosophies, images, and issues. For instance, Weight Watchers International Inc., for a fee, gives its members ideas to help them lose weight and control their eating habits. Other marketers of ideas include political parties, churches, and schools.

3. Another Chapter Excerpt

On pages 95–100 is part of a chapter from a current textbook. Before you read the selection, preview it by answering each question.

1. Read the title. What does it tell you about the contents of this selection?

   The chapter is about health today.

   ____

   ____

2. Read the main headings and the subheadings. On the basis of these headings, what do you think the selection will discuss?

   The selection will discuss what health is and what

   influences health.

   ____

3. Look at the three figures. How do the photographs (Figures 1.2 and 1.4) relate to the chapter? How do the table (Figure 1.1) and the graph (Figure 1.3) relate to the topic of the selection?

Figures 1.2 and 1.4 show healthy, active people.

The opposite of health is shown: death and its causes.

4. What do you think the feature "Health History" tries to do?

give facts about health problems in the past

5. Where do you find a review? What does it tell you? What is the purpose of items 1–4 in the review?

at the end; to remind the reader of the key ideas in the chapter; items 1–4 are questions to see if the reader understands the chapter's concepts

Health Today

You probably know people you would label as *healthy*. They may be active in sports or they may walk to school, jog, or bicycle for exercise. They are likely to be trim and full of energy. They can handle the pressures of everyday activities without showing too much strain, and they project a positive outlook.

These people probably practice good health habits. By making good choices about diet, exercise, and their friendships with others, they are better able to enjoy their lives.

> **Health History**
>
> Childhood diseases were feared killers in the past. Between 1900 and 1904, measles, scarlet fever, whooping cough, and diphtheria together caused nearly as many deaths as cancer.

Health and Wellness

The word *health* can be used in a number of ways. In the past, health meant only the absence of disease or illness. Today, though, health has a broader meaning. **Health** is the state of your well-being that includes how you feel physically, mentally, and socially. **Wellness** is another term that describes this broader view of health. You can understand the need for a broader definition if you think about how health in your life is different from health in your grandparents' lives.

In 1900, the main causes of death were diseases that were spread by bacteria and viruses. If you had lived then, the danger of your dying from pneumonia would have been three times greater than the danger of your dying from cancer. Figure 1.1 compares the leading causes of death in 1900 and today.

The diseases that were most common in 1900 affected people of all ages. It is not surprising, then, that around 1900, the emphasis of health was on freedom from illness. Today many of the diseases that were common in 1900 can be prevented or cured by improved medicines and methods of sanitation. Most diseases now are likely to occur later in life. You as a teenager will probably not have to think about the same threats to your health as your grandparents did.

These improvements in health conditions mean that not only can you now enjoy a better life, but you also have a greater chance of having a longer life. Controlling diseases has increased the life expectancy in the United States. **Life expectancy** is the measure of the average number of years that a group of people may expect to live. Generally, people born more recently have higher life expectancies. Since 1900, the life expectancy in the United States has increased by more than 26 years. It has increased from 47 years for those born in 1900 to 74 years in 1981.

It is important to look also at some numbers that apply only to you. Figure 1.1 lists the main causes of death for people

1900	TODAY	
ALL AGES	ALL AGES	15–24 YEAR OLDS
Pneumonia and flu	Heart diseases	Accidents
Tuberculosis	Cancer	Homicide
Inflammations of the digestive tract	Stroke	Suicide
Heart diseases	Accidents	Cancer
Stroke	Lung diseases	Heart diseases
Kidney diseases	Pneumonia and flu	Birth defects
Accidents	Diabetes mellitus	Stroke
Cancer	Suicide	Pneumonia and flu
Childhood diseases	Liver diseases	Lung diseases
Diphtheria	Atherosclerosis	Diabetes mellitus

FIGURE 1.1 The leading causes of death in the U.S. Tuberculosis, which was the second greatest killer in 1900, was not even in the top ten by the 1980s.

between the ages of 15 and 24. You will see that the first several causes are problems that you might prevent by taking more responsibility for your actions. This includes improving your emotional health and developing good habits such as wearing a safety belt and driving safely.

FIGURE 1.2 Life expectancy has increased steadily through this century. This child has a good chance of living longer than his grandparents.

FIGURE 1.3 Estimated contribution of the four major health factors to U.S. deaths from the 10 leading causes

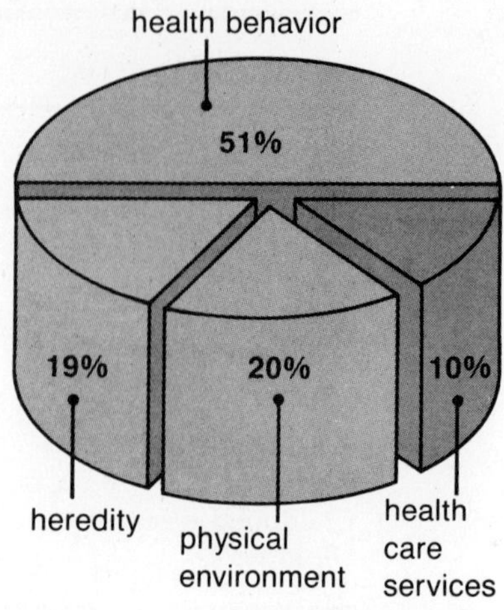

What Determines Health?

The United States Centers for Disease Control has identified four major factors that determine health. They are personal health behavior, biological influences such as heredity, the condition of the physical environment, and the quality of health care services.

FIGURE 1.4 Positive health behaviors, such as regular physical exercise, can lead to a longer, healthier life.

Health Behavior Figure 1.3 shows the estimated percentage that each of these factors contributes to the combined ten leading causes of death. Personal health behaviors are factors in 51 percent of all ten major causes of death. **Health behaviors** are actions you take that affect your health.

A research study of over 7000 individuals reported seven health behaviors that promote good health and tend to increase average length of life. The seven factors are listed below.

1. Sleeping seven to eight hours daily
2. Eating breakfast almost every day
3. Rarely eating between meals
4. Maintaining normal weight
5. Not smoking cigarettes
6. Drinking alcohol in moderation, or not at all
7. Getting regular physical exercise

Those who practiced most or all of these behaviors tended to be in better physical and mental health than those who followed a few or none. People who are in good physical shape are better able to handle the pressures in their lives. People who have good mental health have a good self-concept.

Heredity Sometimes your ability to prevent diseases is limited by heredity and by other personal factors. **Heredity** is the passing of traits biologically from parents to child. If many of your family members have died of heart disease, you may be less able to prevent heart disease than someone whose family members have been free of heart disease. Sometimes a disability can keep you from being able to exercise regularly. Whatever your heredity or physical condition, though, you can improve your chance of having a lifetime of good health by choosing responsible health behaviors.

Physical Environment Your **physical environment** is your physical surroundings — any place in which you live, work, or play. Health threats in your physical environment may affect your personal health. Air pollution may increase your chance of developing lung disorders, or worsen a condition such as asthma. Scientists believe that air pollution might even cause some diseases such as cancer. Too much noise, very crowded living places, and infected food or water are examples of factors in the environment that can affect your health.

Health Care Services The quality of the health care you have available to you also helps determine the quality of your general health. If you can get regular medical and dental care, you may be able to prevent many health problems. Preventing an illness is almost always easier than curing one.

Lesson Review

Your health is a mix of factors in your life — physical, emotional, and social. Being aware of the four major factors that determine health will help you make decisions about positive health behaviors. Even though you cannot control all parts of your health, you can take responsibility for practicing as many positive health behaviors as possible.

1. Define *health*.
2. Explain *life expectancy*.
3. List the four major factors that determine health.
4. List five health behaviors that promote good health.

— Houghton Mifflin Health

5

Using Prereading Warm-ups

Like previewing, "warming up," or prereading, can help you before you read. (*Prereading* means "before reading.") When you warm up, you get yourself ready to do something. To warm up, runners stretch, baseball players bat balls, and golfers swing clubs. Readers can warm up, too.

You can get a general idea of what a reading selection is about from the title, the headings, the illustrations, and other features. (See **3** and **4**.) But it's also important to warm up by trying to think of whatever you know about the selection's topic before you read.

If you explore a topic by thinking about it before you read, you will understand it better when you read. For example, suppose that you are ready to read an essay about dinosaurs. Before you start reading, you should think about whatever you know, remember, or imagine about those huge animals that roamed the earth millions of years ago. Force yourself to do advance thinking. In this way you prepare your mind to accept new information. When you read, you will understand ideas more easily because you did a warm-up.

Many readers like to write down their prereading warm-ups. It doesn't take very much time. Writing your thoughts down before you read lets you add to your thinking as one idea leads to another. When you do a prereading warm-up on paper, don't worry about making mistakes in spelling or grammar. Just get your ideas down.

Of the many ways to write down and organize your warm-ups, one of these may help you:

- Make a list.
- Make a word map.
- Do brainstorming.
- Do freewriting.

5a Making a List

In this prereading warm-up, you simply write down in list form whatever comes into your mind about the topic of your reading.

Look at the example below that a student prepared before reading a selection on dinosaurs.

Dinosaurs
animals
early creatures — prehistoric
lay eggs?
huge bodies, little heads
live in swampy places
none left now (exinct?)
big bones left in mts. (Utah, any other place?)
muzeems put bones back together
dinosaur toys very poplar now
dinosaurs not too smart
movies: King Kong?
Some fly: man eaters?

Notice how the student put down whatever came to his mind about the subject of the reading — dinosaurs. The list includes many different impressions, from dinosaurs in early history to dinosaurs today. Notice the errors: *extinct, museums,* and *popular* are misspelled. But the errors don't matter here. The student is simply trying to record his own ideas, and the list helps him jar loose his thoughts about the topic before he reads.

If necessary, you can reorganize your list later to make it clearer and easier for you to use. Put together any related information.

EXERCISES

1. Making a List

Below you see the title and the headings of a chapter from a college textbook called *Introduction to Psychology* (Sixth Edition) by Clifford T. Morgan, Richard A. King, and Nancy M. Robinson. After you preview (see **3**), use separate paper to make a list of everything you know or think about thinking and language. Don't worry about spelling or grammar.

Chapter 1. Thinking and Language
The Thinking Process
Concepts
Problem Solving
Decision Making
Creative Thinking
Language and Communication
Speech Perception
Psychology of Grammar

2. Checking a List

On page 102 is a list made by a student before he read about dinosaurs. Which items on the list seem related to each other? How could you redo the list so that the related items were close together?

5b Making a Word Map

A word map is a visual warm-up. (See **6.**) When you make a visual as a warm-up, you create a figure that links words and phrases about the topic. The visual is called a *map* because it names areas and connects them. A student made the visual on page 104 before reading a selection called "The Greatest Tightrope Walker" by Robert Kraske. As you can see, a word map links ideas with lines, boxes, circles, or arrows.

There are no rules for developing your own visual device as a prereading warm-up. You simply want to lay out the information in a kind of picture so that you can see your thoughts clearly. The value of the visual is that it helps you keep related information together. Notice how all the circled thoughts connected to the word *circus* are in fact related to the circus: main acts, bicycles, nets, and jugglers. These probably refer to the student's memory of a visit that she made to the circus.

With this "thinking on paper" the student made herself more ready to read. Without knowing it, she put down many words and ideas that the story would deal with. "The Greatest Tightrope Walker" is about Blondin, a Frenchman, who walked tightropes in circuses — and also across Niagara Falls in 1859.

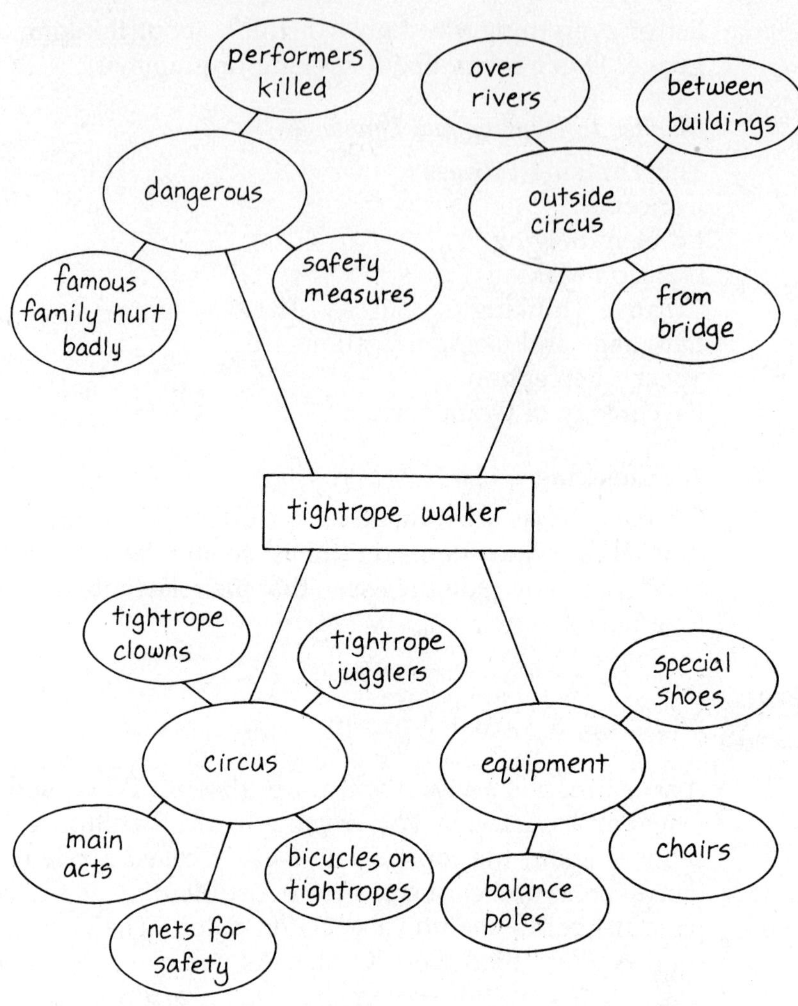

EXERCISES

1. A Prereading Visual

Draw a word map for a chapter called "Public Opinion in American Democracy" from a textbook called *Government in America* by Richard J. Hardy. The author provides this chapter outline on the first page of the chapter:

1. What is public opinion?
2. Many factors shape political opinions.
3. Public opinion is measured in several ways.

Student responses will vary.

2. A Word Map

Look at the word map on page 104. Explain the various areas that are connected.

1. What are the four main areas mapped from the words *tight-rope walker?* **circus, dangerous, outside circus, equipment**

2. What other main area might you add? Look at the areas connected to the main ones. How do they relate to the main group? **They derive from the main heading.**

3. How do the areas connected to the main ones relate to each other? **Student responses will vary.**

5c Brainstorming

Brainstorming is using questions to help you think, "to make a storm" in your brain. When you brainstorm as a prereading exercise, you raise as many questions as you can about a reading selection. Ask *who, what, when, why, where,* and *how*. Or ask any other useful questions.

Remember that you're brainstorming *before* you read. First use as many clues as you can from previewing. (See 4.) Look at the title, headings, drawings, and photographs. Then make a list of questions.

Look at the brainstorming that one student did before she read a chapter in her psychology book, *Developmental Psychology* (Third Edition) by Robert Biehler and Lynne M. Hudson. The chapter was called "Two to Five: Relations with Others." There were three main headings: "Parent Child Relationships," "The Impact of Day Care and Preschool Experience," and "Relationships with Peers."

Who establishes important relationships with the child?
How does the child view his mother at this stage?
What must the mother do or not do?
When should a parent use day care for her child?
How does day care affect the child?
How many child abuse cases at day care are really true?
Are kids in danger at day care centers?
How do kids play together at this age?
Should parents teach kids how to read at this age?
What part do fathers play in raising kids in this age group?

The value of questions in general is that they stimulate thinking and prepare you to find answers. By brainstorming before you read, you prepare your mind to get information. You may not find all the answers to your brainstorming questions, but you'll be reading with much more attention.

EXERCISE

On pages 106–110 is a chapter called "Study Techniques" from *The McGraw-Hill College Handbook* (Second Edition) by Richard Marius and Harvey S. Wiener. On separate paper, do brainstorming on this chapter. Examine the various headings but do not read the selection yet.

After you brainstorm, read the chapter. Which of your questions did you answer? Which did you not answer?

Study Techniques

Develop your study skills by applying techniques for improving your comprehension and retention of what you read. Learn to take useful notes when you read and when you listen to lectures. Studying is an active, continual process that requires planning, repetition, and *writing* to help you remember and use newly acquired information.

First, Plan a Reasonable Study Schedule

Examine your week's activities, and develop a realistic plan for studying. Consider all the demands on your time — eating, sleeping, attending classes, doing homework, exercising, socializing, commuting, watching TV — and set aside time for regular studying. Some students make a weekly chart of their activities so that it's easier to keep track of their hours. If you do block in regular activities and study time on a calendar, leave a number of free periods so that you have time for relaxing and for making adjustments. When exams or special projects come up, for example, you'll need blocks of time over several days, even weeks, to complete your work on time. Try to avoid cramming for tests, because the stress it produces prevents deep learning and memory. If you must cram, try to outline the major points you need to cover and concentrate on learning the central ideas and facts.

Learn and Retain Information by Reading Actively

You can improve your ability to learn and retain material by approaching your reading with a clear plan and by taking various kinds of notes.

1. **Survey your text before you read it carefully.** Surveying — looking at the text for information without reading every word — gives you an outline of the material so that you can focus on what you are about to read. When you survey a book, look for chapter titles and subtitles, headings and subheadings, charts, graphs, illustrations, and words in boldface or italics. Skim the opening and closing paragraphs of a chapter or of chapter sections. Surveying like this can give you the sense of a book very quickly.
2. **Write out questions in advance so that you can read with a purpose.** Once you have looked quickly through the reading material, jot down some questions about it. Writing will help make things stick in your mind, and your written questions will provide a good short review. It is always better to write your own questions about a text you are reading, but if questions do appear at the end of a chapter, consider them carefully before you read. Then let them guide your reading.

   Keeping specific questions in mind as you read will get you actively involved in the material at hand. Your reading then has a purpose: you are trying to find answers to your questions.
3. **Take notes on your reading.** Take notes on what you read. Learn how to make summaries. When you read, try to summarize every paragraph by composing a simple, short sentence. Be ruthless in cutting out the nonessential, and put the author's thoughts into your own words. Don't try to duplicate the style of the book or article you are reading. Putting somebody else's ideas into your own words is a good way of making sure that you truly know those ideas.

Many students underline as they read. Underlining has several disadvantages. Obviously, you cannot underline in a library book; so if you underline material, you will have to own the book. Underlining is also a passive way of learning; it is merely a signpost to tell you that something here is worth remembering. But often, when students come back to passages they have underlined, they cannot remember why they put those lines down in the first place. Often, too, they underline too much, and too much emphasis becomes boring and confusing. Underlining is never as effective as writing down a short summary sentence for each paragraph. Writing a summary sentence ensures that you will reconsider the thoughts in the book, translate them into your own words, and put them on paper.

4. **Look up your reading topic in some reference books.** You can also aid your memory by looking for the same information or closely related information in another source. Your teacher may require you to buy one or more books for the course, and you should read these books and make notes about them. But it is also an excellent idea to check information mentioned in your reading by looking things up in some of the many reference books available in the library. Try an encyclopedia, various dictionaries, and other reference books your librarian may help you find. (Many of these reference books are listed in 35c-3 of this handbook.) When you read the same information several times, presented in slightly different ways, you will find that each source has some details that the others do not have. This seeking of variety in your learning will provide wonderful help to the mind in remembering. If you have taken careful summary notes on the various things you have read, your memory will be all the more strengthened.
5. **Learn to analyze what you read by asking questions about it.** Another skill required in study is the ability to analyze, to tell what things mean, to discover how they fit with other things you know. Here again, writing will help you to study. Many writing teachers advise students to keep a notebook in which they can jot down their notes from sources on one page and then jot down their thoughts about those notes on a facing page. If you ask yourself questions about the things you put down, you will develop your analytical powers. Pay attention to your own feelings. Do you like a book? Make yourself set down

reasons why you like it. Do you dislike a book? Again, write down the reasons for your preference. Whether you feel interested, bored, repelled, or excited, ask yourself what there is in the book (or movie or whatever else you may be studying) that rouses such feelings. Then write your reasons down. Don't think that you have to like a work of literature or art or a study in history merely because someone else does. But you should be able to justify your opinions, not merely to others but to yourself. And as you get into the habit of writing out these justifications, you will find your analytical ability improving steadily.

6. **Look up unfamiliar words, practice using them, and build them into your vocabulary.** With the aid of a dictionary (see 16b-1 through 3), keep a record of new words; write them on index cards or in a notebook. Include correct spelling, pronunciation clues, clear definitions that you write yourself, and a phrase or a sentence using the word properly. Arrange the words in related groups to help yourself study (business words, economics words, psychology words, literature words, and so on). Incorporate new words in your speaking and your writing vocabulary. Here is an example of a word written down for further study.

> puerile (PYOO ar il)
>
> juvenile in a bad sense. People who are puerile are not just children; they are *childish*. He was *puerile* when he refused to let her name appear before his on the program for the play.

7. **Review your notes and your reading assignments.** Immediately after you finish reading, and at convenient intervals thereafter, look over whatever questions, notes, summaries, or outlines you have created from your reading. Don't try to read every word of the original material in the book or article every time you review. Skim over it. You will learn better from many rapid readings than from one or two slow readings. Skimming will help you get the shape of the material in your mind, and as you study your own notes, you will recall many of the supporting details.

   Use your written work to help you complete your assignments. It often helps if you close your book, put away your notes, and try to jot down from memory a rough outline of what you are studying. The more different ways you can write about material you are learning, the more effectively you will learn it.

Learn to Write Useful Notes on Your Lectures, and Compare Notes with Your Classmates

Taking good notes during a lecture is a skill that requires practice. Some students tape-record lectures so they can listen again to what the teacher has said. But even if you have a tape recorder and the teacher is willing to be recorded, writing can still help you understand and remember the lecture.

Never try to write down everything you hear in the lecture as it is going on. Unless you know shorthand, you cannot write as fast as a person speaks, and while you are struggling to get a sentence down, the lecturer will have gone on to another point. In your haste, you may garble both what has been said and what is being said.

Your best bet is to write down words, phrases, and short sentences. Use these jottings to stimulate your memory later on. As soon as possible after the lecture is over, take your notes to a quiet place and try to write down as much of the lecture as you can remember. If you do this regularly, you probably will find yourself remembering more and more of each successive lecture.

Once you have written up your notes, compare what you have with the notes taken by another member of the class. If four or five of you get together to share your notes, you will each acquire an amazingly complete set, and in your discussions of gaps and confusions, you will further your learning.

Take Breaks

Don't try to sit for hours without a break, writing notes about your reading or your lectures. Get up every forty-five mintues or so and walk around the room and stretch. Then sit back down quickly and go to work again. Taking a break will relax your body and perhaps stimulate your mind to some new thought that you can use when you start studying again.

5d Freewriting

With freewriting your purpose is to write freely about the subject of the piece that you are going to read. Do not stop writing for any reason. Write sentences about whatever comes into your mind about the reading selection before you read it. Don't correct words or cross them out. Just get on paper as many ideas as you can think of, no matter how strange or silly they may seem to you.

A student did this freewriting before she read an essay called "Colleges Put a Cork on College Drinking" from *Time* magazine. The article is about efforts by colleges to prevent alcohol abuse among students.

> Colleges and drinking. Drinking at college. I don't drink. My boyfriend sometimes drinks too much. Dorm parties. Tailgate parties. Too much beer. Beer. Drinking too much beer. Students need to drink. It relaxes them, takes pressure off. Can they relax in other ways? Drinking can be a serious problem. Problem. Problem. Drunk driving, of course. But you can hurt your body? In what ways? Maybe if we knew the effects of alcohol. Kids wouldn't abuse it. What can colleges do? Suspend you for drinking. Maybe give courses. My sister belongs to Students Against Drunk Driving at High School. Maybe colleges have groups like that. Just how big a problem is campus drinking?

Do you see how this student put down whatever thoughts came into her head about the reading selection before she read it? She was tapping her own experiences. When she reads, many points in the article will be familiar to her.

EXERCISES

1. Freewriting

On a separate sheet of paper, do freewriting on the following reading selection: Chapter 4, "You and Your Physician — Partners in Prevention," from a textbook called *Alive and Well, Decisions in Health.* **Student responses will vary.**

2. Warming Up on Your Own

Below is a chapter section from the textbook *Spaceship Earth: Life Science* by James E. McLaren, John H. Stasik, and Dale F. Levering. On a separate sheet of paper, do a prereading warm-up for this selection. Use any of the warm-up activities that you learned about in this chapter. **Student responses will vary.**

Chapter 12

World Ecosystems

The English first tried to start towns and farms in North America on the Atlantic coastline. The first settlers arrived in

1584. The group was organized in England by Sir Walter Raleigh. They landed at Roanoke Island off the coast of what is now North Carolina. The next summer, all the people returned to England.

In 1587 Raleigh started a second colony on Roanoke. But he did not send supply ships to the new settlement until 1589. When the ships arrived, the settlers had disappeared. Historians have found evidence that the settlers joined a friendly group of Indians and moved inland. The English had not been able to get a permanent town going.

In 1607 the English tried to settle another place in what is now Virginia. The people traveled several kilometers up the James River and established Jamestown. This was the first English settlement in North America that lasted.

Why was the settlement at Jamestown successful? Why was the one at Roanoke not successful? One factor may have been the environment.

One of the biggest problems at Roanoke was the local plant and animal community. The soil is poor on the island. Scrub pine is one of the few plants that can live in that soil. The scrub pine community provides little in the way of animal food for people, and the soil is not good for growing crops.

The people at Jamestown had great problems of many kinds. They called their third winter "starving time." They had eaten everything they could find, including dogs, cats, mice, rats, and even their shoe leather! One survivor wrote that they had to ". . . searche the woodes and to feede upon Serpents and snakes and to digge the earthe for wylde and unknowne Rootes. . . ." But some people were able to survive.

Jamestown was located at the edge of a forest. There the people could gather nuts and hunt deer and other animals. The forest soil was fertile, so crops grew on cleared land.

The people of Roanoke were living in a natural community that was not right for farming or hunting. The Jamestown settlers found an area where they could get food from the natural community.

Communities and environments differ from place to place. Today people are still learning how to live in many different natural environments around the world. In this chapter you will look at some world communities and environments.

When you have finished this chapter you should be able to:

1. describe the cycles through which water, carbon, oxygen, and nitrogen move.

2. describe what an ecosystem is and give examples of large and small ones.
3. list Earth's major ecosystems and some plants and animals that live in each.
4. explain what climate is, what Earth's climate zones are, and how climate affects ecosystems.
5. tell what soil is, how soils can differ, and how soils affect ecosystems.

Chemical Cycles

12-1 Matter Is Recycled

There is a certain amount of matter on Earth. Most of the matter here when Earth was formed is here now. Very little has been lost. You could say that matter is recycling. To *recycle* something is to use it over and over.

One substance that is necessary for life on Earth has been here for a long time. It is water. Water consists of hydrogen and oxygen. Water makes up about 90% of every living cell. Without water, life as we know it would not exist.

Water is recycled. It moves from Earth's surface to the air by evaporation and then falls back again as rain or snow in the *water cycle*. Some of it moves through organisms also.

Water can be in the form of a solid (ice), a liquid (water), or a gas (water vapor). Water changes from one form to another as it moves between the air and the Earth's surface. For example, water is liquid in the ocean, water vapor in the air as it rises, and ice in a high cloud. Follow the possible pathways of water through the water cycle shown in Figure 12.1.

Water in some places is dirty. For example, soil from a farm field may be washed into a stream. Or what is washed down your kitchen sink drain gets into a lake. When the water evaporates it leaves behind the dirt. Eventually the evaporated water falls back to Earth as rain or snow. The water cycle continually supplies organisms with fresh water. Sometimes the rain or snow is clean; sometimes it picks up chemicals and particles in the air and gets "dirty."

You can create a water cycle and watch how it works.

Materials flask / one-hole stopper with glass tube in hole / dirt / soap / milk / plastic or rubber tubing / beaker / jar / clean water / hot plate / ringstand / clamp

Put some clean water in a flask. Make it dirty by adding some dirt, milk, soap, and other things if you wish. Cap the

FIGURE 12.1 The water cycle. Water falls to the Earth's surface as rain or snow. Eventually, water flows in streams and rivers to lakes and oceans. Water enters the air by evaporation, and plants and animals give off water to the air. Clouds form, and rain or snow falls to the surface of the Earth again.

flask with a one-hole stopper fitted with a long plastic tube. Dip a portion of the long tube in a beaker of cold water, as shown in Figure 12.2. Hang the end of the tube over the edge of a clean jar. Gently boil the water in the flask over a hot plate.

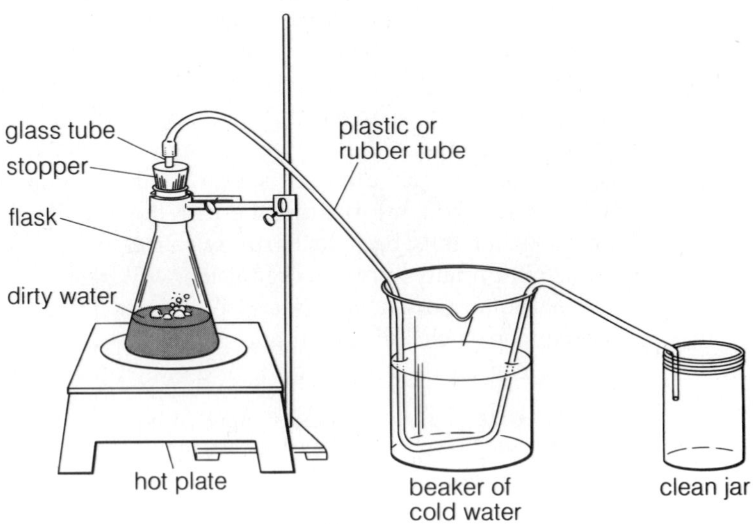

FIGURE 12.2 Use a setup like this to observe a water cycle.

What happens? How does this activity demonstrate a water cycle?

Compare the water you collected to the water you started with. Would you taste the water that dripped from the end of the tube?

The Carbon and Oxygen Cycles

Producers, consumers, scavengers, and decomposers recycle carbon and oxygen. Carbon and oxygen make up carbon dioxide. Remember from Chapter 2 that scientists consider carbon dioxide gas to be an indication that respiration is occurring. Organisms produce carbon dioxide all the time.

Organisms that perform photosynthesis use carbon dioxide in making food. When the sun shines on food-making organisms, carbon dioxide from the air combines with water in cells containing chlorophyll. Sugar and oxygen are produced. The sugar contains the carbon.

Animals eat sugar produced and stored in plants and some protists, and the carbon becomes part of the animals. During respiration, some carbon is released in carbon dioxide. When organisms die, some of their carbon becomes part of the soil. Other carbon is returned to the air as carbon dioxide by bacteria that use the dead organisms for food. Follow the possible pathways of carbon in the *carbon cycle* in Figure 12.3.

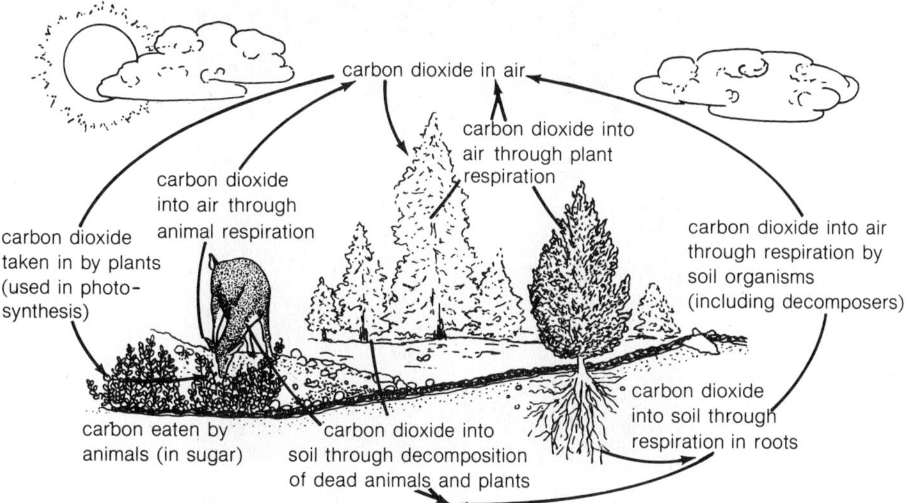

FIGURE 12.3 The carbon cycle on land. Carbon is taken from the air by plants. Some plants are eaten by animals. Some carbon is released as a waste product of respiration and some becomes part of plants' and animals' bodies. Decomposers break down dead plants and animals and carbon enters the soil or the air again.

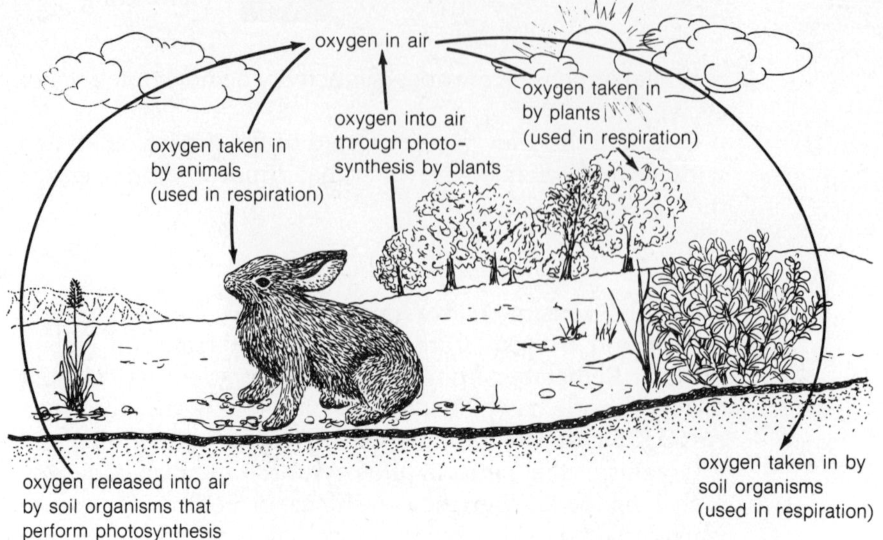

FIGURE 12.4 The oxygen cycle on land. Oxygen released by plants during photosynthesis is taken in by animals and plants and used in their respiration.

FIGURE 12.5 The lumps on these clover roots contain bacteria that change nitrogen gas into large nitrogen-containing molecules that the plant can use. The roots of certain other plants, such as peas, lima beans, peanuts, and soybeans, also contain these lumps.

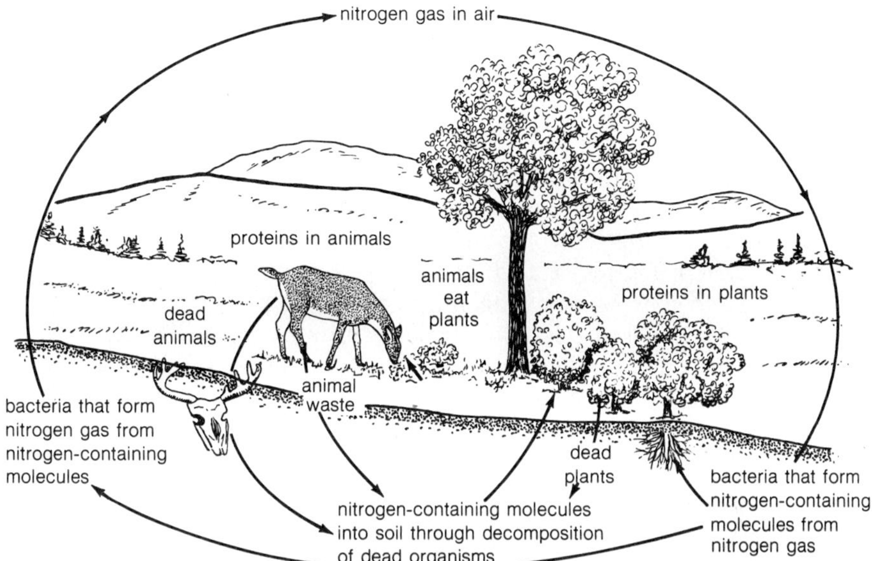

FIGURE 12.6 The nitrogen cycle on land. Nitrogen gas in the air is changed into larger nitrogen-containing molecules by certain bacteria in soil and roots. Plants use the nitrogen in making proteins. Animals eat some plants and the protein enters their bodies. Animal waste material or decaying plant and animal matter return the large nitrogen-containing molecules to the soil. Other bacteria turn the large molecules back into nitrogen gas, which enters the air again.

Oxygen molecules are given off by the organisms that perform photosynthesis and are used by most kinds of organisms during respiration. Figure 12.4 shows possible pathways of oxygen in the *oxygen cycle.*

Respiration produces carbon dioxide and water, which can be used by the producers in making more food and oxygen. In the carbon and oxygen cycles, carbon and oxygen are "exchanged" between producers and consumers.

12.3 The Nitrogen Cycle

About 80% of air is nitrogen gas. Nitrogen is used by organisms in making proteins. Proteins are important parts of all cells.

Substances with nitrogen in them produce one smell of life. If you walk through a barnyard, or parts of a zoo, or anywhere that animals are kept, you may notice a particular odor. The odor is mainly from animal wastes, which contain nitrogen. Decomposing meat and plants smell bad. Much of the odor comes from gases containing nitrogen given off during decay.

Nitrogen gas in the air is in a form that cannot be used by most organisms. Some nitrogen gas is changed into molecules that can be used by most plants. Certain bacteria that live in the roots of some plants, especially members of the pea family, and other bacteria in soil can change nitrogen gas into larger nitrogen-containing molecules that can be used by plants (Figure 12.5). Other bacteria can change larger molecules containing nitrogen into nitrogen gas.

Follow the possible pathways of nitrogen in the *nitrogen cycle* shown in Figure 12.6. You can see that nitrogen used by plants comes from waste material of animals and from the decay of waste and dead material by bacteria. Another source of nitrogen is nitrogen-containing molecules formed from nitrogen gas by bacteria in soil and roots.

Using Visual Aids

Information in print may appear in more than just words and sentences. Writers often use illustrations — that is, drawings, photos, charts, graphs, and tables — as *visual aids.* (*Visual* refers to what you can see; an *aid* is a helper.) You often see sentences and visual aids used together, for example, in advertisements, cartoons, cookbooks, maps, and repair manuals. These and other print forms communicate with both words and pictures.

Why do writers use illustrations? Sometimes you can understand a difficult point more easily with a picture or a drawing. Illustrations are really helpful, for example, when you're trying to figure out how to do or make something. If you've ever put together a stereo unit, a bookcase, or a child's toy, you know how useful an illustration can be. And to make the meaning of numbers visual, other aids — such as charts and graphs — can present data briefly and to the point. Using sentences and paragraphs alone might make the explanation longer and more complicated than necessary. Sometimes a cartoon or a photograph adds an element of delight or surprise that keeps readers interested and involved.

Good readers, adults and children alike, always use visual aids to help them understand written words. As you build your reading skills, rely on photos and drawings to fill in anything that you're not sure of. Visual aids often supply very important information that the words themselves do not supply.

Most of us probably learned to recognize words by connecting them with visual aids. As a child you could read *STOP* from a red-and-white six-cornered sign on the corner. The familiar shape and color of the sign helped you learn the word. In a similar way, children today learn to read *McDonald's* because of the golden arches, *Band-Aids* because of the picture on the box, and *Coca-Cola* from the white script letters and red can or label.

Using Visual Aids to Help You Understand What You Read

- *Do not ignore visual aids.* Many inexperienced readers think that pictures, charts, or other illustrations are there just to make the page look good! As a result these readers do not look at the visual aids carefully. But if you skip over an illustration, you might be skipping information that is important in understanding what you are reading.
- *Read carefully the captions, titles, or notes that help explain the illustrations.* A caption is an explanation in words for a picture. Often a group of words or a sentence or two will tell why the illustration is important. In newspapers, photographs usually have captions that name the people in the pictures or give other information. Captions and titles for charts, graphs, and tables often highlight the main point of a drawing. In addition, charts and graphs often have notes to explain what certain figures and symbols mean. Look at those notes carefully.
- *Try to connect the words that you are reading with the illustrations.* You may look at the picture before you read, or you may read and then study the picture. However, when an illustration appears with a selection, readers most often use the words and pictures together. You read a few paragraphs and then you examine the illustration to connect it to what you've read so far. Then you continue reading, returning now and then to the illustration. The point is to try to put together the illustration with the sentences. Ask yourself questions: What is this visual information showing me? What does the illustration have to do with what I'm reading? Why has the writer included the picture? What does the picture tell that the words do not?
- *State visual information in your own words.* Illustrations do give information. Try to state that information in your own words. A graph, chart, or table, for example, puts information in visual terms. This makes it easier to look at lots of data quickly. From the information you can make comparisons on your own. Yet unless you try to state comparisons in your own words, you can miss the point of the graph, chart, or table.

Look at the graph below about estimated numbers — an *estimate* is a rough guess — of illegal aliens in America. Illegal aliens are people who are not permitted to enter a country but who go there and stay anyway against the law. Answer the questions after you study the graph. Then check your answers in the explanation that follows the questions.

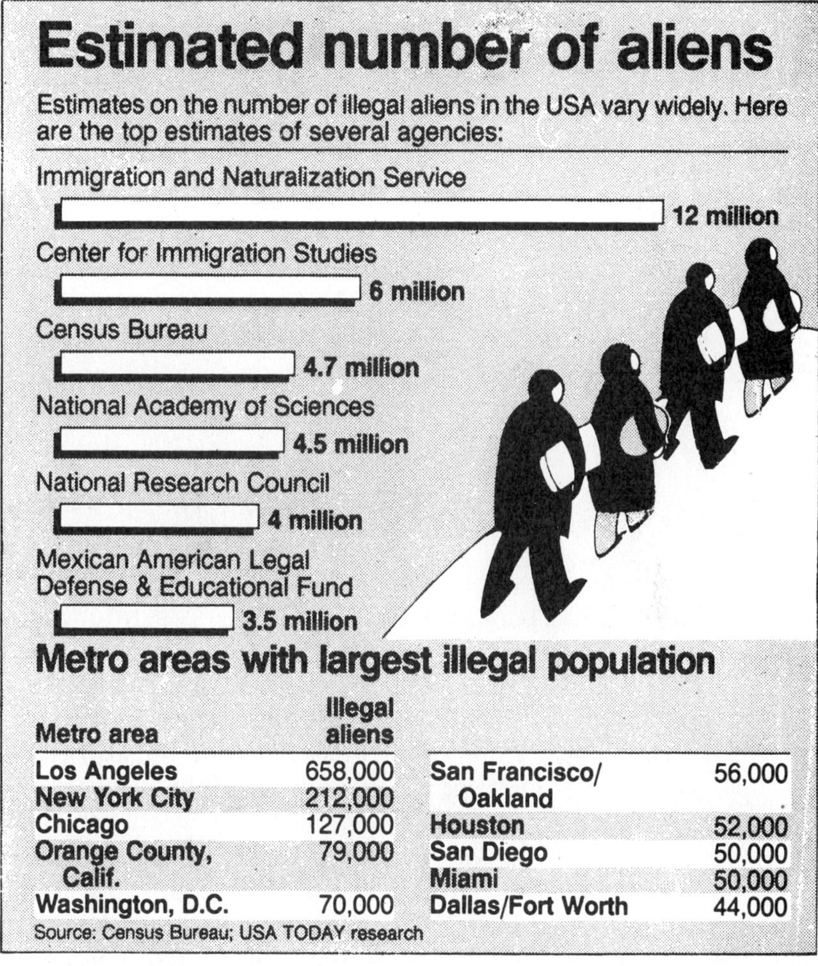

Metro area	Illegal aliens	Metro area	Illegal aliens
Los Angeles	658,000	San Francisco/ Oakland	56,000
New York City	212,000	Houston	52,000
Chicago	127,000	San Diego	50,000
Orange County, Calif.	79,000	Miami	50,000
Washington, D.C.	70,000	Dallas/Fort Worth	44,000

Source: Census Bureau; USA TODAY research

d 1. The word *agencies* that appears on line 3 probably means
   a. groups of people carrying their belongings.
   b. U.S. populations.
   c. estimates.
   d. groups that gather information or take actions on behalf of others.

a 2. The white bars that you see in the graph show the
a. numbers of aliens estimated by different agencies.
b. working conditions for aliens.
c. millions of dollars spent by agencies for aliens.
d. cities with large illegal populations.

d 3. The U.S. agency that estimates the smallest number of aliens in this country is the
a. Dallas/Fort Worth Census Bureau.
b. National Research Council.
c. Immigration and Naturalization Service.
d. Mexican American Legal Defense and Educational Fund.

c 4. Houston, Miami, San Diego, and San Francisco/Oakland
a. have fewer illegal aliens than Dallas/Fort Worth.
b. have more illegal aliens than the other cities listed in the graph.
c. have between 50,000 and 60,000 people considered as illegal aliens.
d. have a higher number of illegal aliens than Orange County, California.

For question 1, you should have guessed the meaning of the word *agencies* from clues in the graph. You could guess that each name appearing above a bar is the name of a group concerned with aliens. Perhaps you knew from your own experience of the work of the Census Bureau. Perhaps the word *research* in "National Research Council" told you that the group investigated data. Using those clues, you should have chosen *d* as the correct answer. Choice *a* is wrong, even though the illustration shows people carrying their possessions. The graph makes no connection between the word *agencies* and that drawing. Choice *b* is incorrect; it's too broad, and, further, there's no reason to make that choice based on the graph. Choice *c* is wrong, too. Although the word *estimate* appears three times on the graph, it has nothing to do with the word *agencies*.

The only correct answer for 2 is *a*. From the title of the graph, you know that the illustration will deal with estimates of aliens. To the right of each bar, you can see a number and the word *million*. Those clues should tell you that each bar represents a certain number of people. The longer the bar, the higher the estimate is. The shorter the bar, the lower the estimate is.

If you chose answer *c* for 2, the word *million* beside each bar tricked you into thinking about money. But the graph has nothing to do with costs or expenses. It also has nothing to do with working conditions. Therefore, choice *b* is also wrong. Finally, *d* is incorrect, too. Although a part of the graph does compare cities that have large illegal populations, the bars have nothing to do with specific cities. Only the table called "Metro Areas with Largest Illegal Population" compares cities.

For questions 3 and 4, you must use the graph to make comparisons on your own. For 3, only *d*, the Mexican American Legal Defense and Educational Fund, is correct. How do we know that this group makes the smallest estimate? First, we look at the length of the bar. Then we compare its length to the lengths of the other bars. Clearly the bar under the Mexican American Legal Defense and Educational Fund is the smallest. Our second hint is the numbers beside the bar. The 3.5 million figure is the smallest among the figures for all the agencies. But the key to reaching the right answer here is making the comparison in your own mind. The graph does not say outright which group's estimates are bigger or smaller than another's. You have to make the judgment yourself.

For question 4, only *c* is correct. Looking at the numbers, you can see that each of the four cities named in the question has between 50,000 and 60,000 illegal aliens. The number 60,000, however, does not appear anywhere on the graph. But you can reach that fact for yourself. Both San Diego and Miami have 50,000 illegal aliens. Houston has 52,000. San Francisco/Oakland has 56,000.

Answer *a* is incorrect. Dallas/Fort Worth has the smallest number at 44,000. Answer *b* is wrong, too, because many other cities (such as Los Angeles and New York) have higher numbers of illegal aliens than Houston, Miami, San Diego, and San Francisco/Oakland. Answer *d* is obviously incorrect, too. Orange County, California, has 79,000, a much higher figure than any of the four cities named in the question.

EXERCISES

1. Visual Aids

Look at the illustration on page 86. Read the caption beside the picture. What does the visual tell you about the product that the caption alone does not?

Student responses will vary.

____

____

____

____

____

2. Visual Aids

Look at the illustration on page 129 and read the caption below it. What information do the pictures give you that the caption does not give?

Student responses will vary.

____

____

____

____

____

3. Words and Pictures for Meanings

Look at the selections on pages 126, 127, 129, 131, and 133. They all contain words as well as pictures. Use the sentences and the illustrations to answer the questions after each selection.

1. Try to figure out the definition of each word from the selection on pages 126 and 127. Write the letter of the correct choice in the blank space.

a 1. discard
   a. throw away
   b. eat
   c. cook
   d. slice

d 2. joint
   a. bad place
   b. marijuana cigarette

c. wing
d. point of contact between bones

c ______ 3. reserve
a. throw away
b. prepare carefully
c. save
d. put salt on

b ______ 4. additional
a. less
b. extra
c. fatty
d. poor quality

b ______ 5. expose
a. decorate
b. show
c. pose
d. make clear

a ______ 6. sever
a. separate by cutting off
b. cook under high heat
c. add spices to
d. never

d ______ 7. repeat
a. cut
b. remove the bone
c. remove the leg
d. do again

a ______ 8. incision
a. deep cut
b. mark
c. line
d. view

d ______ 9. trim
a. slim
b. width
c. open
d. cut away

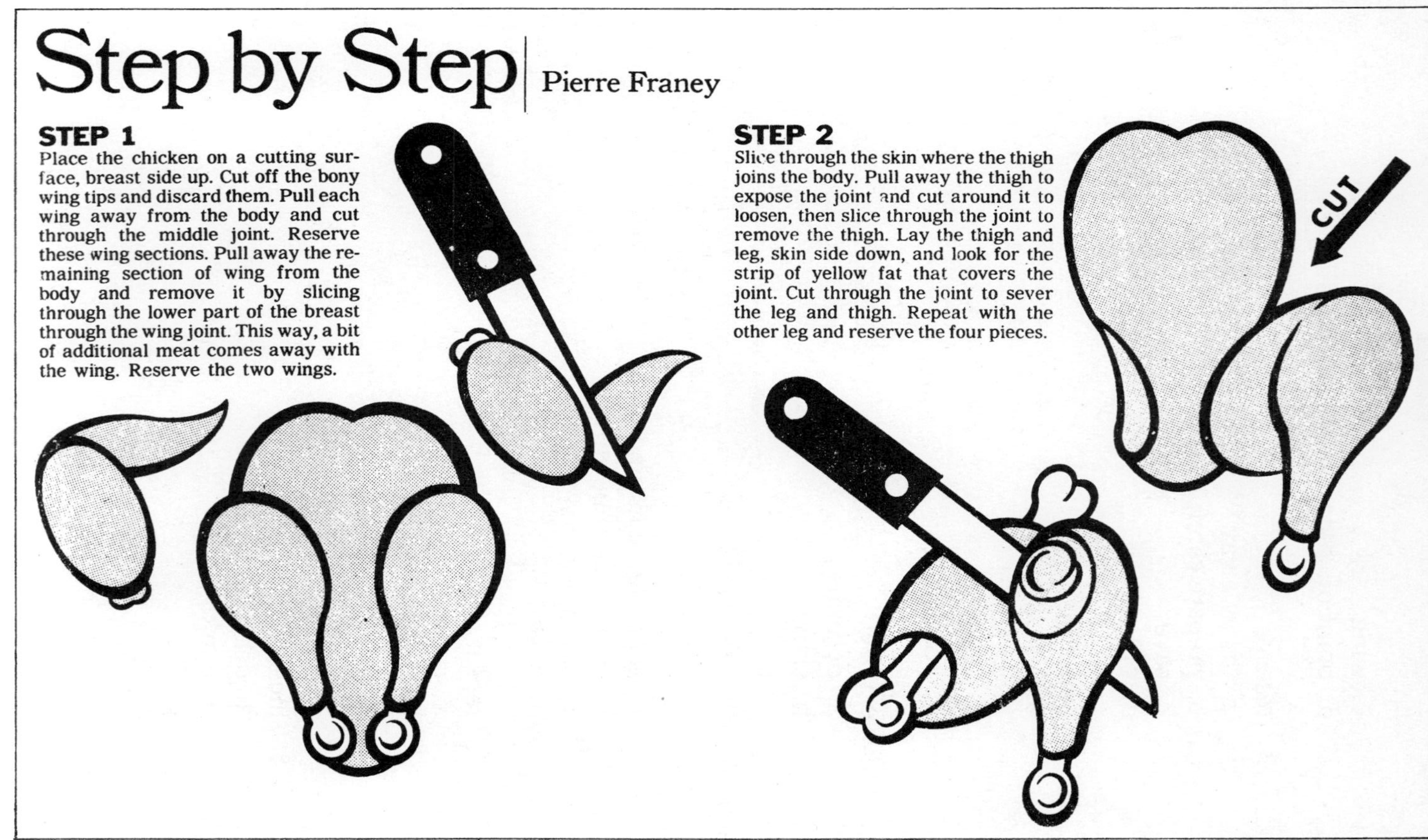

Step by Step

Pierre Franey

STEP 1
Place the chicken on a cutting surface, breast side up. Cut off the bony wing tips and discard them. Pull each wing away from the body and cut through the middle joint. Reserve these wing sections. Pull away the remaining section of wing from the body and remove it by slicing through the lower part of the breast through the wing joint. This way, a bit of additional meat comes away with the wing. Reserve the two wings.

STEP 2
Slice through the skin where the thigh joins the body. Pull away the thigh to expose the joint and cut around it to loosen, then slice through the joint to remove the thigh. Lay the thigh and leg, skin side down, and look for the strip of yellow fat that covers the joint. Cut through the joint to sever the leg and thigh. Repeat with the other leg and reserve the four pieces.

Cutting A Chicken

THIS country consumes more chicken per capita than any other kind of meat. Not only is chicken still among the most economical of foods, it is also extremely versatile. For those reasons, I have devised more recipes for chicken over the years than for anything else. Using a chicken in parts extends the cooking possiblities to include casserole dishes, such as paella, and sautéing and braising. Moreover, small pieces of chicken cook faster and more evenly than large ones.

STEP 3
Make a long incision along one side of the backbone, beginning at the neck and running to the hind section. Repeat this action until the breast meat is removed. Do the same on the other side.

STEP 4
Trim excess skin and fat from the breasts. If desired, slice the breasts in half widthwise.

Drawings by Doug Taylor

2. Now answer each question about the selection on pages 126–127.

c 10. In the first picture, the knife is showing
a. how to cut a chicken.
b. how to remove the wing from the chicken.
c. how to cut the wing at the middle joint.
d. how to reserve the wing section.

a 11. When you cut the wing from the chicken, you should slice through the lower part of the breast through the wing joint because
a. extra meat comes off with the wing.
b. the breast will be discarded.
c. the bony tips should be reserved.
d. the wings are too tiny.

d 12. To remove the thigh and the leg, you should first
a. cut through the joint to sever the leg and the thigh.
b. look for the strip of yellow fat over the joint.
c. cut the skin where the body and the thigh meet.
d. expose the joint.

d 13. You should chop through each side of the backbone from the neck to the hind section in order to
a. discard the wing tips.
b. reserve the neck.
c. reserve the backbone.
d. remove the breast meat.

3. Give the correct answers based on the selection on page 129.

c 1. To open exit windows,
a. call one of the crew members.
b. push a button at the base of your chair.
c. grasp the two handles on the exit window and pull.
d. push the window out of the airplane.

b 2. The exit windows open onto the
a. propeller.
b. wings.

TO OPEN DOOR EXITS AND INFLATE SLIDES

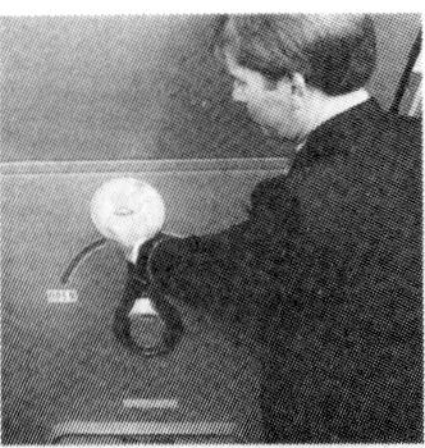

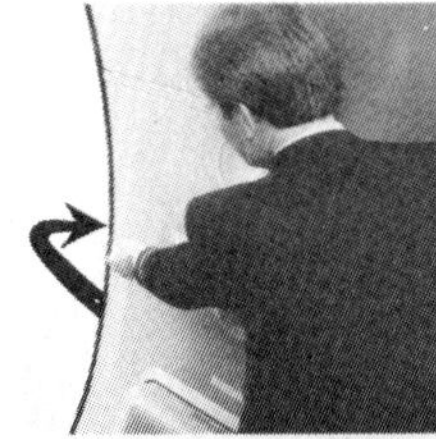

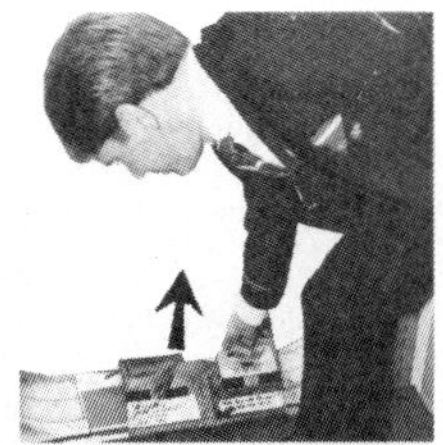

TO OPEN WINDOW EXITS

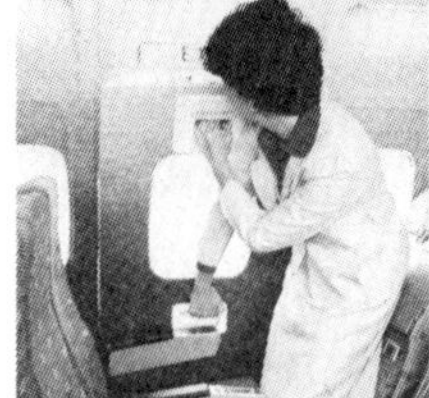

CREW MEMBER WILL OPEN REAR STAIR DOOR AND LOWER STEPS

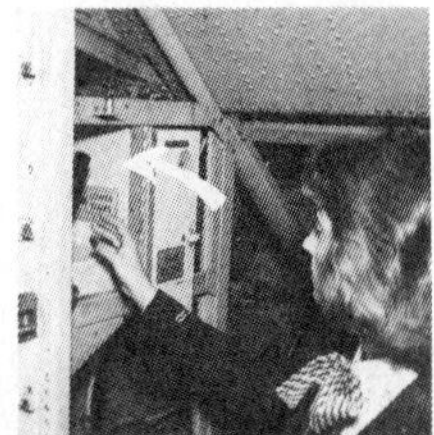

BRACE POSITIONS

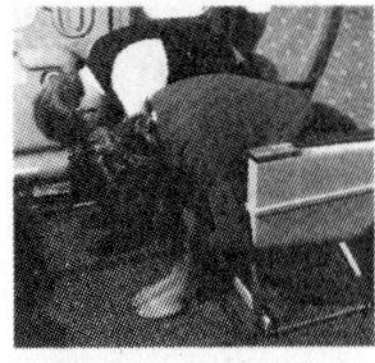

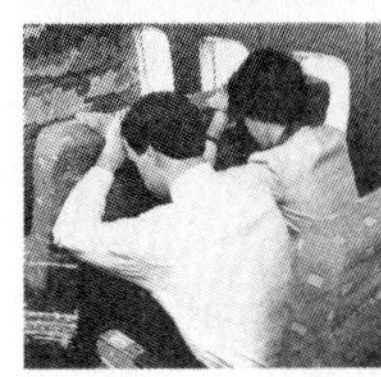

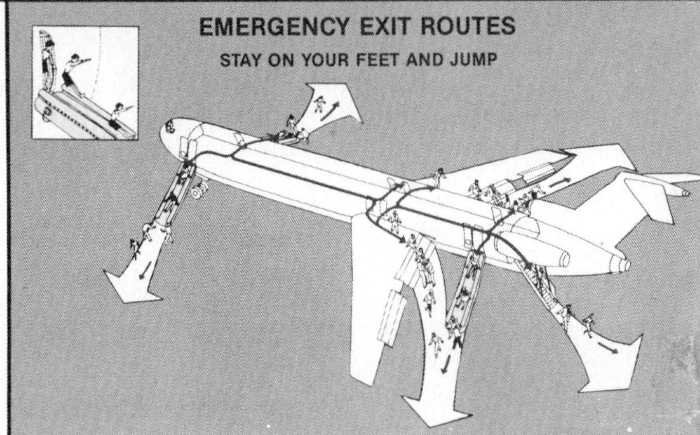

c. door exits.
d. slides.

a
______ 3. In order to inflate the slides,
a. swing open the door and pull a marked handle.
b. blow hard into the special tubes.

c. get into the brace position.
d. lower the rear door steps.

d _______ 4. To use the emergency exit routes, you should
a. lie on your stomach and slide down slowly.
b. lie on your back and guide yourself down with your hands at your sides.
c. wait until the captain uses them first.
d. remain standing and jump.

a _______ 5. To open the stair at the back of the plane and lower the steps,
a. call a crew member.
b. push hard against the door.
c. do nothing because it opens by itself.
d. read the instructions posted near the rear stair door.

4. Answer the following questions about the selection on page 131.

c _______ 1. The sentence "Caution: Dinosaurs on the Loose!" here means that
a. dinosaurs have escaped from their special cages at the Field Museum.
b. people should be careful not to step on the dinosaurs roaming free at the museum.
c. at the museum there are lots of enjoyable activities involving dinosaurs.
d. dinosaurs are dangerous animals.

a _______ 2. The words *Dinosaur Days* refer to
a. October weekends given over to stories, films, and crafts about dinosaurs.
b. the period in history that dinosaurs walked the earth.
c. fun days when museum visitors dress up as dinosaurs.
d. weekends when dinosaurs walk freely through the city.

c _______ 3. The illustration shows that the advertisement is supposed to be
a. very serious.
b. very intelligent.
c. humorous.
d. sad.

Field Museum of Natural History

Caution: Dinosaurs on the Loose!

During Dinosaur Days

Every weekend in October is filled with dinosaur fun for all ages. See funny plays about silly dinosaurs. Make dinosaur hats and masks to wear. Enjoy dinosaur stories, films, crafts, and tons more.

It's all FREE with Museum admission. For details, call (312)322-8854.

Dinosaur Days - a prehistoric adventure the whole family will enjoy.

Field Museum of Natural History
Roosevelt Road at Lake Shore Drive
Chicago, IL 60605

Illustration by Tamar Rosenthal

b ______ 4. To enjoy Dinosaur Days,
a. take a scooter to Lake Shore Drive.
b. visit Chicago's Field Museum of National History in the fall.
c. call the museum for details.
d. contact the illustrator, Tamar Rosenthal.

5. Look at the chart at the top of page 133 and choose the best possible answer.

b ______ 1. This graph is trying to show
a. how serious colds are for Americans of all ages.
b. the number of colds that people get according to their age groups.
c. some effective ways to treat colds.
d. how often sneezes and sniffles strike young people.

a ______ 2. The word *sniffles* probably means
a. breathe noisily through the nose.
b. sneezes.
c. statistics.
d. very young people.

d ______ 3. About 30 percent of which age group had at least one cold in a year?
a. toddlers and infants under age five
b. senior citizens
c. middle-age men and women older than age twenty-five but younger than age forty-four
d. people less than age twenty-five but age eighteen or older

c ______ 4. Which statement is true based on the graph?
a. Children under age five have the fewest colds in a year.
b. Colds generally strike people at the same rate no matter what their age group.
c. As people get older, they get fewer colds in a year.
d. People between ages forty-five and sixty-five have more colds than those in any other age group.

d ______ 5. The two age groups that have very close to the same rate of colds per year are

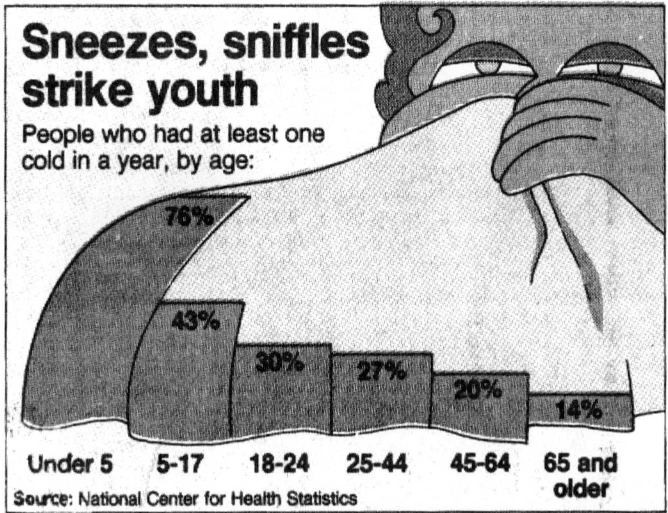

a. under age five and ages sixty-five and older.
b. ages five to seventeen and ages forty-five to sixty-four.
c. ages twenty-four to forty-four and ages forty-five to sixty-four.
d. ages eighteen to twenty-four and ages twenty-five to forty-four.

4. Visuals from Textbooks

The following visual aids come from textbooks in a variety of courses. Examine each visual and any words that go along with it. Then answer each question.

1. *Business Economics*

WORKERS EMPLOYED IN THE UNITED STATES IN 1984

Industry	Number of Workers
Mining	1,002,000
Construction	4,380,000
Manufacturing	19,744,000
Transportation and Public Utilities	5,179,000
Wholesale and Retail Trade	21,775,000
Finance, Insurance, and Real Estate	5,677,000
Services	20,692,000
Government	15,931,000

1. What is the chart trying to show? **how many workers are employed in different industries in the United States in 1984**

2. Which three types of employment had the largest number of workers? **manufacturing, wholesale and retail trade, and services**

3. Approximately how many people worked in 1984? **ninety million**

2. *American Government*

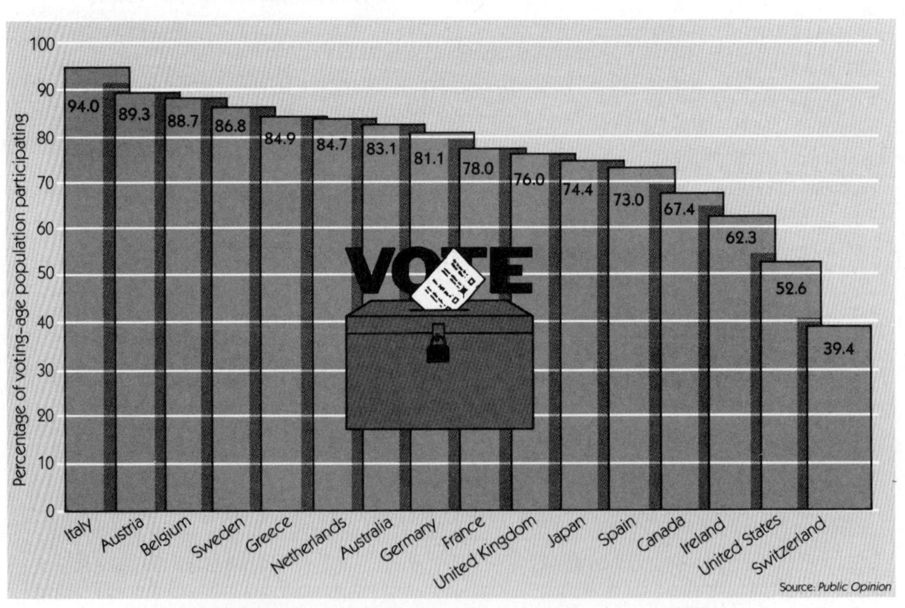

FIGURE 11.5 Voter turnout in democratic nations. Voter turnout in the United States is lower than that in most other democratic nations.

1. What do the numbers on the left side of the graph represent? **percentage of voting-age people who voted**

2. Which country has the largest percent of voters?

Italy

Which country has the smallest percent?

Switzerland

3. What point does the caption make about voting in the United States? What evidence could you give to support that point? **Voter turnout in the United States is lower than voter turnout in most democratic countries. In this figure it is lower than voter turnout in all countries except Switzerland.**

3. *Health*

The Cerebrum The largest and uppermost part of the brain, which regulates your thoughts and actions, is the *cerebrum* [*SER uh brum*]. The cerebrum is responsible for the highly developed intelligence of human beings. As you can see in Figure 13.4, the surface of the cerebrum looks like a wrinkled walnut with many grooves. These grooves follow a pattern in normal brains. The patterns are used to identify specific regions of the brain. Some regions receive messages about what

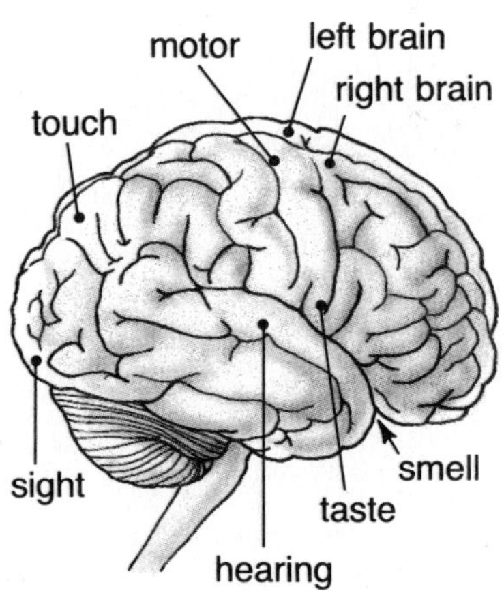

FIGURE 13.4 Control centers of the brain.

you see, hear, and smell, or how you move. Other parts control your ability to think, write, talk, and express emotions. Figure 13.4 identifies different regions of the brain.

1. What does the illustration show? **the control centers of the brain**

2. Why is the illustration necessary to the paragraph? **It helps you visualize the brain and locate the control centers.**

3. What do the labels indicate? **the different activities controlled by parts of the brain**

7

Using SQ3R

SQ3R is a technique or method that helps you understand what you read. It gives you a useful series of steps that can improve your comprehension. You may recognize parts of SQ3R because they were discussed under different names in earlier chapters, but SQ3R pulls together five different steps into a whole system. You can use the system for your reading, especially in textbooks, newspapers, and magazines.

What is SQ3R? The letters stand for the following activities:

*S*urvey
*Q*uestion
*R*ead
*R*ecite
*R*eview

The *S* in SQ3R is for *survey*. The *Q* is for *question*. The *3R*'s stand for three words that begin with an *R*: *read, recite, review*.

7a Survey

When you survey, you preview. Do you remember previewing from chapters **3** and **4?** If not, look back for a quick review.

Survey means the same as *preview*. Its purpose is to give you information about what you are reading *before* you actually begin. When you survey, you do the following:

- read the sentences that introduce the chapter
- read the main headings and the subheadings (look for **boldface** or *italic* print)
- look at the illustrations and the photos and read all the captions (sentences that explain the pictures)

- read the checklists and the questions at the end of the selection
- read the introductory sentences at the beginning of the chapter

In surveying, don't read all the material. Your purpose is *not* to read the complete piece. You want an overview. Take only a few minutes to survey.

EXERCISE

Take a Survey

Look at the English textbook selection "Giving a Talk" below. Survey it, but do not read the whole piece.

1. What do the two introductory paragraphs tell you?
2. What are the headings?
3. What questions or activities appear after the selection?

Giving a Talk

Giving a talk or a speech might bring butterflies to your stomach, make your knees knock and your palms moist, and give you a dry mouth. People who normally have no trouble talking, often search for words when they are speaking in front of an audience.

How can you overcome your nervousness and be a good speaker? Remembering these five *P*'s should help — Prepare, Plan, and Practice, Practice, Practice.

Prepare

1. Choose a topic that is interesting to *you*.
2. Choose a topic that you can research if necessary.
3. If appropriate, add humorous or interesting details or personal stories that will keep your audience interested.

Plan

1. Be sure that you know exactly what you want to say. Make notes or an outline on note cards or slips of paper that you can look at during your talk. Write only key words on your cards that will help you recall your main points and details. You do not want to read your speech.

2. If you are using illustrations or pictures, be sure they are large enough for your audience to see.
3. Ask your family or friends to set aside some time for you to practice your talk in front of them.

Practice

1. Find a quiet place to practice your talk out loud.
2. Read over your notes until you have them almost memorized. Then practice your talk by just glancing at your note cards occasionally. Find the key word, and look up again as you continue with your talk.
3. Practice in front of a mirror so you can see how you look. Your hands are busy with your note cards, but how are you standing? Are you rocking back and forth? Are you pacing like a caged lion? Try standing with your feet slightly apart so that you are comfortable. If you feel yourself getting tense, take a deep breath, and relax.
4. Listen to yourself as you practice out loud. Are you talking loudly enough without shouting? Are you stressing your main points and details? Let your voice show your feelings. Look at one or two spots while you practice. When you give your talk, replace these spots with actual people.
5. Practice in front of your family and friends. Time yourself. If you are over or under your time limit, speed up or slow down or change the length of your talk. Practice using your illustrations. Ask for comments when you finish.

If you follow the five *P*'s, you will feel confident in front of your audience. You will know that your talk is interesting and that your presentation is strong. Try to enjoy yourself.

Activity

Write notes or a short outline for a five-minute talk on one of the following topics, or choose one of your own.

a strange pet I would like to own
my favorite activity
somewhere I would like to visit

— *John Stewig and Shirley Haley-James*

7b Question

In the SQ3R process, the *Q* for *Question* means that you actually produce your own questions. You identified the main headings and the subheadings when you surveyed. Now look again at the headings (usually in boldface print). Turn each heading into a question. Write the questions down.

To construct your question, you might want to use one of these word groups:

- Why is (are)?
- How do (did)?
- When did?
- Why did?
- What is (are)?
- What does (do)?

For example, look at the headings taken from a chapter called "Six to Twelve: Relationships with Others" in a college psychology text. They appear in the left column. Then look at the right column for some possible questions prepared from those headings.

Headings	*Questions Made from the Headings*
1. Relationships with Parents	What are a child's relationships with his or her parents?
2. Reactions to Child-Rearing Styles	What are some reactions to child-rearing styles? How do children react to the different styles that parents use in bringing up their children?
3. The Impact of Divorce	What is the impact of divorce on a child?
4. The Impact of Maternal Employment	What is the impact of maternal employment? How does a mother's working affect a child?

EXERCISE

Develop Questions

Look at the selection "Giving a Talk" on pages 138 and 139. Write your own questions using the title and the three head-

ings. (Do not write a question for the heading "Activity.")
Student responses will vary.

1. Question for the title "Giving a Talk":

____

____

____

2. Question for the heading "Prepare":

____

____

____

3. Question for the heading "Plan":

____

____

____

4. Question for the heading "Practice":

____

____

____

7c Read

The first *R*, *Read*, means that now you read the selection from one heading to the next heading and stop before going on. While you read, try to find the answer to the question that you've made up from the heading — from the *Q* step in SQ3R.

Reading in this way gives you a purpose. It keeps you

focused on segments (short pieces) of the text. You do not read the whole selection at once.

When you read the sentences from one heading to the next, stop before you continue. Your purpose is to read in order to answer the questions you wrote. After you answer each question, go on to read down to the next heading. Keep repeating the process.

7d Recite

The second *R, Recite,* means that after you've read from one heading to the very next one, you stop reading and try to answer the question.

When you first start using SQ3R, recite your answers out loud. As you gain more experience, say the answers to yourself. Remember that the key here is the following:

- Look at the question that you made up from the heading.
- Read only from one heading to the next.
- Stop before going on.
- Recite the answers to the questions.

After you answer the question, read down to the next heading. If you can't come up with an answer, read the sentences under the heading again.

EXERCISES

1. Read and Recite

Look again at the selection "Giving a Talk" on pages 138–139. Follow the instructions below carefully.

a. Read the question that you wrote from the title "Giving a Talk" (see "Exercise," pages 140–141).
b. Now read the two paragraphs beneath the heading and try to find out the answer to your question. After you complete that step, *come back to read step* c *below before going on*!
c. After you read to look for an answer, recite your answer aloud. If you can't answer your question, read the paragraph again.

2. Read and Recite

With the same selection, "Giving a Talk," pages 138–139, consider only the sentences from the heading "Prepare" to the heading "Plan." Follow the instructions below carefully.

a. Read the question that you wrote for the heading.
b. Now read the sentences beneath the heading to find out the answer to your question. Come back to read step c below before going on.
c. After you read to look for an answer, recite your answer out loud. If you can't answer your question, read the sentences again.

3. Read and Recite

Continue reading in the selection "Giving a Talk."

a. Read from the heading "Plan" to the heading "Practice." Follow exactly steps a, b, and c in Exercise 2 above.
b. Read from the heading "Practice" to the heading "Activity." Follow exactly steps a, b, and c in Exercise 2 above.

7e Review

After you read the whole selection, *review* your reading. *Review* means "look again." What is the best way to look again at what you've done? Simply go back and read your questions another time. Try to answer the questions.

This time, however, do not read the material under each heading. Now you're trying to remember what you read by thinking about each question and giving an answer. If you can't answer a particular question, then reread only the material under the heading that will answer your question.

EXERCISE

A Review of Your Reading

Return to the selection "Giving a Talk," pages 138–139. Look first at all the questions that you wrote from the headings. Try to recall what you read and answer your own questions. Write the answers below.

1. **Student responses will vary.**

2.

3.

4.

On pages 144–149 is the introduction to the third unit — "Television" — of a college basic reading textbook. To see how SQ3R can help you read carefully, follow the instructions on pages 137–143 before you read the selection.

Introduction

The Age of Television

For better or worse, television is an integral part of American society. We are citizens of the television age. When it was publicly introduced at the 1939 World Fair in New York, a reporter for *The New York Times* wrote, "The problem with television is that the people must sit and keep their eyes glued on a screen: the average American family hasn't time for it. Therefore, the showmen are convinced that for this reason, if for no other, television will never be a serious competitor of broadcasting." Looking back at the last four decades, we can be amused by this reporter's comments. Not only has television caught on; it now plays a central role in the life of the typical American household.

The 1970 census revealed that 96 percent of the homes in the United States have one television set and that over a third have two or more. In his book *The Cool Fire,* Bob Shanks comments that there are more television sets than bathtubs. According to the latest statistics, the average American family has the television set on almost seven hours a day. The average child will spend more hours watching television than in the classroom. Jeff Greenfield speculates that, by the early twenty-first century, it is possible that we will watch television even more than we sleep or work.

Television is ever-present and easily accessible. It conveys new ideas and helps us escape from our troubled surroundings. It entertains, informs, and persuades and is the way many people, young and old, spend their leisure time. More than entertainment, television is a powerful force that has a strong influence on the way many of us think or act. The power of the medium can be illustrated by its ability to attract a multitude of people to experience a single event simultaneously. For example, more people watched the final episode of "M*A*S*H" than voted for Reagan and Carter combined in

"Don't Blame T.V., blame yourself!
According to them, they're giving you what you want!"

the 1980 presidential election! Children who have not yet learned to read can tell you about "ring around the collar" and admonish you not to "squeeze the Charmin." Slogans made popular by television shows easily become incorporated into our daily expression.

Asking Ourselves Questions

Because of television's pervasive presence in our lives, it is important for us to stop and reflect on how it might affect our views, values, expectations, and behaviors and to consider how the medium might be influencing and shaping our society. One way we can assess television's impact on us is by posing a series of questions. Answering these questions is not easy, because the issues are complex and opinions vary. Ultimately it will be up to each of us to weigh the factors involved and arrive at our own conclusions.

What Would We Do with Our Time If We Weren't Watching Television?

Because television occupies so much time in the life of the average American, it is interesting to consider what people might be doing if they weren't watching television. Would children play more, use their imaginations, build, create, read, draw, and interact with their peers? Or would they sit, brood, and sulk? Obviously, children spent their time differently before the age of television. Similarly, if adults weren't watching the tube, how would their behavior be altered? Would they socialize more, go places, visit friends, and pursue intellectually stimulating activities? Or would they remain isolated and inactive?

Does Television Isolate Us or Bring Us Together?

In its very early years, when it was a relatively new phenomenon, television viewing was a special occasion. Members of the family and invited guests would gather around the only available television set to watch a limited number of programs. Does this pattern apply to today's society? Are enough programs viewed by most Americans to give us a shared experience?

Close to 40 percent of households have more than one television set. What does this suggest about family viewing patterns? With numerous channels available and various programs being broadcast at any given hour, how likely is it that families as a unit watch a particular program as part of their evening activity? When a show is viewed in common, does a discussion follow wherein family members participate and share ideas? Approximately 45 percent of American households have the television set turned on during dinner time. What does this suggest about family communication?

Does Television Make Us Active or Passive?

Television is a form of communication, but, unlike the telephone or speech, it reaches only one way. With the typical television sets currently in use in the average American home, we only receive information and cannot respond or communicate with the sender. The ideas and images portrayed don't come from within us (from our minds) but rather from the outside (from the tube). Does television stimulate our minds or inhibit our thinking? Does it open our eyes to new worlds and ideas, or does it dull our imagination? Does our constant viewing of the screen inhibit our ability to become self-activated? What happens to the behavior of an active toddler who, after playing and exploring his or her environment, is gradually introduced into the world of television? As regular viewers, are we able to make use of our ability to form and develop our own ideas and viewpoints, or do we tend to adopt the views expressed on the screen? In watching television frequently, do we withdraw from the outside world or become more active participants?

Does Television Reflect Real Life or Distort It?

Television can be a source of confusion because it alternates between reality and fantasy. Much of what is shown on television is shaped to fit rigid time constraints. Does what we view on television give us a picture of true life, or does it tend to distort reality? Should television programs accurately represent the real world, or is that not their purpose? Because of built-in time limits to programs and commercials, stories are developed and concluded in a relatively short period on most television shows (the exception being the popular soap operas). Television often presents us with the 60-minute or the 60-second solution. This means that even the most difficult problems are usually solved within the time limits of the program. Does this typically occur in real life? Do you think people want to see a realistic approach to problem situations?

Is watching television as a source of escape from real-world problems any worse than reading comics, listening to the radio, or going to the movies?

Making Connections

As you read and study this unit and begin to formulate answers to many of the questions posed, it should become clear that this unit can be connected to the previous two units. "Reading and Literacy" and "Work and Careers," and to the next unit, "The Family." Many of the issues raised in this unit are related to the ideas presented in the other units.

Here are some broad issues posed as questions to consider as you begin to work with this unit and relate it to the other units. There are many other questions that can be asked, but these should serve as a start. You will be presented with several opportunities to make connections as you work with the text.

"Television" and "Reading and Literacy"

How can television and reading be compared and contrasted? Does one medium influence the other? Can television stimulate people to read and become more literate? Or does it promote anti-reading attitudes and foster lower literacy levels? Does television viewing require the same effort as reading a book? If students are taught to be critical readers, can they (and should they) be taught to become critical television viewers?

"Television" and "Work and Careers"

Does television present an accurate view of the working world? What types of occupations and careers are portrayed on television? Are certain careers and occupations over-represented on television in proportion to their true numbers in the real world? What work values are emphasized on television? What kinds of work-related decisions are people shown making? Are women seen as gainfully employed? Are union members represented on shows? What picture of work and careers emerges from most television shows?

"Television" and "The Family"

How has television's portrayal of families changed over the years? Does television present an accurate picture of the American family today? What family values are stressed, and which ones are not emphasized? Are the families that you see on the TV screen similar in behavior to yours, or are they different? Do you expect or want your family life to resemble the life of families portrayed on TV?

Gearing Up for the "Television" Unit

Television consumes a great deal of our time and undoubtedly will continue to do so in the future. Because of this fact, we must examine our relationship with it, understand what we see, and become aware of the medium's potential effects. Just as we are urged to become critical readers of texts, so must we become critical viewers of television. Taking a critical look at this phenomenon in our lives requires us to become active — to explore, react, challenge, and understand. We must decide for ourselves how to use television and comprehend the positive and negative aspects of the medium. Finally, we must place the television experience in perspective so that, in the words of Ben Logan, a broadcast producer and freelance writer, "it does not become more important than one's real life, other persons and issues that confront our communities and the world."[1] Before reading this unit, respond to the following situations:

1. Imagine that you have returned from the doctor after having had a complete checkup. The doctor has informed you that you have a strange disease that requires special attention. You must stop watching television. No television at all is allowed. Write about how your life would be affected by this news. What kind of adjustments would have to be made? What, if anything, would change?
2. Imagine that you met a hermit — a person who lives alone, isolated from society. This hermit lived in a cave, and his only connection with the outside world was television. His entire view of society was shaped by television. What would the world be like to this hermit? What image of our society would he have formed on the basis of his television viewing?

1. Survey

Take only about three minutes to survey the reading. Read the first paragraph. Look at the illustration. Read the caption. Examine all the headings and the subheadings.

---

[1] Ben Logan and Kate Moody (eds.), *Television Awareness Training* (New York: Media Action Research Center, Inc., 1979), p. v.

What does the first paragraph tell you? You learn from the first paragraph about the important role of television in American life since it was introduced in 1939. Also, you see that people did not at first think that television would be as popular as radio was.

What does the illustration show? Did you realize that the cartoon was giving a humorous comment about what appears on television? Many people complain about the poor quality of the programs. The cartoon shows that if we continue to watch the programs now on the air, we can expect more of the same in the future! In other words, we ourselves are at fault for bad television shows.

Did you notice the four main headings in boldface italics? Write each heading in the left column.

1. ______________________ ______________________

______________________ ______________________

______________________ ______________________

2. ______________________ ______________________

______________________ ______________________

______________________ ______________________

3. ______________________ ______________________

______________________ ______________________

______________________ ______________________

4. ______________________ ______________________

______________________ ______________________

______________________ ______________________

Did you see the four subheadings under "Asking Ourselves Questions"? Write each subheading at the top of page 151.

1. ______________________________

2. ______________________________

3. ______________________________

4. ______________________________

Did you see the three subheadings under "Making Connections"? Write each of these subheadings in the left column.

1. ______________ ______________

______________ ______________

______________ ______________

2. ______________ ______________

______________ ______________

______________ ______________

3. ______________ ______________

______________ ______________

______________ ______________

Did you see the questions numbered 1 and 2 at the end of the selection — under the "Gearing Up for the 'Television' Unit" heading? The questions help you focus on the major issues that the writers will deal with later in the chapter.

2. Question

Now turn each of the four main headings that you wrote into a question on page 150. Write your questions on the blank lines in the right column next to the headings. After you've written your questions, come back to this point and read the next paragraph.

Do your questions look like these?

1. What are the features of the age of television?
2. What questions can we ask ourselves about television viewing?
3. What connections can we make between television and other issues?
4. How can we gear up for studying the television unit in this textbook?

The subheadings under "Asking Ourselves Questions" are already in question form.

Now turn into a question each of the three subheadings under "Making Connections" that you wrote on page 151. Write your questions on the blank lines in the right column next to the headings.

3. Read

Return to the selection. Read *only* the paragraphs under the first heading, "The Age of Television." Come back to this point and continue to read only after you finish those paragraphs.

4. Recite

Now look at the question that you wrote for the first main heading. Try to answer the question aloud. If your question was "What are the features of the age of television?" you should have found some of these answers:

- The age of television is our current age.
- The age of television means that TV plays a major part in the American household.
- Ninety-six percent of us have at least one television set; 33 percent of us have two or more sets (1970 census).
- Kids spend more time watching television than in school.
- Television informs, entertains, and persuades.
- Television can attract large numbers of people to the same event at the same time.

Now return to the selection again. Read *only* the paragraphs under the second main heading, "Asking Ourselves Questions." When you finish reading that section, try to answer aloud the question that you wrote for the main heading. Then try to answer aloud the question in each subheading.

Repeat these steps one section at a time until you finish the chapter introduction. *Recite* the answer to your own question for each main heading and subheading. In other words, *Read* and *Recite* for each section before you go on to the next.

5. Review

After you finish reading the introduction to the chapter "Television," go back to the questions that you wrote for the headings. Try to answer each question again without looking back. If you can't answer a question, reread the section that has the answer.

EXERCISE

Review of SQ3R

Look at the selection below. Use SQ3R on your own to read the selection. Follow all the steps explained in **7a, b, c, d,** and **e.**

For *Q, Question,* write down the questions you make up for the headings. For *Review* write down answers to those questions.

Tips on Taking a Test

With the right preparation, you shouldn't have to panic when the teacher passes out a test. Here are some tips to help you while you're taking a test:

1. **Plan your time wisely.** Before you begin working, quickly look over the whole test. See how many items there are, and give yourself a set amount of time to do each one. As you go through the test, first answer the items you are sure of. Then go back and do the items you aren't sure of. Sometimes an answer in one part of a test will give you a clue to another answer you didn't know the first time.
2. **Follow the directions carefully.** Read the directions for each section completely and carefully. If there is an example, work through it. If there is something you don't understand, ask your teacher.
3. **Answer the question that is asked.** Read each item carefully. Watch for "tricky" wording to be sure you know exactly what kind of answer is called for. For example, look at the three questions below. They look very much alike, but each one calls for a different answer.

- Which city *is* the capital of Mexico?
- Which city *was* the capital of Mexico?
- Which city *is not* the capital of Mexico?

4. **Check your work.** Leave time, if you can, to go over your answers. Check to see that you have followed the directions correctly. Also check for careless mistakes. When you're in a hurry, it's easy to write an *a* instead of a *d*. Be sure that you check for misspellings, too.

Different Kinds of Tests

There are many kinds of tests. Each can be a little different and requires a different approach.

1. **Essay.** These tests usually require you to explain something in a paragraph or more. The test items check to see how well you understand the idea of a lesson. Often you are asked to explain why or how something has happened.

   Example:

   > *Answer the following question in two paragraphs or less.
   >
   > How did Cortez manage to conquer the Incas?

2. **Short answer.** These tests usually check your knowledge of facts. The answers you give should be short.

   Example:

   > *Write your answer on the line following each item.
   >
   > In what year was Martin Luther King, Jr. born?
   >
   > ______________________________
   >
   > What were the last words Julius Caesar said before he died?
   >
   > ______________________________

3. **Fill in the blanks.** These tests require you to write an answer of one or more words.

Example:

*Fill in the blank spaces with the correct word or words.

A body of land surrounded by water is an

____.

The half of the earth that is south of the equator is the

____________________ ____________________.

Tips: Read each sentence carefully. Look for clues to the right answer. For example, in the first item, the word *an* appears before the blank. This means that the answer begins with a vowel. In the second item, two blanks need to be filled in. This means that your answer should have two words in it.

4. **Multiple choice.** Multiple-choice tests ask questions or make incomplete statements; then they give you several possible answers from which to choose.

Example:

*Write the letter of the correct answer on your answer sheet.

Which is the largest continent?
a. Australia b. Africa c. Asia

A country that is not entirely in Asia is ____________.
a. Turkey b. China c. India

Tips: Be sure you read the directions carefully so that you understand exactly what you're expected to do. You may be asked to show your answer by underlining, circling, or writing a letter.

Multiple-choice tests often give you the chance to make "educated guesses." You can rule out the answers you know are wrong and choose the best from those left over. Only do this, however, if you know that extra points will not be subtracted for wrong answers.

5. **Matching.** Matching tests are usually set up in two columns. You are asked to match the items in one column with those in the other.

Example:

*In the blank on the left, write the letter for the definition in Column B that goes with the word in Column A.

	Column A	Column B
_______	1. citadel	a. wedge-shaped writing
_______	2. cuneiform	b. area protected by walls
_______	3. silt	c. soil in water

Tips: Again, reading the directions carefully is very important. In matching tests, you may be asked to write the letter or number of each matching item, as in the example, or you may be asked to draw lines connecting the items.

Answer the items you are sure of first, and mark them off on the test. You may be able to figure out the other matching items by a "process of elimination"; that is, by choosing the best answer from those that have not been used already.

6. **Labeling or categorizing.** In these tests, you have to tell what something is. There are many different kinds of labeling tests.

Examples:

*Read each book title. Write *N* if the book is nonfiction and *F* if it is fiction.

_______ The Cheetah: Nature's Fastest Racer

_______ Tartu's Jungle Dream

*Read each country name. Write *1* if the country is in Europe, 2 if it is in Asia, and 3 if it is partly in Europe and partly in Asia.

_______ Turkey _______ Iran

_______ Mongolia _______ Italy

*Read each question. Decide which is the best reference book to use for finding the answer. Then write *dictionary, atlas, almanac,* or *encyclopedia* after the question.

a. How do you pronounce *plateau?* _______________

b. What is Spain's main industry? _______________

Tips: As you can see, following directions is also important in labeling tests. You may have to write an abbreviation, a letter or number code, or a whole-word answer. If you have trouble remembering a code, write it on a separate piece of paper and refer to it during the test.

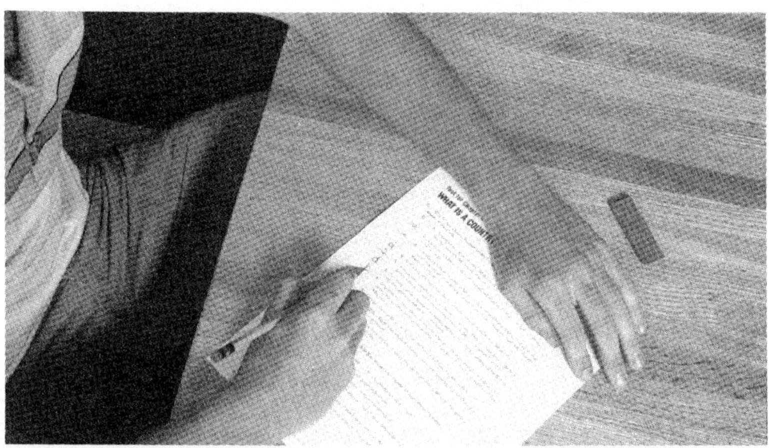

7. **True/false.** In these tests, you read statements and decide whether they are true or false.

Example:

> *Write *T* if the statement is true and *F* if the statement is false.
>
> ______ Mount Kilimanjaro is higher than Mount Kenya.
>
> ______ Rain forests in Africa always get 50 inches of rain a year.

Tips: The important thing to remember about true/false statements is that if one part of the statement is not true, the whole answer should be marked false. Watch out for words such as *always, never, no,* and *all.* These words allow no room for exceptions. Whenever you see one of these words, read the statement very carefully to be sure it is true all the time.

Also, when you are asked to write *T* or *F* for an answer, write clearly so that there will be no confusion as to which letter you wrote.

8. **Standardized tests with computerized answer sheets.** These tests are given to students in all parts of the country.

Usually Standardized Tests come in the form of booklets with computerized answer cards or sheets. Instead of circling, underlining, or writing an answer, you fill in a space in the test booklet or on a separate answer card or sheet.

Examples:

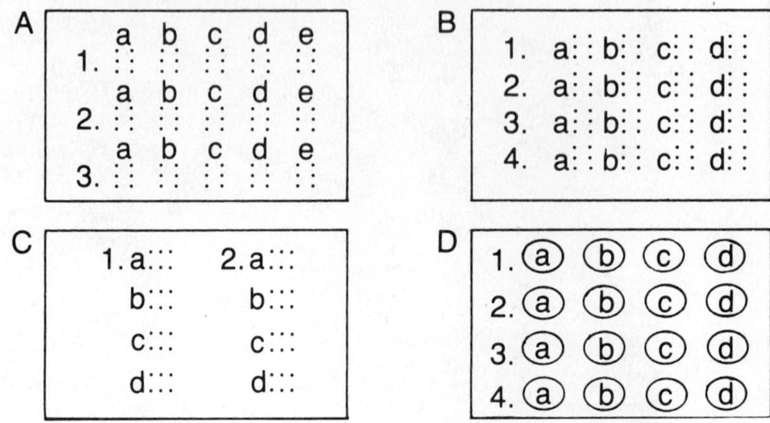

In examples A, B, and C, you must fill in the space between two dotted lines. Notice that the choices are arranged and labeled differently. In D, the answer space to be filled in is an oval.

Tips: Since computerized answer sheets are scored by machine, you must be very careful about how you mark your answers. (You can't explain a wrong answer to a machine!) Here are some things to keep in mind as you mark your answers:

a. Use only a soft-lead pencil. The machine will not score marks made with pens, felt-tip markers, or colored pencils. If you're not sure you have the right kind of pencil, ask your teacher.
b. Make dark marks that completely fill in the answer space. The machine will not pick up light marks.
c. Do not make any other marks on your answer sheet. The machine might score these as wrong answers.
d. Don't cross out an answer. Again, the machine will score any pencil marks. If you want to change an answer, erase the old one completely.
e. Be sure you fill in the correct space. Always check the number of the question with the number on the answer sheet. It's easy to skip an answer. If you do, all the answers that follow will be in the wrong places.

Questions

1. There are four things you can do while actually taking a test that should help you do better. What are those four things?
2. If you had a choice of taking an essay test, a fill-in-the-blank test, a multiple-choice test, or a true/false test, which would you prefer? Tell why you would choose that one.
3. What is a matching test?
4. If you mark the wrong answer space on a computerized answer card what steps should you take to change your answer to the correct space?

— *J. M. Stanchfield and Thomas G. Gunning*

Unit Three

Understanding What You Read

8

Reading for the Main Idea

A piece of writing often presents many ideas, yet these ideas usually relate to one important idea. In order to understand how these ideas fit together, you need to spot the main idea that gives an overall meaning to the reading.

Ideas come in different sizes. Some are sentence-length ideas. These sentence-length ideas build a larger paragraph-length idea. And then a number of paragraph-length ideas build an essay, an article, or a book chapter.

Here we start by finding the key ideas in sentences. Then we will see how sentences add up to the larger ideas in paragraphs.

8a Finding Key Ideas in Sentences

Each sentence, no matter how long it is, usually contains one key idea. The rest of the sentence then gives more information about that key idea. The key idea is usually about one of the following:

- What a person or object is
- What a person or object does

For example, look at this sentence:

> A computer sends me bills.

Now look at this sentence:

> Every month a broken computer at the telephone company sends me outrageous bills for telephone calls I never made.

The key idea of both sentences is the same. The second adds more details to let you know more about the computer and its bills. Both sentences tell you that the computer is sending bills to someone. That key idea is important because it helps you understand the importance of all the other details. Why do you care whether the telephone calls were made? Because someone is being billed for them. Why is the computer called broken? Because it sends incorrect bills. Why are the bills outrageous? Because they are being sent incorrectly. What happens every month? This outrageous bill is sent.

To find key ideas in sentences, do the following:

- Ask *who* or *what* the sentence is about.
- Ask what the person or object is doing or what is happening to the person or object.
- Separate the minor details that simply add information to the key idea. These details often tell *when, where, why, what kind,* and *how.* By taking away the minor details, you can see the main idea more clearly.

Look at how this method works in the following sentence:

> The old discount supermarket at the Faded Gold Shopping Center has been clean from top to bottom for a week because the Health Department threatened to close the store.

First, let's take away the minor details:

When: for a week
Where: at the Faded Gold Shopping Center
Why: because the Health Department threatened to close the store
How: from top to bottom
What kind: old discount

With those details crossed out, what is the sentence about? *The supermarket.*

And what happened to the supermarket? *It is clean.*

So the key idea is: *The supermarket is clean.* The rest of the sentence simply gives more details about this miracle.

EXERCISES

1. Key Ideas in Sentences

In each of the following sentences, underline the words that give the key idea. Here is an example:

> In today's world reading is necessary for all kinds of daily jobs.

1. On the job, your boss will give you a list of things to do before the day is finished.
2. Complex directions, printed in small type, appear with most new things you buy at the store.
3. Even at the supermarket, the brightly colored packages will get you very confused unless you can read the labels.
4. People of any age who cannot read well often need tricks to get help and to hide their problem.
5. Even though learning to read when you are an adult is hard, the hard work pays big rewards.

2. Key Ideas in Newspaper Sentences

Write the key idea of each sentence in the space provided after that sentence. Look at this example:

> The captain of a cargo ship involved in a fatal crash with a fishing tug will be arrested on negligent homicide charges when his ship docks, an official said Saturday.

The captain will be arrested.

1. Back this week for its final flurry of business, Congress finds itself facing the problem of the budget deficit, which is the same issue that has troubled it all year.

   Congress faces the deficit.

2. It took no time at all in this opening game for top-ranked Oklahoma to hit mid-season form.

   Oklahoma hit mid-season form.

3. Since the beginning of the year, at least sixteen people have died in the city after using cocaine, usually in combination with other drugs, according to Medical Examiner Dr. Janice Siner.

   Sixteen people have died.

4. Rural mail carrier Alberta Morley of Somers knows not only the names of all those on her route but also what they look like, what cars they drive, what dogs they own, where their kids go to school, and whether they will be away from home during any given week.

   Alberta Morley knows all about the people on her route.

5. Houston Manager Hal Lanier had one more wish Saturday after José Cruz's two-run home run lifted the Astros to a seven-to-six victory over the St. Louis Cardinals.

   Hal Lanier had a wish.

6. There were more than 5,400 mishaps at nuclear power plants — including sixty-eight at the two reactors at Indian Point — that could have led to serious accidents during 1984 and 1985, according to a report by Public Citizen, a consumer advocacy group.

   More than 5,400 mishaps occurred at nuclear power plants.

3. Key Ideas in Newspaper Stories

The headline of a news story generally states the main idea of the story. The headline has been removed from each brief story in a recent newspaper. Read each story and decide on its key idea. Then select the correct headline from the list on page 167 and write it on the blank.

1. **Westmont Teen Honored**

   A Westmont teenager wins a $20,000 Westinghouse scholarship for her genetic research into cancer.

2. **Ex-City Aide Closes Case**

   James D. Montgomery, former Chicago corporation counsel, ends his part of a lawsuit against Las Vegas police; Montgomery said he quit his city job to complete the case.

3. **Mistake Blows City Away**

   In a transmission error, the National Weather Service falsely reports that tornados destroyed Rockford.

4. **Marchers Lose Sleep**

   A residents' group pickets O'Hare airport to protest an airline's new program of late-night flights.

5. **Villa Park Slate Back**

A Du Page County judge reinstates a Villa Park board slate that had been thrown off the April 7 ballot.

Headlines

Villa Park Slate Back
Ex-City Aide Closes Case
Westmont Teen Honored
Mistake Blows City Away
Marchers Lose Sleep

— Chicago Tribune

4. Key Ideas in Fact Sentences

On the blank lines write in your own words the key idea of each statement.

1. Honolulu, Hawaii, contains the only royal palace in the United States, the Iolani Palace built in 1882 for King Kalakaua and Queen Liliuokalani.

   The only royal palace in the United States is in Honolulu.

2. The northernmost part of the United States, except for Alaska, is in Lake of the Woods County, Minnesota.

   Minnesota contains the northernmost part of the United States.

3. The number of Indians in the area that was to become the United States was over one million one hundred thousand in 1492, when Europeans first learned about the New World.

   One million one hundred thousand Indians lived in the United States in 1492.

4. The first skid row was in Seattle, where lumberjacks named the run-down part of town "skid road" after the greased log paths, on which logs were slid down to the river.

   The first skid row was in Seattle.

5. Because its climate is too cold for flies to reproduce in, Alaska is the only state without houseflies.

Alaska has no houseflies.

8b Stating Paragraph Topics

Several sentences grouped together form a paragraph. Each paragraph has a *topic,* a general point that the paragraph deals with. You should be able to state simply in just a few words the topic of a paragraph.

Look at this paragraph from a computer textbook. What is the topic?

> To be productive and to participate fully in the Information Age, individuals must become computer literate. There has been some debate, particularly in educational circles, over what computer literacy is and how students and others should be prepared for a society that is entering an Information Age. Should students learn to write computer programs? Do students need to know how to operate a computer but not how to write programs? How much does a computer-literate person need to understand about the role of computers in society?
>
> — *Ronald E. Anderson and David R. Sullivan*

Did you state the topic of the paragraph as *computer literacy*? (*Literacy* here means being educated; a *literate* person is an educated person.) The general topic is about becoming computer educated. All the sentences contribute to that topic.

You might be tempted to say that the topic of the paragraph is *computers* or *students.* Certainly the paragraph deals with those ideas. However, the topic is more exact than just *computers* or *students.* These are too general. The paragraph is about becoming educated in computer use. You wouldn't say that the topic is the *Information Age.* Even though the words appear in the paragraph, the point is too narrow. Nothing else in the paragraph develops the point.

When you state the general idea of a paragraph, avoid *too* general a statement. Also avoid any statements that are too specific.

Look at the following paragraph from a sociology textbook. What is the topic of the paragraph?

> Sociologists reserve the term *small group* to refer to a group small enough for all members to interact simultaneously, that is, to talk with each other or at least be acquainted with each other. Small groups such as work groups and families are the intermediate link between the individual and the larger society. This intermediate position defines their importance in terms of attitudes, values, and behavior. For this reason, sociologists are interested in what happens when people get together in small groups, whether it is to share gossip, reach a decision, or even play card games.
>
> — *Richard T. Schaefer*

The topic here is *small groups*. The sentences in the paragraph build that topic. You wouldn't say that the topic is the *individual and society*, even though those words appear in the paragraph. They state the topic too generally. You also wouldn't say that the topic is *sharing gossip* or *playing card games*. Those words appear in the paragraph too, but they make too narrow a point to be the topic of the paragraph.

Read this paragraph from a book called *This Fascinating Animal World*. What is the topic of the paragraph?

> To what use does a kangaroo put its great heavy tail? It leans back and props itself on it, as a man does on a shooting stick. Many lizards use their tails that way too. The original monster lizards, almost certainly, swung their tails as weapons, in a carry-over from the tail-swinging technique of fish. And today? Is it true that a crocodile uses its tail as a weapon? Yes. It can knock a man over with one wallop. Do any warm-blooded animals do the same sort of thing? Yes again. Take an ant bear. It thwacks with its tail as powerfully as a bear with its forepaw.
>
> — *Alan Devoe*

The topic here is *the ways some animals use their tails*. By explaining about kangaroos, lizards, crocodiles, and bears, the paragraph tells us how they use their tails. The topic is not *animals* because that topic is too general. Yes, the paragraph deals with animals — but with only one feature of only some animals. That feature, of course, is the animals' tails and how they are used. You also couldn't say that the topic is *crocodiles' tails as weapons*. Even though the paragraph mentions this idea, it is too narrow a point to be the topic of the paragraph.

Stating Paragraph Topics

- Read the sentences carefully. Ask yourself these questions: What is the paragraph about? What general point is the paragraph trying to make?
- Do not state the topic in terms that are too general.
- Do not state the topic in terms that are too specific, or narrow.
- State the topic in a few words. Draw on the key ideas in the paragraph to state the topic in your own words.

EXERCISES

1. Paragraph Topics

Read each paragraph and try to determine its topic. Then look at the three choices for stating the topic. Put a *C* next to the choice that you think best states the topic. Put a *G* next to the choice that you think is too general. Put an *S* next to the choice that you think is too specific.

1. We discovered our first vampires in the cave of Los Sabinos, about 200 miles south of the border. At the time this was the northernmost colony of vampires ever reported, although since then another colony has been found 50 miles closer to the United States. The village of Los Sabinos consisted of half a dozen thatched huts deep in the jungle, a few people, and several sheep, pigs, and goats. I spent some time talking to the Indians as I was curious to find out what sort of people would voluntarily live next to a community of vampire bats. The villagers discussed the bats as calmly as New Jerseyites would talk about mosquitoes. The bats came every night to feed on their stock — and on them. The villagers retired to their huts as soon as the sun went down and carefully filled in every chink. If anyone forgot a chink, when he awoke the next morning he was dripping blood from half a dozen little wounds. When the animals got bitten so badly they became weak, the villagers took them into the huts too.

   — *Daniel P. Mannix*

G ______ a. protecting against vampire bats

C ______ b. vampire bats and the people of Los Sabinos

S ______ c. bats south of the border

2. At first the movement for public schools met the resistance of voters who refused to approve the necessary taxes. Some people objected to the idea of public education itself, thinking it might make working people too independent. As the benefits of education became clear, however, the idea of supporting schools through taxation took hold. By the mid-1800's most white children in northern states could obtain a free elementary education. The 1850 census reported that the country had about 80,000 primary schools, attended by almost 3,500,000 young people.

— *Henry F. Graff*

C ______ a. the start of tax-supported public education in the 1800s

S ______ b. resistance to taxes for public education

G ______ c. education in America through the 1850s

3. My day begins officially at 7:00, when all inmates are required to get out of bed and stand before their cell doors to be counted by guards who walk along the tier saying, "1, 2, 3 . . ." However, I never remain in bed until 7. I'm usually up by 5:30. The first thing I do is make up my bed. Then I pick up all my books, newspapers, etc., off the floor of my cell and spread them over my bed to clear the floor for calisthenics. In my cell, I have a little stool on which I lay a large plywood board, about 2½ by 3 feet, which I use as a typing and writing table. At night, I load this makeshift table down with books and papers, and when I read at night I spill things all over the floor. When I leave my cell, I set this board, loaded down, on my bed, so that if a guard comes into my cell to search it, he will not knock the board off the stool, as has happened before. Still in the nude, the way I sleep, I go through my routine: kneebends, butterflies, touching my toes, squats, windmills. I continue for about half an hour.

— *Eldridge Cleaver*

G a. life in prison

S b. guards counting inmates in prison

C c. one prisoner's morning activities in his cell

2. Paragraph Topics

On the first blank line below each paragraph, write the topic of the paragraph in your own words. (You'll return to use the remaining blank lines for exercise 3 on page 192.) Most of these paragraphs come from textbooks.

1. How does a sociologist study interactions within small groups? In a sense, he or she must develop useful instruments for such investigations, just as natural scientists rely on microscopes and telescopes. Few methods of studying groups are as clearly devised or widely utilized as the "*Interaction Process Analysis*" (IPA) developed by Robert F. Bales (1950a, 1950b, 1968, 1970). The IPA is a technique for classifying every gesture, remark, and statement that occurs within a group in order to analyze the group's structure and processes. It permits observers to draw conclusions about how a group establishes norms, confers leadership on members, performs ceremonial tasks, and solves problems.

   — *Richard T. Schaefer*

Topic: **sociologists' methods**

Main idea: **The Interaction Process Analysis is one of the methods most widely used by sociologists.**

2. Crying is the most powerful way — and sometimes the only way — that babies can signal to the outside world when they need something. It is, therefore, a vital means of communication and a way for infants to establish some kind of control over their lives. Those babies whose cries of distress do bring relief apparently gain a measure of self-confidence in the knowledge that they can affect their own lives. This can be inferred from the findings that by the end of the first year, babies whose mothers respond promptly to their crying with tender, soothing care cry less. The more the mother ignores, scolds, hits, commands, and restricts the baby, the more the baby cries, frets, and acts aggressively.

   — *Diane E. Papalia and Sally Wendkos Olds*

Topic: **babies' crying**

Main idea: **Babies' crying sends messages to other people.**

3. At many colleges, contributions are up in nearly all categories — including alumni gifts, corporate and foundation grants, and planned giving. Several colleges recorded sizable increases in overall giving, ranging from 15 per cent to more than 50 per cent, and a few went over the $100-million-mark for the first time.

— *Liz McMillen*

Topic: **college contributions**

Main idea: **Contributions are up at many colleges.**

4. In addition to reciting, you can improve your memory for material by reviewing it several times. Many students wait until just before a test to review. Then they find that there is too much material to review thoroughly, and they have to stay up all night to cover it all. However, if they would take that "cramming" time and spread it out over the term, reviewing a little bit at a time, they would remember much more and do better on the test. Reviewing is based on two final learning principles: further consolidation or reduction, and distributing study time.

— *Sherrie L. Nist and William Diehl*

Topic: **reviewing as part of learning**

Main idea: **Reviewing can improve your memory for material.**

5. Even in sports where Blacks predominate as athletes, we are routinely passed over as candidates for top coaching and sports-administration jobs — often despite having the combination of both academic preparation in physical education and substantial practical experience at the *assistant* level in major athletic programs. Hence, there are only two Black athletic directors, three Black head football coaches, and fewer than 30 Black head basketball coaches at major Division I, NCAA colleges and universities. There are no Black head

baseball coaches at such institutions today. And in the professional ranks, circumstances relative to Black access to top positions are even more dismal.

— *Harry Edwards*

Topic: **Black coaches and administrators**

Main idea: **Blacks are routinely passed over for top sports coaching and administration jobs.**

6. The periodicals section of most libraries contains much useful information on jobs and careers. Trade journals and professional magazines provide current information. Besides these publications, more popular periodicals regularly feature articles on careers and job hunting. Getting a job and getting ahead in the working world are frequent topics. Even if the local library has a limited supply of trade or professional publications, it will very likely have a good supply of popular magazines. In addition, periodicals have the advantage of being more timely than books or other reference materials. Some magazines feature articles on careers, training, aptitude testing, applying for jobs, and opportunities in small business for all job hunters. Others, such as *Working Woman* or *Black Collegian,* are geared toward specific groups.

— *Gail Martin*

Topic: **career information in periodicals**

Main idea: **Library periodicals have much useful information.**

7. Like their elders, most of today's parents care deeply about their children's growth. They want to share in it — and shape it. They know that early experiences make a great difference in what will happen later. While parenting is often fun, it is harder to be a parent today than ever in the past. We have to deal not only with the age-old dilemmas of toilet training and sibling rivalry — but with aspects of massive and rapid change: the loss of a known world, the sexual revolution, the drug culture, and the ever-present flickering of zillions of television sets.

— *Kate Moody*

Topic: **parents' concerns**

Main idea: **Parents care deeply about their children's growth.**

8. Summer employment can be very useful in areas besides financial ones. Both summer and part-time jobs are opportunities for you to try out what it means to work, to experience what it means to have other people rely on you and to develop an understanding of why others behave as they do. In addition, part-time and summer jobs provide firsthand experience to add to information obtained through books, newspapers, family, friends, and counselors. Probably the most difficult thing about a summer job is finding it. Although more summer jobs are available during good economic times than bad, there never seem to be enough for all the students who want them.

   — *Bruce Shertzer*

Topic: **summer jobs**

Main idea: **Summer jobs can help you learn many things in addition to offering you money.**

9. When you complete a textbook chapter, you may wish to construct an outline to represent the overall organization of the material. Check this outline with the subheadings in the text. You might also try writing a brief summary of each chapter. Refer to your own marginal notes and then write a single sentence that crystallizes your understanding of the chapter. Then record explanations and illustrations of that major idea. Through these means you are saying: "Here is what I think is going on. How does that sound?"

   — *Elaine P. Maimon et al.*

Topic: **outlining and summarizing textbook chapters**

Main idea: **Outlining and summarizing textbooks can help you see the meaning of your reading.**

10. The Civil Rights Act of 1964 was one of the most far-reaching laws ever passed by Congress. Among its most important provisions, it (1) prohibited discrimination in public places such as theaters, restaurants, and hotels; (2) insisted on identical voting requirements for blacks and whites in all states; and (3) prohibited discrimination on the basis of race or sex by all employers, unions, and employment agencies engaged in interstate commerce. The new law also offered financial aid to school districts that needed help in beginning desegregation programs and required that federal funds be denied to districts practicing segregation.

— *Henry F. Graff*

Topic: **the Civil Rights Act of 1964**

Main idea: **The Civil Rights Act of 1964 fought discrimination and segregation in several important ways.**

8c Finding Main Ideas in Paragraphs

Once you know the general topic **(8b)**, you should be able to state the *main idea* of a paragraph. The main idea holds the paragraph together. Each sentence relates to the main idea and helps build the paragraph's meaning. The main idea of a paragraph is more than the general topic. To find the main idea, you start with the topic, of course; but you must figure out what the paragraph is saying about the topic.

Sometimes the main idea of a paragraph is directly written down, often at the beginning of the paragraph. Then, to find the main idea, all you have to do is to find the one or two sentences that sum up the paragraph.

Some paragraphs do not state the main idea in a few direct words. Then you must put together the different parts of the idea to see what they add up to. The idea that they add up to is the main idea of the paragraph.

Look again at this paragraph that you examined in **8b:**

To be productive and to participate fully in the Information Age, individuals must become computer literate. There has been some debate, particularly in educational circles, over what computer literacy is and how students and others should be prepared for a society that is entering an Information Age. Should students learn to write computer programs? Do students need to know how to operate a computer but not how to write programs? How much does a computer-literate person need to understand about the role of computers in society?

— *Ronald E. Anderson and David R. Sullivan*

You know the general topic to be *computer literacy* or *becoming educated in computer use.* But the paragraph does more than name the topic. To find the main idea, ask yourself what the paragraph is saying about the topic of *computer literacy.* The paragraph says that *There is no agreement on what computer literacy really means.* The second sentence here gives you the main idea of the paragraph. The rest of the sentences support the main idea.

8c(1) *Stated Main Ideas*

If one sentence states the main idea of a paragraph, we usually call that main idea sentence a *topic sentence.* The topic sentence can appear almost anywhere in a paragraph — at the beginning, the middle, or the end. Most often, though, it appears at the beginning, as one of the first few sentences.

Look at the following examples of paragraphs from a book of consumer advice. In each paragraph the topic sentence is marked in italics.

Main Idea at the Beginning

Supermarkets rip you off when they cut meat. They say, "It's fair, we're just charging for labor." Maybe, but then they must pay their butchers $500.00 per hour. You're better off buying a big piece and cutting it yourself. Examples: At my supermarket, boneless chuck costs $2.09 per pound, top chuck costs $1.69. Yet plain chuck steak costs only $1.09 per pound, and when you cut it in half you get top chuck and boneless chuck. It's even more impressive with the expensive cuts. Filet costs $6.69. Shell steak costs $4.29. Yet you get both filet and shell if you cut a porterhouse steak in half. Porterhouse costs $3.29. A cookbook which gives detailed instructions on how to cut down larger cuts of meat can pay for itself in less than a month.

— *John Stossel*

The general topic of this paragraph is *meat cutting in supermarkets.* Use that topic to figure out the main idea. The main idea of the paragraph is *Supermarkets rip you off when they cut meat.* All the remaining sentences in the paragraph give more information, such as the supermarket's excuses, examples, and how to avoid the rip-off.

Main Idea in the Middle

> During the first cold snap, I usually go over to the American Automobile Club's towing headquarters and tag along as they go out to rescue motorists who can't get their cars started. Amazingly, seldom do the AAA mechanics have to do anything mechanical to the car. Most often, the mechanic simply hops in the car and starts it. The driver stands there looking foolish and says something like, "I can't understand it . . . I tried it a dozen times and it just wouldn't start." *Most often, the driver's mistake is pumping the gas pedal.* That's how I was taught to start a car in cold weather, but pumping is dead wrong. The correct way: Depress the gas pedal *once* (that sets the choke). Let the pedal all the way up. Then turn the key.
>
> — *John Stossel*

The topic of this paragraph is *problems in getting a car started in the cold.* The main idea of the paragraph is *Most often, the driver's mistake is pumping the gas pedal.* The earlier part of the paragraph lets you know about the problem that this mistake causes. The later part of the paragraph lets you know how to avoid the problem.

Main Idea at the End

> How fresh is canned food? Is your baby food older than the baby? Some companies now print pull dates on cans. A Hellmann's mayonnaise jar will say in plain English, "Buy before July 10, 1982." Good for Hellmann's. A Campbell's soup can will say "September, 1981." That's the pull date. This is helpful, to a point; 1981 means Campbell's says the soup is good at least until then. You don't know if the soup was packed last year, or perhaps ten years ago. In Campbell's case, the company believes the soups have a shelf life of three years. Different companies have different beliefs about shelf life. Worse, some companies print the dates in code: 7-1-9-3-0-1 on a box of Duncan Hines cake mix means the mix was packed in July, 1977. *Knowing the pack date is the most useful; that tells you exactly how old the food is.*
>
> — *John Stossel*

The topic of this paragraph is *canned food freshness.* The main idea of this paragraph is *Knowing the pack date is the most useful; that tells you exactly how old the food is.* All the sentences before this part of the paragraph were leading up to the main idea by explaining the difficulty in knowing how old canned food is.

Finding Stated Main Ideas in Paragraphs

- Decide on the general topic of the paragraph. (See **8b.**)
- Ask yourself: What is the paragraph saying about the topic?
- Find the sentence(s) that states what the paragraph is saying about the topic.
- Sometimes the main idea sentence will use a word such as *it* or *he* or *she.* Or, the main idea sentence can be made clear only by referring to another sentence in the paragraph. Feel free to use the words from other sentences when you state the main idea, even when you identify one sentence as the main idea sentence. For example, look at the textbook paragraph below this box.
- Stated main ideas always appear as sentences, not as questions. Sometimes a paragraph will introduce a topic by asking a question, but the *answer* to that question is usually the main idea.

> A copyright is also a kind of protection. In this case, the protection is for authors or creators of books, plays, software, movies, and musical compositions, as well as for photographers, painters, and sculptors. This protection extends for the lifetime of the person or persons who produce the item, plus fifty years. Copyright is also a kind of right to property and a protection against persons copying what others have already made. Publishers, music recording studios, and movie studios are all examples of businesses that may be involved with copyrights.
>
> — *Betty J. Brown and John E. Clow*

Here, the topic is *copyrights.* The main idea sentence is the second sentence of the paragraph. But did you notice that the second sentence does not even state the word *copyright*? You have to return to the first sentence for that word. Thus, even though the second sentence states the main idea very closely, you should draw on information in the first sentence to state the main idea: *A copyright is protection for authors or creators of books, software, movies, and musical compositions, as well as for photographers, painters, and sculptors.*

EXERCISES

1. Stated Main Ideas

For each paragraph, first write the topic in your own words on the appropriate blank. Then underline the sentence that tells the main idea of the paragraph. Finally, write the main idea in your own words on the appropriate blank.

1. Recent scientific studies have demonstrated that the wolf is not particularly ferocious. Basically he is friendly and more sensitive than the dog, with a complicated and subtle social organization. Wolves do not customarily hunt in large packs. Their howling is not a hunting cry, and does not frighten other animals. Like all animals they get their food the easiest way they can, and with the least risk. Thus much of their prey is mice, squirrels, and rabbits; but also, unfortunately from man's point of view, lambs and calves. It is chiefly in winter that wolves form packs to hunt larger game. The pack is of moderate size — very often merely a family group consisting of an old couple and their mature offspring.

   — *Tom Burnham*

Topic: **the ferocity of the wolf**

Main idea: **Wolves are not as fierce as we think.**

2. Why don't buildings collapse? How can they stand with all the weight pushing down on them? The reason is the buildings push up as much as other things push down. If your feet push down on the floor, the floor pushes up on your feet. A force cannot get lost, but it must be balanced by an opposite and equal force. If the forces are not balanced, something will be pushed one way or another. And then the building may collapse.

Topic: **why buildings stand**

Main idea: **Buildings stand because the upward and the downward forces balance.**

3. The idea of birthstones came from old superstitions about precious stones. Certain stones were thought to bring health and long life. Others were supposed to make the wearer brave and strong. Some other stones would protect you from fire and lightning. By wearing a special stone for their month of birth, people thought that they would have special luck or qualities.

Topic: **birthstones**

Main idea: **Old superstitions about the powers of stones stand behind the use of birthstones.**

4. The first automobile accident happened in 1769, in France. A steam carriage travelling at less than three miles an hour overturned while making a turn. Half a century later in England steam carriages would travel the roads between cities at a speed of five miles an hour. In 1885, in Germany, Gottlieb Daimler mounted a small gasoline engine on a bicycle and Karl Benz used a gasoline engine to power a three-wheeled car. The idea of using an engine to turn the wheels of a vehicle was around long before the modern automobile was invented.

Topic: **the idea of an automobile**

Main idea: **Engines were used to power vehicles for over a century before the modern automobile was invented.**

5. Most Americans believe that Abner Doubleday invented baseball in 1839, at Cooperstown, New York. This is not true. Many books printed before 1839 mention baseball, including books from England. The main character in the novel *Northanger Abbey*, for example, enjoys both cricket and baseball. Jane Austen, the famous British novelist, wrote *Northanger Abbey* in 1798. The "fact" that Doubleday invented baseball was made up by a three-person commission in 1908. The commission wanted to show that baseball was an all-American game, having nothing to do with foreign influences.

Topic: **baseball's beginnings**

Main idea: **Doubleday's invention of baseball was made up.**

6. One approach to reading is similar to the way in which a sponge reacts to water: ABSORB IT! This commonly used approach has some clear advantages. First, it is relatively passive. The reader's job is finished after discovering what the writer said. Little thinking is required by readers who use the sponge method. Thus, reading like a sponge is quick and usually easy. The primary mental effort required is concentration and memory. Another advantage of the sponge model is that it can be a useful thinking style. If you absorb a lot of information, you have a knowledge base that can help you do more complex thinking at a later time.

   — *M. Neil Browne and Stuart M. Keeley*

Topic: **the sponge approach to reading**

Main idea: **The sponge approach to reading has many advantages.**

7. You can usually blame a bad essay on a bad beginning. If your essay falls apart, it probably has no primary idea to hold it together. "What's the big idea?" we used to ask. The phrase will serve as a reminder that you must find the "big idea" behind your several smaller thoughts and musings before you start to write. In the beginning was the *logos,* says the Bible — the idea, the plan, caught in a flash as if in a single word. Find your *logos,* and you are ready to round out your essay and set it spinning.

   — *Sheridan Baker*

Topic: **the primary idea for an essay**

Main idea: **The primary idea for an essay helps hold the essay together.**

8. (1) Daydreaming once was considered a waste of time. Psychologists regarded it as evidence of maladjustment, an at-

tempt to escape from reality. They warned that habitual daydreaming could reduce a person's effectiveness in real life and hamper his ability to cope with problems. Even the more indulgent psychologists considered daydreaming a childish habit which caused students to get bad grades and adults to fail at their jobs.

— *Eugene Raudsepp*

Topic: **daydreaming**

Main idea: **Daydreaming was thought to be no good.**

9. After peace had been restored between Spaniards and Amerinds in New Mexico, the two cultures existed side-by-side in relative harmony. The fact that religion and the family were the foundations upon which both Amerindian and Spanish society rested contributed to a common outlook. Over the years, each group came to adopt some customs of the other. The colonists borrowed ideas from the Amerinds in the fields of farming and architecture. The Amerinds, for their part, learned to use domesticated animals and new foods. While they did not completely abandon their old ways of worship, they incorporated the white man's God into their own religious beliefs.

   The success of the missions, pueblos, and *presidios* (forts) soon drew other colonists to New Mexico. These people were, for the most part, peace-loving farmers and ranchers. Distrust of foreigners made the settlers cling together and discourage outsiders. The area remained untouched by outside influence until the 1800's.

   —*Gilbert Martinez and Jane Edwards*

Topic: **Amerinds and Spaniards in New Mexico**

Main idea: **Amerinds and Spaniards in New Mexico got along well together for many years.**

10. Most of the activities of the United States Department of Agriculture (USDA) relate in one way or another to matters affecting the consumer. One of the more important duties of the department is protecting and maintaining standards of quality in the daily food supply of the nation. It does this

through inspection of meat and poultry products in particular. In addition, the USDA grades meat and meat products, eggs and butter, and both fresh and canned fruits and vegetables. Grade labels, labels that indicate levels of quality, help consumers to judge the products. The standards for grades are set by the USDA. For example, *U.S. Prime* is the best quality of beef, followed by *Choice, Good,* and *Standard*. The USDA also furnishes numerous pamphlets, booklets, and other printed materials on agricultural programs and on products and services for consumers.

— *Betty J. Brown and John E. Clow*

Topic: **the USDA**

Main idea: **The USDA is concerned mostly with consumer issues.**

2. Stated Main Ideas in Textbooks

For each textbook paragraph, put a checkmark beside each sentence (or sentences) that tells the main idea of the paragraph. In the blank space, write the main idea in your own words.

1. From a very early age, infant memory is a powerful tool for ✓ organizing the child's world. Babies as young as 5 months of age who have seen a face for only two minutes will still remember some things about it two weeks later (Fagan, 1973, cited in Cohen, 1979). In another study, 5-month-old infants who saw a three-dimensional Styrofoam figure remembered the shape of the figure 24 hours later (Strauss & Cohen, 1978). Ten minutes after they had first seen the figure, they had remembered its color. Its size and orientation in space, however, were the two aspects they forgot almost immediately. Apparently, even from infancy, we remember certain aspects of our surroundings more distinctly than others.

— *Diane E. Papalia and Sally Wendkos Olds*

Main idea: **Infants have strong memories.**

2. It is in the interest of all countries to wipe out disease. The World Health Organization (WHO) is an agency whose pur- ✓ pose is to improve the health of people in all countries. Its main functions are to support research, to set up health cen-

ters, to help countries conduct health surveys, and to administer vaccination programs.

Among the greatest successes of the World Health Organization has been the campaign against communicable diseases. The number of people suffering from such diseases as tuberculosis, malaria, cholera, and yellow fever has been greatly reduced. One very important victory came in the fight against smallpox. Throughout history, hundreds of millions of people have died from smallpox, a virus that spreads from person to person through the air. In 1967, WHO began a program to rid the world of smallpox. The organization sent over 700 doctors, nurses, scientists, and administrators to more than 30 countries in Africa, Asia, and South America. They vaccinated everyone who had been in contact with the disease. In 1978, WHO announced that the world's last known smallpox case had been located in the East African country of Somalia. No one else caught the disease from that person. Through cooperation, one of the world's most dreaded diseases had finally been wiped out.

— *Arthur Getis and Judith M. Getis*

Main idea: **WHO serves to improve the health of all people of the world.**

3. Reynolds, a Mormon living in Utah, was convicted of marrying two women, thus breaking a federal law. Because the Mormon church at that time approved of polygamy (having more than one spouse), Reynolds contended that the law violated his religious freedom. In this case, the Supreme Court ruled that religious freedom does have its limits. The ✓ Court held that "It was never intended that the First Amendment . . . could be invoked as protection for the punishment of acts inimical to the peace, good order, and morals of society."

— *Richard J. Hardy*

Main idea: **Religious freedom does have limits according to the Supreme Court.**

4. Occupational choice begins when we first become aware that ✓ an occupation can help meet our needs. As we develop, we recognize that certain activities give us satisfaction whereas others are unpleasant. We tend to seek enjoyable experiences and to avoid painful ones. As we become aware of a variety of

occupations, each of us gradually comes to realize that certain occupations provide experiences that are satisfying, whereas others require unpleasant activities. Some jobs attract and others repel. At this point, occupational choice actually starts for each of us.

— *Bruce Shertzer*

Main idea: **Being aware of how jobs fill our needs helps us choose our occupations.**

8c(2) *Implied Main Ideas*

Sometimes a writer does not directly tell you the main idea of a paragraph. Instead the writer *implies* (suggests) the main idea through the combination of information in the paragraph. You, the reader, must draw on that information to see how it fits together. You take some words from one sentence and some words from another sentence to help you construct the main idea. But basically, when you see the overall picture of the paragraph, it is then up to you to state the main idea in your own words.

The main idea that you have to put together yourself is called an *implied main idea.* Here is an example from a textbook of consumer advice:

> A lot of people assume it's nutritionally better to buy dark breads. We tend to believe that white bread has the nutrients processed out, while dark bread still has them inside. Not necessarily true. Dark bread is sometimes simply white bread, dyed dark. There's no definite data on what bread may be better for you, but consider this: Consumers Union bought thirty-three brands of bread and fed them to laboratory rats. Then they weighed and measured to see how much each rat grew or did not grow. The study found it made no difference whether the rats ate dark or white bread. It also made no difference whether the bread was "enriched." The bread companies that I called said the test was ridiculous, since no one eats only bread. Nutritionists I called said if you want a more nutritious bread, buy whole wheat. Whole wheat has more nutrients left in. The word "wheat" alone, or "health food" bread doesn't mean anything.
>
> — *John Stossel*

What is the topic of this paragraph? Clearly, the writer is talking about the nutritional value of breads. Knowing the topic helps you figure out the main idea. But in this paragraph, the writer never directly tells you the main idea of the paragraph: *White bread is probably just as nutritious as most dark breads, except for whole wheat.* You have to figure that out from the various details the writer gives you.

Finding Implied Main Ideas

- Look at all the ideas and details in the paragraph.
- Ask if the ideas and details all relate to a single person or object. What is that single topic? Then check all the sentences of the paragraph (not just the first few) to make sure that they really are all about your suggested topic. If not, try to find a topic that fits all the sentences. As you have seen, all the sentences in the example on page 186 discuss how much nutrition different breads have.
- Ask what point all these ideas and details are making about that topic. Then write a complete sentence that (1) names the person or thing and (2) tells what that person or object is doing. Again check all the sentences of the paragraph to make sure that they fit your main idea sentence. If they do not, you must make your point broader so that it will cover everything in the paragraph. The sentence "Whole wheat bread is nutritious" would not cover the whole example paragraph above.
- Make sure that your implied main idea sentence is not too general. Can you make the topic more specific, or can you say something more specific about that topic and still be describing all the sentences in the paragraph? If you can, then you should make your sentence more specific. If your sentence covers all the sentences in the paragraph and cannot be made any more specific, then it is correct. The topic sentence "All breads have some nutrition" would be too general for the example. Only the sentence given is not too narrow or too general: *White bread is probably just as nutritious as most dark breads, except for whole wheat.*

Look again at this paragraph, which you examined in **8b**:

> Sociologists reserve the term *small group* to refer to a group small enough for all members to interact simultaneously, that is, to talk with each other or at least be acquainted with each other. Small groups such as work groups and families are the intermediate link between the individual and the larger society. This intermediate position defines their importance in terms of attitudes, values, and behavior. For this reason, sociologists are interested in what happens when people get together in small groups, whether it is to share gossip, reach a decision, or even play card games.
>
> — *Richard T. Schaefer*

You know that the topic here is *small groups*. But what point is the writer making about small groups? What is the main idea of the paragraph? The writer implies it; he doesn't state it directly. Using the pointers explained in the box on page 187, you should be able to state the main idea in your own words. You might say something such as this: *Sociologists study small groups because they are important in understanding how people relate to each other.*

EXERCISES

1. Implied Main Ideas

In each selection, the main idea is implied. Read each selection and the statements that follow. Then put a checkmark next to the statement that you think gives the main idea most clearly. Be prepared to discuss why the other choices are not correct.

> Too often young women use work as a stopgap between high school and marriage. The idea is to keep themselves afloat until Mr. Right comes along. Then they can marry and have children. Being a wife and mother is a perfectly valid occupation, but no woman should allow it to cancel out her ability to be self-supporting. Life plays too many tricks. Mr. Right doesn't come along. Mr. Right doesn't earn enough to support the family and you have to work. You find housewifery boring and you want to work but you have no skills. The marriage doesn't last and you have to go back to work. Your children grow up and don't need you so much. You must be prepared.
>
> — *Greta Walker*

√ ______ 1. Young women should consider their careers seriously.

______ 2. Life does not always turn out as we hope.

______ 3. Being a housewife is an absolutely secure career.

______ 4. Mr. Right is bound to be a disappointment.

It is widely believed that if an electric chair or gas chamber should fail to operate, or the rope breaks during a hanging, the prisoner must go free because he cannot twice be put in jeopardy for the same offense. But this is a confusion between the *trial* and the *sentence.* A man cannot, under the Constitution, be tried twice for the same offense. But once he has been convicted and sentenced, then the sentence must be carried out, malfunctioning equipment or no, if the law is to be followed.

— *Tom Burnham*

______ 1. Electric chairs and gas chambers sometimes do not work correctly.

______ 2. If a prisoner is not executed on the first attempt, he or she should be set free.

______ 3. A trial is different from carrying out a sentence.

√ ______ 4. Even if an execution attempt fails, the prisoner still must be executed.

Parents and teachers sometimes tell their charges, "If you say 'I haven't got none,' then you are *really* saying 'I *do* have *some.*' You should be more logical." Double negatives once held, in fact, an honorable place in our language; as witness Chaucer's immortal lines describing the Knight in the Prologue to the *Canterbury Tales:* "He never yet no vileynye ne sayde/In al his lyf unto no maner wight." Or, in modern English, paraphrased freely but quite accurately: "He never said nothing bad in all his life to nobody." The argument that a double negative "cancels itself out" is borrowed, apparently, from elementary algebra, the rules of which have nothing to do with grammar.

— *Tom Burnham*

______ 1. Chaucer, a famous poet, used a double negative.

______ 2. Double negatives are useful.

√_____ 3. The rules of algebra, not grammar, are the source of our thinking that double negatives are illogical.

______ 4. People long ago wrote differently.

2. Implied Ideas in Your Own Words

The main idea in each paragraph is implied. On the blank lines, write the main idea in your own words.

1. A Wisconsin law once required all parents to send their children to high school. This law brought protests from the Amish, a Protestant group whose centuries-old religious beliefs compel them to remain apart from modern society. In 1972 the Supreme Court declared that the state of Wisconsin could not require Amish children to attend school past the eighth grade (*Wisconsin v. Yoder*). The Court ruled that the law interfered with the Amish people's freedom to put their religious beliefs into practice. Similarly, in *Sherbert v. Verner* (1963), the Court ruled that a Seventh-Day Adventist could not be denied unemployment benefits because she refused to work on Saturday (her Sabbath day).

— *Richard J. Hardy*

Main idea: **The Supreme Court has ruled to protect religious freedom.**

2. Economists believe that job earnings influence choice of occupation. They acknowledge that people place varying emphasis on income, but point out that workers tend to move from one occupation to another because of changes in salaries. In 1931, H. F. Clark, an economist, stated that "proper information regarding wages, if sufficiently impressed upon people, will lead to correct choice of occupation and correct number (of people in an occupation), provided barriers to occupations have been removed." This means that the supply of and demand for workers have much to do with wages, which in turn influence people to choose certain careers. However, all barriers to occupations will have to be removed before career choices can be explained by economics alone. There is little

question that economic factors have some influence on choice of an occupation. But to picture them as the major or most important reason goes against the soundest of folk wisdom: "Man does not live by bread alone."

— *Bruce Shertzer*

Main idea: **People do not choose their jobs primarily on the basis of earnings.**

3. Social scientists have used the objective method in studies of the prestige of occupations. The term *prestige* refers to the respect with which an occupation is regarded by society. "My daughter the physicist" has a very different connotation from "my daughter the waitress." Prestige is independent of the particular individual who occupies a job, a characteristic which distinguishes it from esteem. *Esteem* refers to the reputation that a specific person has within an occupation. Therefore, one can say that the position of president of the United States has high prestige, even though it has been occupied by persons with varying degrees of esteem.

— *Richard T. Schaefer*

Main idea: **Prestige refers to the respect given to a position, while esteem refers to the respect given to an individual.**

4. According to one sociologist, Theodore Caplow, the accident of birth often plays a large role in determining what occupation people choose. Children follow their parents' occupations: farmers are recruited from farmers' offspring, teachers from the children of teachers. The parent "passes" an occupation on to the child. Furthermore, such factors as time and place of birth, race, nationality, social class, and the expectations of parents are all accidental, that is, not planned or controlled. They all influence choice of occupation.

— *Bruce Shertzer*

Main idea: **Accidents of birth influence occupational choice.**

5. Let's consider that you want an automobile to get to work. Is it possible to get to work on the bus or with a friend while

saving money for a car? Or do you need the car now? You must decide whether obtaining the car *now* is worth the extra cost of buying on credit. Thousands of decisions like this are made all the time because buying a car on installment is the most common use of credit in our economy. Appliances such as television sets, refrigerators, and washing machines are usually sold on installment. The costs of electric guitars, pianos, and other expensive musical instruments also are usually spread over a number of payments. Some of the things you buy from door-to-door salespeople are customarily bought on installment plans too. These are such items as reference book sets, vacuum cleaners, home repairs, and photography service sold to you in your home.

— *Betty J. Brown and John E. Clow*

Main idea: **We buy many items on credit.**

3. Paragraph Topics and Main Ideas

Return to the exercise on pages 172–176. You have already written the topic for each paragraph. Now determine the main idea of each paragraph and write it on the remaining blanks. Some of the main ideas are stated directly; others are only implied. In either case, write each main idea in your own words.

4. Stated and Implied Main Ideas

In some of the following paragraphs, written by sports stars, the main idea is stated; in others, the main idea is implied. On the blanks below each selection, write whether the main idea is stated or implied. If the main idea is stated, underline the main idea sentence. If the main idea is implied, write your own main idea sentence.

1. You can have the best coach in the world, someone who knows the game inside out and is an excellent teacher. But he or she can only help to a certain point. After that, it's up to you to produce the mental side, to carry out what the coach has said. My dad taught me how to play the game, but I taught myself to win. Embracing his belief that the one who works the hardest will do the best started me on the road.

   — *Chris Evert Lloyd, tennis*

stated

2. The thing about growing up poor is that you really don't have any sense that you are in fact growing up poor. It was just the way things *were*. I didn't know anything else. I was a Jackson, and my father worked real hard, and there were always meals on the table. Never any food in the fridge, though. There was no such thing as eating between meals, but we did always eat. What was brought home at night was what we had for dinner, and then I went to bed. We never ate breakfast except for special Saturdays and Sundays when Dad cooked. That experience was the only experience. Like with haircuts. My father had these old military clippers, and when my hair would get too long, he'd run those clippers over my head three or four times and that would be that until the next time. He didn't worry about it looking funny or weird. He just cut it to the scalp so he wouldn't have to be cutting it all the time.

— *Reggie Jackson, baseball*

stated

3. Team athletes on the road take their place in a long line of males in flight from domesticity and its responsibilities of one woman and family. The road symbolizes the same thing for a basketball player as the forest, frontier, or sea did for some of America's greatest writers: Like Rip Van Winkle who escaped through sleep, or the Pathfinder who blazed trails through a wild environment, or Nick Adams who escaped through fishing, the pro player escapes through a life of games on the road. Being away with the fellas makes up an essential part of the job.

— *Bill Bradley, basketball*

implied; Being on the road is a kind of escape for team athletes.

4. The public tends to think most athletes are stupid. I first started running into that in the classroom, in college, when teachers would automatically give me a poorer grade than the

other students in the class just because I was an athlete. It wasn't that they didn't like athletes in general — or me in particular. They just assumed that anyone who participated in sports must not be very smart, and they graded athletes accordingly. People think that because we use our bodies to make a living, we must have empty heads. They don't realize how much you have to use your mind to be really successful, year after year, in professional sports.

— *Wilt Chamberlain, basketball*

stated

---

5. I'd been to Los Angeles before, and I'd even performed inside Pauley Pavilion, the basketball arena where the Olympic gymnastics events were going to be held. But this time the whole atmosphere was different. The American team was staying in dormitory rooms at the University of Southern California with runners and swimmers and fencers and cyclists and thousands of athletes from all over the world. You could walk around the campus and see people from China and Brazil and Romania and dozens of other countries who'd all been working just as long and hard as you had and who had the same dreams. And all of them were on different schedules. Some were competing on the first day, others had to wait more than a week. So the cafeteria and infirmary and game rooms were open around the clock, buses were coming and going at all hours, and there were chain-link fences and security guards everywhere to protect us.

— *Mary Lou Retton, gymnastics*

implied; The Olympics created an exciting atmosphere.

---

5. Main Ideas in Paragraphs

In each paragraph, the main idea is either stated or implied. If the main idea is stated, underline the sentence that states it, then write the main idea in your own words on the blanks provided. If the main idea is implied, simply write the main idea in your own words.

1. The popular notion that witches were burned in Salem is quite false. In fact, no witches were burned at any time in

Salem or anywhere else in America. Nor were witches by any means all women; in fact, they were not all even human beings. Two dogs were actually put to death in Salem for "witchcraft." The means of execution in all cases, including the unfortunate dogs, was by hanging, with one exception: an old man named Giles Corey. Corey, in an instance of bravery under torture scarcely paralleled in American history, "stood mute," or refused to plead either yes or no to the charge against him. Under the law, this meant that his heirs would not be deprived of his property, which would have been sold at auction had he confessed or been found guilty. (Had he denied the charge, he would almost surely have been convicted.) Corey's death was by "pressing"; heavy stones were placed upon his chest in an attempt to force him to plead. He was crushed to death; it is said that his last defiant words were "More weight!"

— *Tom Burnham*

implied; Witches in America were usually hanged instead of burned.

2. It is very difficult to produce and maintain extreme cold because heat energy constantly seeks to fill in the low places. A boiled egg will always cool off to room temperature when it is taken off the stove. The heat in its molecules rapidly leaks away by contact with air and by radiation. If the egg is wrapped in a woolen cloth it stays hot longer, since the cloth acts as *heat insulation.* But it cools eventually, because nothing stops the flow of heat altogether. It always keeps on leaking till its source has the same temperature as its surroundings. The problem of taking the heat out of a substance such as air, and keeping it out, makes it difficult to study extremely cold temperatures. When there is a large difference in temperature, such as 300 or 400 degrees, even the best insulation is only partially successful.

— *David O. Woodbury*

It is hard to make something very cold and keep it very cold.

3. It would be nice if once you have a job everything would go along perfectly. It never happens that way. Life is filled with problems, and very often they are job-related. Sometimes

they loom as insoluble. This is usually because problems can create panic, and panic tends to blot out the various choices that are usually available to you. Other times you might let things slide because the difficulty doesn't seem very important. You hope that it will go away or somehow resolve itself. The opposite usually occurs — the problem gets bigger and more unwieldy. So when difficulties occur remember two things: view your problems as calmly as possible; take action immediately.

— *Greta Walker*

implied; When job problems occur, you should face them calmly.

4. Let us face it. Nothing blows the mind more than a precise statistic. Ninety-nine and forty-four one-hundredths percent pure! That's hard to beat. But I must be honest with you. I have pulled a few classics in my time. On the average of 1.73562 times each year, a student will interrupt my lecture with a question such as: "Professor, is it true that we use only ten percent of our brain during the course of a lifetime?" Now I ask you, how do you answer a question like that? For years, my approach has been to break down that statement. What do you mean by *use*? How does a person use his or her brain? Unless we can come up with some satisfactory definition of this word, the rest of the statement is sheer gobbledygook. Even assuming that we can agree on definition, we're not much better off. How do we measure the proportion of the brain that gets "used" in a lifetime? Could we stick thousands of electrodes on various parts of the brain to determine whether the underlying nerve cells are firing? The question is unanswerable and any attempt to provide a statistic is a fake, no matter how well intended.

— *Richard P. Runyon*

Precise statistics are convincing, even if they are false.

6. Main Ideas in Textbook Excerpts

The following paragraphs come from textbooks. After you read each selection, put a checkmark next to the statement that best states the main idea. Remember that some main ideas are stated and that others are only implied.

Computer Science

If you go to a picnic, you later have memories of it. You may remember the taste of the food, the excitement of the games, and the names of friends who were there. With the passage of time, however, you will probably forget some of the details. A computer's memory is different. No matter how you program it, the computer cannot remember such things as the taste of food or the feeling of excitement. But it can remember names. Your computer will easily keep track of the names of everyone who attended the picnic. Of course, the computer doesn't already know the names. You have to tell it the names of the picnickers. Once you supply it with that input, the computer's memory, unlike yours, will never forget. The list will always be complete and always correct — as long as the computer is turned on.

— *Barbara L. Kurshan, Alan C. November, and Jane D. Stone*

______ 1. People are more forgetful than computers are.

______ 2. People remember tastes and feelings.

______ 3. Computers remember details that they are told.

__√__ 4. Computer memory is different from human memory.

Anthropology

Bedouin live in a traditional society. This means that they live in much the same way their ancestors did. Customs and beliefs have changed very slowly. People who live in traditional societies have strong ties to the past. They fear that changes will make their lives worse rather than better. Values are passed with few changes from one generation to the next. Yet changes do take place. Bedouin life at the time of Muhammad was different from what it was in ancient times. All cultures change, but they change more quickly at some periods than at others. In very recent years, changes have taken place very quickly everywhere — including the deserts of Southwest Asia and North Africa.

— *Merwyn S. Garbarino and Rachel R. Sady*

_____ 1. The life of the Bedouin people is changing.

_____ 2. Bedouin society has strong ties to the past.

__√__ 3. Bedouin people must now face change even though they fear it.

_____ 4. Bedouin life was different at the time of Muhammad than it is now.

Biology

The earthworm has strong muscles under its skin and tiny bristles on its underside. When the earthworm moves, certain muscles squeeze and stretch out the front part of the body, while the rear part stays in place. Now the worm looks long and thin. The bristles on the front end stick out into the soil. Then the bristles on the rear end let go. Other muscles squeeze and pull the rear end forward while the front end stays in place. The worm now looks short and thick. The rear bristles catch the soil and the front bristles let go. The front end is stretched out again and the motions are repeated. In this way, the earthworm slowly tunnels through the soil.

— *James E. McLaren, John H. Stasik, and Dale F. Levering*

_____ 1. The earthworm moves slowly even though it is strong.

__√__ 2. The earthworm moves by squeezing and stretching its muscles.

_____ 3. The earthworm has a very difficult and funny way of moving.

_____ 4. The earthworm uses its bristles to catch the soil.

Astronomy

It is not just the sun's great size that makes it fascinating. Something is always happening to the sun! One great sunspot after another, whole families of them sometimes, appear on the sun's disk. Sunspots are regions of gases that are cooler than the rest of the sun's surface, so they look dark.

Vast solar flares shower space with intense radiations that can be dangerous for space travelers. Hundreds of areas of seething gases, up to 800 km in diameter, make the sun's surface look like a pot of boiling breakfast cereal. Streamers of exploded gases rise hundreds of thousands of kilometers above the surface.

— *Joseph H. Jackson and Edward D. Evans*

√_____ 1. Many interesting things appear on the sun's surface.

_____ 2. Sunspots look dark because they are cooler than the rest of the sun's surface.

_____ 3. The sun's surface is constantly exploding.

_____ 4. The sun sends out dangerous radiation into space.

Music

Man probably used his own voice to produce the earliest music, and music through the ages has developed with reference to the voice. It seems likely that primitive human beings, discovering that their voices were capable of certain timbres and pitches, would have had a natural interest in similar sounds encountered by accident: a plucked bow string, wind blowing across the reeds in a brook. This natural tendency to relate new sounds to the human voice makes the voice the most fundamental of musical sounds.

— *Richard L. Wink and Lois G. Williams*

_____ 1. The earliest music was voice music.

_____ 2. People compare musical instruments to voices.

√_____ 3. The voice is the most fundamental of musical sounds.

_____ 4. Voices are capable of making different sounds.

7. Textbook Main Ideas in Your Own Words

In each textbook paragraph below, the main idea is either stated or implied. Write the main idea on the blanks after each selection.

1. You may not think of the post office as a place to go with a consumer complaint. But anything having to do with a mail-order problem is a matter for the United States Postal Service. The mails cannot be used to cheat people. If you order by mail and do not receive your order, ask the Postal Service for help. If you have been cheated by a company, the Postal Service may take legal action to get your money back. On this and other matters, it has a special department to help protect your rights.

— Betty J. Brown and John E. Clow

Main idea: **The post office can help you if you have been cheated by a mail-order company.**

2. John Whitney, Sr., is a man who imagined a new world and then invented the means to get him there. Mr. Whitney experimented with new computer technologies to find new ways of creating images. One of the new ideas he developed was the slit-scan camera, which gives a sense of depth on films. This camera is the ancestor of the cameras used to create special effects in movies like *Star Wars*.

— Donald J. Guerrieri, F. Barry Haber, William B. Hoyt, and Robert E. Turner

Main idea: **John Whitney, Sr., used computers to create images in new ways.**

3. To influence the conduct of the government in a significant way, citizens need organizations. Organizations are important for anyone who wishes to influence government, but they are particularly crucial for those who lack great individual resources. By banding together and pooling their small resources, including votes, citizens who would be politically ineffectual alone can gain influence by acting jointly. In this way, organization can be a resource that helps members of a group to compensate for their lack of individual resources.

— Robert A. Dahl

Main idea: **Through organizations citizens can band together to influence government.**

4. The many forms of plant and animal life may at first glance appear chaotic, but the biologist sees in them a high degree of

order. This order is due to an elaborate system of classification. All life is first grouped into a few primary divisions called phyla; each phylum is in turn subdivided into smaller groups called classes; each class is subdivided into orders; and so on down through the family, the genus, the species, the variety. This system brings order out of chaos, enabling the biologist to consider any plant or animal in its proper relationship to all the rest.

— *Louise E. Rorabacher*

Main idea: **A classification system helps biologists see the order of forms of life.**

5. As the economy limped into the 1930s, statistics began to tell the story of a national tragedy. Between 1929 and 1933 a hundred thousand businesses failed; corporate profits fell from $10 billion to $1 billion; and the gross national product was cut in half. But what happened to America's banks — and savings — illustrates especially well the cascading nature of the Great Depression. Banks tied into the stock market or foreign investments were badly weakened; some failed. When nervous Americans made runs on banks to salvage their threatened savings, a powerful momentum — panic — took command. In 1929, 659 banks folded; in 1930 the number of failures climbed to 1,350. The next year proved worse: 2,293 banks shut their doors; another 1,453 ceased to do business in 1932. By 1933, 9 million savings accounts had been lost.

— *Mary Beth Norton, David M. Katzman, Paul D. Escott, Howard P. Chudacoff, Thomas G. Paterson, William M. Tuttle, Jr., and William J. Brophy*

Main idea: **Between 1929 and 1933 many banks and businesses lost money and went bankrupt.**

6. Always speaking in the same tone of voice, never moving or gesturing, using monotonous grammatical structure, an overly predictable pattern of speech, and lots of clichés — all these are good ways to lose an audience's attention. Variety has motivational effects. Rosenshine (1971a) found that a lecturer's changes in the form of movement and gesturing correlate positively with student achievement. Whatever the lecturer can change fairly often, without making the change so

extreme that it distracts students from the subject of the lecture, probably helps students to pay attention.

— *N. L. Gage and David C. Berliner*

Main idea: **Variety in speech and gesture helps audiences pay attention.**

7. As the technology of microscopy improved, scientists obtained more accurate views of cell structure. By 1824, sufficient observations had been made to prompt the French biologist Dutrochet to establish the first of three major principles composing the modern cell theory, namely, that all living things are composed of one or more units called cells. The other two principles were not established fully until 1858, when, in a widely read publication, Rudolf Virchow argued forcefully, first, that cells were capable of independent existence and, second, that new cells can arise only from preexisting cells.

— *Paul B. Weisz and Richard N. Keogh*

Main idea: **Improved microscopes led to new knowledge about cells.**

8. What do you think when you hear the word *taxes*? Many people have negative feelings about taxes, because taxes take away some of their money. Realistically, we must pay income taxes to support our government and its programs. Taxes reflect the democratic ideal that the people control the government. Nevertheless, workers often lose sight of this ideal when they see how much money is taken out of their paycheck each week or think of the complex tax forms they must fill out every year. You may never have earned enough to fill out an income tax return, but if you have held a job, taxes were probably withheld from your paycheck.

— *Richard J. Hardy*

Main idea: **Taxes support our government, even though we do not like to pay them.**

9. The density of water is another reference standard. It relates metric units of volume (milliliters) to metric units of mass

(grams). At 4°C, water has a density of 1 gram per milliliter (1 g/mL). This means that 1 gram of water at 4°C will occupy a volume of 1 milliliter. If we measured out exactly 1 mL of 4°C water, we would find that it had a mass of 1 g (Figure 12.5).

Water has intrigued humanity since the days of the ancient Greeks. One of its most interesting properties is the way in which its volume changes when its temperature is changed. Suppose we start with a certain amount of water at room temperature. If we warm it, the volume of the water increases. If we cool the water below room temperature, its volume at first decreases. This is exactly the behavior we would expect from a liquid. However, as we cool the water below 4°C, the volume of the water starts to *increase.* And its volume continues to increase until it freezes at 0°C. This behavior is very unusual, because the volumes of most liquids decrease continuously as the liquids are cooled.

— *Alan Sherman, Sharon Sherman, and Leonard Russikoff*

Main idea: **Water has maximum density at 4° C and expands as temperatures go either up or down from that point.**

10. When a person wonders whether to tell the truth or tell a falsehood in order to get out of trouble, he is engaged in the process of weighing the pros and cons of each alternative action. In short, he is "deliberating." Deliberation always has to do with future actions that are within our power. We do not deliberate about the past. Nor do we deliberate about those actions about which we have no choice. Deliberation means that we are considering what we should do. Sartre speaks of the young woman who deliberates over whether to remove her hand or leave it resting in her companion's. She also deliberates about whether she wants to be involved in the actions that leaving her hand there would make possible. Deliberation means asking the question "Should I do it?" or "What ought I to do?" To a certain extent, we know in general what we want to achieve through our actions — we want to achieve a sense of well-being, of happiness. What we deliberate over is how we shall achieve that end, or as Aristotle says, it is "the mark of a man of practical wisdom to be able to deliberate well about what is good and expedient . . . about what sort of things conduce to the good life in general." Certainly, deliberation has to do with action, and that is why Aristotle calls deliberation "practical wisdom." That is what

we mean when we say a person made a conscious, deliberate choice.

— *Samuel E. Stumpf*

Main idea: **Deliberation means considering what we should do.**

8d Main Ideas in Long Selections

Individual paragraphs build the meaning of an entire selection. As you read the paragraphs of a long piece and consider their main ideas — whether directly stated **(8c1)** or implied **(8c2)** — you should be thinking about the main idea that all the paragraphs together are developing. Often called a *thesis,* the main idea of a long selection is the major point that all the sentences contribute to.

In some long works the main point is clearly stated in the first paragraph, or introduction. Thus, the main idea of the first paragraph is also the main idea of the whole selection. All the other paragraphs expand and support this main idea.

In other selections you have to develop the main idea on your own, as you do when the main idea is implied in a paragraph. To figure out the main idea of the long piece, you need to use the individual paragraph main ideas, of course. But you do not simply add these points together; your main idea sentence would be too long and detailed. Instead, you develop a short, direct statement that includes the major points from the various paragraph main ideas.

The following is a selection from a science textbook. The main idea sentence appears beside each paragraph.

Why Is There No Life on the Moon?

Now that people have actually explored the surface of the moon, we have learned many new things about it. One thing we knew, though, before anyone ever reached the moon is that there's no life on it. — **Paragraph 1 Main idea:** ***Even before people explored the moon, we knew it had no life on it.***

The moon has no atmosphere, which

means that there is no air around it to protect it from the sun's powerful rays. Earth's atmosphere, on the other hand, screens out dangerous radiation from the sun and still allows Earth to receive heat and light. Without that heat and light, life on Earth would not be possible.

— **Paragraph 2**
Main idea: ***Unlike the moon's, the Earth's atmosphere screens out the sun's harmful rays, allowing life.***

Because there is no atmosphere on the moon, its surface is either extremely hot or extremely cold. As the moon rotates, the side of it that is lighted up by the sun becomes very hot. The temperature there reaches more than 260 degrees Fahrenheit. That's hotter than boiling water! The hot lunar day lasts two weeks.

— **Paragraph 3**
Main idea: ***The side of the moon lighted up by the sun is extremely hot.***

It is followed by a night that is also two weeks long. At night the temperature drops to more than 260 degrees below zero. That's more than twice as cold as temperatures reached at the Earth's South Pole!

— **Paragraph 4**
Main idea: ***During the moon's long night, temperatures are extremely cold.***

Under these conditions, it's no wonder that life as we know it here on Earth could not exist on the moon.

— *Arkady Leokum*

— **Paragraph 5**
Main idea: ***Such extreme conditions prevent life on the moon.***

How would you state the main idea of the whole selection?

First determine the topic. (See **8b**.) You could state the topic as *why life on the moon does not exist.* Certainly the various paragraphs deal with that issue, and the title provides a good clue to the topic.

Next figure out what the whole selection says about the topic. Consider the information in the individual paragraph main idea sentences. You should come up with a sentence such as this: *Life cannot exist on the moon because the moon has no atmosphere to support living things.*

The main idea tells what the whole selection is about. It draws on information given in the separate sentences of the paragraphs. Yet the main idea statement does not include *all* the specifics from those separate sentences. The main idea sentence developed for the selection — clearly expressed in a few important words — makes a more general statement than the individual sentences make.

Stating Main Ideas for Long Selections

- *Define the topic.* What is the selection about? Use what you know of the topics in the individual paragraphs to state the selection topic in your own words. Often, the title of a selection helps you with the topic. In the reading on pages 204–205, "Why Is There No Life on the Moon?" is the title. It states much of the topic neatly as a question.
- *Define what the selection is saying about the topic.* The main idea usually asserts something about the topic; that is, the main idea expresses an opinion or a position on the topic. In the selection on pages 204–205, the main idea asserts something about the topic, why life on the moon does not exist. It says that life does not exist on the moon *because the moon's harsh conditions prevent life from developing.*
- *Use the information you gather from the main ideas of the various paragraphs.* Note how the individual paragraph main ideas in the selection on the moon help you develop the main idea of the whole selection. Not all the information from the separate paragraph main ideas must appear in the selection main idea. In fact, only the main idea in the first two paragraphs provides the words for the selection main idea statement. Still, the main ideas of the other two paragraphs do support the selection main idea. They provide important specific details, but those details do not have to be included here. The selection main idea covers the points they make in general terms.
- *Develop a brief statement that highlights the general meaning of the selection.* There are no rules about the length of the main idea statement that you develop for a whole selection. You may choose to include more specific information in the main idea statement, and you may need more than one sentence to express the key point. For example, you might have stated the main idea for the selection "Why Is There No Life on the Moon?" in one of these ways:

  1. Life cannot exist on the moon because the moon has no atmosphere, and its surface is either too hot or too cold to support living things.
  2. Life cannot exist on the moon because the moon's harsh atmospheric conditions cannot support living things; its surface is too hot or too cold for living things.

  You have many options in stating the main idea of the selection. In any case, you should aim for a relatively short statement that states the point of the reading.

Look at this selection from a health education textbook. On the blank lines beside each paragraph, write the main idea. Then look at the discussion that follows to help you determine the main idea of the whole selection.

Sleep Problems

Most people sleep seven to eight hours a day. The normal amount of sleep varies from person to person. The inability to sleep your usual amount is called *insomnia.* Insomnia is a problem for an estimated 75 million Americans. (1)

— ***Main idea of paragraph 1:*** __________

Often to get a good night's sleep, doctors advise avoiding foods or medications that keep you awake. These include many drinks that contain caffeine, such as coffee, chocolate, and cola drinks. Exercise during the day often helps people sleep better. Establish a regular bedtime and go to bed only when you are tired. If you just cannot sleep one night, get up and read a book or do work on some project. Remember that not being able to sleep well occasionally happens to everyone. Constant insomnia is serious and should be treated by a doctor. It can be a sign of a physical or mental illness. (2)

— ***Main idea of paragraph 2:*** __________

Some people may have problems staying awake during the day, even though they get a full night's sleep. Extreme daytime sleepiness may indicate a disorder called narcolepsy. *Narcolepsy* is a disorder in which people fall asleep suddenly even while doing something such as talking or driving. The cause of these sleep attacks is often unknown. (3)

— ***Main idea of paragraph 3:*** __________

Sleep apnea is a condition in which breathing stops periodically during sleep. It may stop because of a blockage of the upper airway or by the brain in-

— ***Main idea of paragraph 4:*** __________

terrupting its signals to breathe. When this happens, the sleeper partly awakes, gasps for breath, and then falls back to sleep. This may happen many times during the night, leaving the person feeling very tired by day. (4)

— *Bud Getchell, Rusty Pippin, and Jill Varnes*

Your main idea sentences for the separate paragraphs should look something like these:

Paragraph 1: Insomnia is a sleep disorder for many Americans.
Paragraph 2: People can improve the way they sleep by following some simple recommendations.
Paragraph 3: Narcolepsy is a sleep disorder in which people fall asleep suddenly during the day.
Paragraph 4: During sleep apnea, breathing stops periodically.

How would you state the main idea of the whole selection?

First determine the topic. You know from the title and from what you have read that this passage is about *sleep problems.* What is the passage asserting about sleep problems? You can tell from the various problems explained here that sleep disorders are varied and that they affect many people. The various topic sentences support that point with specific information about different sleep problems. To state the main idea of the selection, you need to make a short, general statement that covers the major point expressed here.

Try your hand at stating the whole selection's main idea. Write it in your own words on the blanks below.

____

____

____

You should have written something such as this: *Various problems can affect people's normal sleeping patterns.*

Do you see how the main idea statement for the whole selection reflects the general point of the passage? It states the topic, *sleep problems,* and asserts something about the topic.

These problems *can affect people's normal sleeping patterns.* Note how the separate paragraph main ideas help you develop the main idea for the whole selection. However, few of the specific details in those paragraph main ideas appear in the selection main idea. To cover all these details, you needed to produce a general statement.

EXERCISE

Main Ideas in Long Textbook Selections

Read each textbook selection. Each paragraph is numbered. On separate paper, write the main idea of each paragraph of each selection. (Remember that the main idea may be stated or implied.) Then write the main idea of each whole selection in the blanks.

1. *Organized Labor*

There are many organizations or associations of workers employed in the same types of jobs. Doctors may belong to the American Medical Association, secretaries to the Professional Secretaries International, and lawyers to the American Bar Association. It may be that the organization sets or recommends standards that individuals must meet before entering the occupation. There are many, many such organizations. (1)

The purposes of these organizations vary quite widely. Some provide continuing education for their members through journals, magazines, and even classes. Others try to get elected officials to pass laws that would benefit their members. Some try to get members to work together on a project or activity. During elections, some organizations actively campaign to help elect people who favor their goals. (2)

A labor union is an organization that is formed to represent workers, often in the same type of occupation. Sometimes a union or many unions together are referred to as *organized labor.* Like other organizations of workers, unions engage in a variety of activities. However, there is one activity that is unique to a labor union. That activity is collective bargaining, the coming together of union members and their bosses, or management, to discuss basic issues that arise between them. In the course of collective bargaining, representatives of the union and management sit down to bargain about issues. Some of those issues might be pay, working conditions, and hours of work. (3)

A union is somewhat like a small democracy in action. That is, the union members elect other members to represent them in dealing with the management of a business. The union members send their demands to the union representatives. The union representatives, in turn, work toward getting those demands accepted by management. The whole process of collective bargaining is an important one in our economic system. We'll look at it later in this chapter. (4)

— *Betty J. Brown and John E. Clow*

Main idea: **Unions, like other organizations, serve the particular needs of their members, but unions also represent their members in bargaining with management.**

2. *Nursing Occupations*

The field of nursing includes registered nurses; licensed practical nurses; and nursing aides, orderlies, and attendants. Nursing accounts for about one-half of total employment among health service workers. Nursing personnel perform a variety of duties in caring for and comforting the sick, the injured, and others requiring medical services.

Registered nurses (RN's) carry out the treatment prescribed by physicians, but must often make independent judgments in providing nursing services. Some RN's, after advanced training, become *nurse practitioners* and perform services, such as physical examinations, that traditionally have been handled by physicians. Those nurses who become head nurses have responsibility for all nursing services of a specified area of a hospital — for example, a pediatrics ward.

Licensed practical nurses (LPN's) provide skilled nursing care to sick, injured, and convalescent patients. They work under the general supervision of physicians and registered nurses, and may sometimes supervise nursing aides, orderlies, and attendants.

Nursing aides, orderlies, and *attendants* make up the largest group of nursing personnel. They serve meals, feed patients, and do other tasks that free RN's and LPN's for work that requires professional and technical training.

Persons who wish to become RN's, LPN's, or nursing aides, orderlies, or attendants need to like working with people. They must also be reliable and able to keep a level head in emergencies.

— *Alan Sherman, Sharon Sherman, Leonard Russikoff*

Main idea: **Nursing ranges from the highly trained work of registered nurses and nurse practitioners, through the skilled work of licensed practical nurses, to the general services of aides, orderlies, and attendants.**

3. *Regulating Interest Groups*

In the early years of the republic, presenting gifts to or bribing willing legislators were not uncommon ways of influencing the passage of a specific bill. Indeed, in the early 1800s, as prominent a senator as Daniel Webster was on retainer to the Bank of the United States, which was fighting for its survival. Webster wrote to the bank president: "My retainer has not been renewed or refreshed as usual. If it is wished that my relation to the Bank should be continued, it may be well to send me the usual retainer."

Despite their reputation for bribery and corruption, most interest groups function within the law. Nevertheless, Congress has found it necessary to pass laws regulating the groups and their representatives.

In 1887 Congress first required lobbyists to register with the House of Representatives. Additional laws mandate that lobbyists file reports listing their clients, as well as describing their activities and recording the amount of money spent on them. The 1946 Federal Regulation of Lobbying Act is the most recent comprehensive attempt to regulate the groups. Efforts to add further restrictions have not succeeded.

Under the 1946 act, lobbying is vaguely defined and the regulations are minimally enforced. Of the estimated twenty thousand lobbyists active in Washington, D.C., only fifty-five hundred are actually registered. One reason is a loophole in the law: only individuals paid to lobby for someone else must register. Thus, for example, an official who works directly for a corporation and lobbies for the interests of that company need not register. In addition, only lobbyists who have direct contact with members of Congress must register. A great deal of the lobbying that goes on, however, targets the staff people who work for and advise members of Congress.

In the more than forty years since the law was enacted, it has been violated only six times. Whether this fact reflects the vagueness of the statute or the honesty and rectitude of contemporary lobbyists is anybody's guess.

— *Alan R. Gitelson, Robert Dudley, and Melvin L. Dubnick*

Main idea: **Interest groups have always tried to influence legislators despite laws that have tried to restrict lobbyists.**

4. *Getting the Most Out of a News Story*

Why do people read the newspaper? Some people read it for entertainment; they enjoy sections like the comics or the sports. Others look for things to buy or sell; they might look mostly at the advertisements. Most people, though, read the newspaper for news!

The news is reported in news stories, which can be found throughout the newspaper. Unlike the comics or the advertisements, news stories report facts. In this article, you will learn some hints about how to get the most out of a news story.

Many news stories have the following elements: headline, by-line, dateline, and lead. The *headline,* which is above the story, tells what the story is about. The size of the headline depends on the importance of the news — important news would get a large, bold-typed headline. The *by-line* tells who wrote the story. Not all news stories have by-lines. The *dateline,* which some news stories also do not have, usually names the place where the story originated or where the news happened and the date on which it happened. The *lead* is the first paragraph; it gives the most important details in the story by telling *who, where, when, why,* and *how.*

— *J. M. Stanchfield and Thomas G. Gunning*

Main idea: **A newspaper story has a headline, a by-line, a dateline, and a lead.**

5. *Barriers Made by People*

Transportation and communication networks bring people together. Yet sometimes people themselves create barriers to transportation and communication.

In some countries, laws stop people from moving freely from place to place. Over the centuries, many groups of people have been denied the freedom to travel because of their race, religion, or nationality. In the Middle Ages, for example, Jews were often forbidden to move about freely within certain cities. Modern South Africa's government has required black Africans to carry passes when they travel within the country. Some governments require all citizens to carry identification papers and to report to government officials whenever they move.

Countries set up customs posts at their borders. Foreign travelers must go through a customs inspection before they are allowed to travel in the country. Usually travelers have to carry special papers such as passports and visas (VEE-suz). Some countries even limit the number of visitors to their country each year. Others allow tourists to visit only certain areas of the country, or they may require that travelers be with an official guide at all times during their stay.

Many of those barriers to travel also act as barriers to communication. When two governments disagree with each other on important matters, they usually do not want their citizens to exchange news or ideas freely. Countries often try to keep military or industrial information secret.

Today, people have the ability to travel, to communicate, and to transport goods more quickly and easily than ever before. Natural barriers that were difficult or dangerous to cross a hundred years ago can now be crossed easily. The barriers that people themselves make are not so easy to overcome. But in spite of all the different kinds of barriers, people continue to enjoy travel and the exchange of goods and ideas.

— *Arthur Getis and Judith M. Getis*

Main idea: **Laws and policies have limited transportation and communication within and between countries.**

6. *The Environment*

Rachel Carson was a biologist whose words shook the world. She wrote several popular books about the creatures living in and around the sea. But she is best known for one book, *Silent Spring*.

Carson knew how chemical poisons damaged or destroyed organisms in addition to the insects or plants they were meant for. She believed that the public should be informed of these effects, so that they could make wise decisions about the use of pesticides and other dangerous chemicals.

Silent Spring, published in 1962, described the effects of chemical poisons on the environment. Almost all the birds in one town were killed by the pesticides meant for insects that were damaging trees. After another spraying project, cows and sheep became sick, chemicals showed up in the milk farmers sold, and pigs stopped giving birth or produced small and sickly offspring. As pesticides spread through the environment, many wild birds, such as eagles and cranes, stopped laying eggs. Fish were killed in streams and lakes.

People were affected by pesticides, too. Some people who lived near sprayed areas became ill after the spraying. Food and water supplies were contaminated by the chemicals. Even today, babies are born with small amounts of chemicals in their bodies.

People who believed that pesticides could be safely used in large amounts tried to prove Carson wrong, but could not. Her book created so much attention that President John F. Kennedy formed a group to study pesticide spraying. Some pesticides were banned in several countries. Tighter rules were placed on the use of others. People began to look for ways to control harmful insects and plants without chemicals. Today, many years after *Silent Spring* was published, people still argue about pesticide use.

In a television interview made before her death in 1965, Rachel Carson said, "We still talk in terms of conquest. We still haven't become mature enough to think of ourselves as only a tiny part of a vast and incredible universe. Man's attitude toward nature . . . is important . . . because we now have the power to alter and destroy nature."

— *James E. McLaren, John H. Stasik, and Dale F. Levering*

Main idea: **Rachel Carson warned us about the dangers of pesticides.**

9

Reading for Information

The main idea of a selection gives you an overall picture of what the writer is saying. But the remaining details complete the picture. In order to make sense of the full picture in a paragraph, you need to do the following:

- Find the facts presented.
- Understand the order, or the sequence, that the writer puts them in.
- Separate the major facts and details from the minor ones.

Each of these steps will help you with the others. We will look at each step separately. When you actually read, you may follow a different order, or you may do several steps at the same time.

All these steps, however, will help you see the details in relation to the overall meaning of your reading. Information that is just a collection of odd bits and pieces will do you little good and will be very hard to remember. On the other hand, information that fits in with a larger meaning will make more sense. As you come to see the whole picture, each detail will fit into its own special place.

9a Finding Facts

To find and remember the facts from a reading passage, you must be a wide-awake, active reader. Here are six ways to help you locate facts:

- Know why you are reading. Have a definite purpose for reading. When you read a cookbook that you plan to buy, you check to see if the ingredients are expensive, if the dishes are easy to cook, and if the results sound tasty. When reading the same cookbook while you are cooking a particular dish, you look for the exact amounts of ingredients, the order of steps, and the cooking times and temperatures. Even if you are reading an assigned textbook to complete a homework assignment or to prepare for an exam, you will remember more if you have a definite purpose in mind. Are you reading your math book to find out how to do a particular kind of problem? Are you reading your history book to find out why the United States got into the war in Vietnam?

- Know the overall meaning of the reading. Read for the main idea. If you recognize the main idea, the facts that support that idea will stand out. (See **8.**)
- Look for information in groups or units. Facts often appear together in clumps.
- Question yourself as you read. Stop to think and let the facts sink in before you rush on to other information. Ask yourself "What does that mean?" or "What does that information tell me?" or "Why is this information here?"
- Use the five *W*'s: *who, where, when, what, why*. These five words will give you specific questions to ask about the facts.
  1. Ask yourself, "Who?" Then look for the name of someone or something.
  2. Ask yourself, "Where?" Then look for a place.
  3. Ask yourself, "When?" Then look for a date (a day, a month, or a year) or a time of day or year.
  4. Ask yourself, "What happened?" Then look for an action.
  5. Ask yourself, "Why?" Then look for an explanation.
- Think about the questions that someone might ask you about the information you have read. Then go back over the passage to make sure that you have the answers to those questions.

To see how these ways of locating facts can help you, read the following passage about an oil billionaire. The first step in helping you to become an active reader and to remember facts is to consider *why* you are reading. Your first reason for reading is to see how the passage serves as an example of the idea discussed in this chapter. That is, you will be reading to see how details help make a full picture of the man's life. But you might also find that the story of how Jean Paul Getty got rich is interesting in itself. Life stories of rich people, such as Getty, fascinate us for many personal reasons.

Jean Paul Getty, who in 1957 sadly philosophized that "a billion dollars isn't worth what it used to be," was born in Minneapolis on Dec. 15, 1892. His father was a lawyer who made millions on Oklahoma oil. J. Paul was educated at the University of Southern California, the University of California at Berkeley, and Oxford, from which he went to Tulsa (site of his father's Minnehoma Oil Company) in 1914, determined to make a million dollars within two years. He bought and sold oil leases with great success and — true to his resolve — was a millionaire by 1916.

After taking a few years off from the moneymaking grind to enjoy spending his earnings on women, Getty returned to Oklahoma in 1919. During the 1920s he added about $3 million to his already sizable estate. His succession of marriages and divorces (three during the 1920s, five throughout his life) so distressed his father, however, that J. Paul inherited a mere $500,000 of the $10 million the senior Getty left at his death in 1930.

Through shrewd investment during the Depression, Getty acquired Pacific Western Oil Corporation, and he began the acquisition (completed in 1953) of the Mission Corporation, which included Tidewater Oil and Skelly Oil. In 1967 the billionaire merged these holdings into Getty Oil.

His most daring business venture began in 1949, when he paid Ibn-Saud $9.5 million in cash and $1 million a year for a 60-year concession to a tract of barren land near the border of Saudi Arabia and Kuwait. No oil had ever been discovered there, and none appeared until four years and $30 million had been spent. But from 1953 onward, Getty's gamble produced 16 million barrels a year, which contributed greatly to the fortune that made him the richest person in the world.

He died on June 6, 1976. Getty owned the controlling interest in nearly 200 businesses, including Getty Oil, and associates put his overall wealth at between $2 billion and $4 billion.

— *David Wallechinsky and Irving Wallace*

When you considered your reasons for reading, did you read actively? Do you recall some details of Getty's life? Reading with a purpose in mind can help you remember information.

Another way to find facts is to figure out the overall meaning of the passage. This will help you see how the details support that meaning. The main theme of this piece is that Getty became rich through clever buying and selling of oil properties.

Within this framework, you can now place the various details of the different oil deals.

You can also find facts if you learn to look for clumps of information. In the above passage, facts about Getty's birth and family are in the middle of the first paragraph; facts about his final wealth are at the end. In the middle are clumps of facts about his various ventures.

Still another way to find facts is to ask yourself about puzzling points in the reading. For example, you may wonder why the passage begins with a strange remark that Getty said in 1957. Why do you think the quotation is here? And why is it given a date? The quotation shows that by that time Getty was so rich that he could think a billion dollars was not worth much.

The five question words — *who, where, when, what happened,* and *why* — can shed light on each paragraph.

The *who* throughout is mainly Jean Paul Getty.

The *where* is the oil fields of the United States and Arabia.

The *when* is throughout his life, with different periods mentioned in each paragraph.

The *what happened* is the gain of wealth through different deals. Each paragraph gives the details of each deal.

And the *why* is to get richer, supported by specific dollar amounts given at each stage of the story.

Finally, you might ask yourself some questions to help you locate facts. In addition to the obvious questions of how he got rich or how rich he was, you might also ask other questions. You might ask, "How important was inherited money to him?" or "Was he so busy making money that he didn't have a chance to enjoy it?" Now go back over the passage with these questions in mind. Which details now seem important to answer these questions? Details about Getty's father's wealth and his inheritance now become more striking. So do the details about his romances in the second paragraph.

In these ways you can build up a much more detailed picture of this story. You can learn much more than the simple fact that Jean Paul Getty was a rich man.

EXERCISES

1. Finding Facts

Reread the selection on page 217. Then answer each question.

1. How rich did Jean Paul Getty become?

   He had between two billion and four billion dollars.

2. When and how did he make his first million dollars?

   between 1914 and 1916, by buying and selling oil leases

3. Did Jean Paul Getty do anything else besides make money?

   He spent his money on women and was married five times.

4. What different places was Getty involved with in his life?

   California, Oxford, Oklahoma, Saudi Arabia

5. Write down three of the most important facts.

   Getty did not inherit any money until he had built his own fortune.

   Getty made money through dealings with oil companies.

   His largest gamble with Arabian oil made him the richest man in the world.

6. Write a question that you think this passage answers.

   How did Getty build his fortune?

2. Finding Facts

Read the following selection about the wide use of asbestos until recently. Asbestos is a fireproof material used in homes and buildings. Then answer each question.

> "Asbestos" is a general term used to describe minerals formed out of fibers. Ancient Greeks first found the mineral "magic" more than 2,000 years ago, when they wove it into handkerchiefs and napkins that they cleaned by throwing into fire and burning off the stains. (The name asbestos

comes from the Greek term for *indestructible.*) But it wasn't until the 19th century, and the wide use of steam power, that the world began mining huge quantities of the heat-resistant, flexible and durable substance.

Throughout the 20th century, the use of asbestos rapidly increased. By the end of World War II, asbestos had become a primary building material. Not only schools, but public buildings, ships, hospitals and even homes contained it.

Insulators sprayed it onto steel girders in buildings and onto walls and ceilings as both a fire retardant and a sound absorber. Millions of feet of pipes were wrapped with asbestos-containing insulation and thousands of boilers were covered with it. It was mixed with plaster and also was an ingredient of construction board and ceiling tiles.

Irons, hairdryers, toasters and many other everyday products also contained the substance — including a papier-mâché mix that children used in art class.

But as its use grew, the body of evidence also grew that asbestos can be dangerous, and even deadly.

— Sunday Herald-Times

1. Who or what is the main subject?

   asbestos

2. What is the main idea of this passage?

   Asbestos was widely used before it was found to be dangerous.

3. Where was asbestos first used?

   Greece

4. When was it first used?

   over 2,000 years ago

5. What happened as time went on?

   It became used more widely in machinery and buildings.

6. Why was asbestos used for so many things?

   It would not burn in fires.

7. How does the last sentence change your view of the whole passage?

   It makes you think that asbestos is not as wonderful as you had thought.

8. Why might people be interested in finding out the facts presented in this passage?

   Since asbestos is now considered dangerous, people might wonder how its use first became so widespread.

3. Finding Facts

Read the following selection about the native Americans of New Mexico. Then, on the blanks, write five questions about the facts in the selection and answer each question.

> The first people to live in sunny New Mexico were the ancestors of today's Pueblo Indians. Their origin legends tell them they have always been here. Archeologists say they wandered across the Bering Strait from Asia many thousands of years ago.
>
> Prehistoric hunters left their dart (*atlatl*) points at Blackwater Draw near Clovis, New Mexico, about 11,500 years ago.
>
> They imprinted rocks all over New Mexico with their subtle pictographs (rock drawings) and petroglyphs (rock carvings).
>
> The ancestors of today's Pueblo Indian tribes were the Anasazi, the Ancient Ones. The ruins of their towns, each contained in one large, crescent-shaped, multistoried enclave, bespeak an advanced civilization. These small walled towns, silent now, evoke a strange excitement.
>
> By the year 1000, as do today's Pueblo people, they grew crops by irrigation, crafted beautiful pottery and jewelry, traded with distant peoples, and had a rich religious life, embellished by ceremonial dances performed in splendid costumes. Around 1200 A.D., they migrated to the Rio Grande and other scattered sites, where the Spaniards found their pueblos in the 16th century.
>
> A later people, the Athabascans, wandered into New Mex-

ico some 600 to 800 years ago. One group of them learned from the Pueblo people they raided, settled down after a fashion, and became the Navajos. They built more or less permanent hogans, became weavers and did minimum farming, always scattered in small groups among the canyons, forests, and deserts of a big bold land, as most of them still are.

The other group continued to roam and became the Apaches. The bands now grouped as the Jicarilla Apaches hunted and raided in the northern mountains and plains. All Apaches wove fine baskets, which served their mobile lifestyle as pottery served the stable Pueblos. The Jicarillas still make fine baskets.

The bands now known as the Mescalero Apaches staked out the mountains, plains, and deserts of the southern half of the state. When the Spaniards came, the Apaches took to the horse as if they had been born for it and became great guerrilla fighters. They were the last of the Southwestern Indian people to settle on reservations.

— *New Mexico Tourism and Travel Division*

Questions and answers will vary. Examples:

1. **Who were the first people to live in New Mexico?**

   ancestors of the Pueblo Indians, called the Anasazi

2. **How long did they live there?**

   at least as far back as 11,500 years ago

3. **What things did the Anasazi accomplish?**

   They irrigated crops, made pottery and jewelry, carried on trade, and had a rich religious life.

4. **Who were the Athabascans?**

They were a more recent Indian people who split into

the Navajos and the Apaches.

5. **Who were the different groups of Apaches?**

the Jicarilla and the Mescalero

9b Noting Sequence

Writers put all of a paragraph's ideas and information in an order, or a sequence. Readers can then see how the details fit together in an overall pattern. The more you notice the pattern that a writer uses, the better you can understand and remember the information.

The most widely used patterns are time order, space order, and order of importance. Once you can notice these patterns, you can see how different paragraphs are organized.

Writers do not, however, always follow these simple patterns. Sometimes they combine patterns. In those cases you can often notice the patterns that you are familiar with as part of the combined pattern. When writers use more complex patterns, they also often give the readers clues about the patterns.

If you pay attention to paragraph patterns, you will usually be able to see what the pattern is. Unless you are reading a mystery story, the writer will not try to confuse you. Although fitting the parts of a paragraph together may be something of a puzzle, the writer will want to make that puzzle easy to solve, so that you can get the right picture.

9b(1) Noting Time Order

Some paragraphs put details of an event in the same order that they happened. In this way it is easy for you to see how one detail follows another. Time order is very useful for telling stories, explaining how something happens, or describing how to do or make something. Time order is sometimes called *chronology*.

Time Order Clue Words

Time words help you know that time order is being used and how events follow one another: *now, then, before, after, soon, next, one day, in a few days, meanwhile, first, second, third, suddenly, finally*.

Notice how the following story about the beginnings of coffee uses time order. Pay attention to the clue words.

> According to Arab legend, a lone shepherd named Kaldi was roaming the hills with his herd of goats sometime around A.D. 850. One day he found his usually quiet herd behaving very strangely: old and young alike frolicked and danced, scampered up and down the rocky slopes bleating excitedly. The bewildered shepherd then hid and watched them nibbling the berries of shrubs scattered over the hillside. Soon he was overcome with curiosity and sampled the fruit. The effects were similar. He joined the dancing goats. An *imam* [holy man] passing by noticed Kaldi, and soon he too ate the berries and joined the party.
>
> The *imam* returned to his monastery with the powerful shrub, but neither he nor the monks could identify it. They next sought advice from Mohammed. As the prayers dragged on, the *imam* dozed, and Mohammed appeared to him advising him to boil the berries of his plant in water and drink it — this, Mohammed said, would keep him awake enough to pray! The monks immediately followed this command and called the new drink *qahwah,* which means both "life-giving" and "wine." Their monastery soon became famous for its long and lively prayer meetings.
>
> — *adapted from* How Did They Do That? *by Caroline Sutton*

9b(2) *Noting Place Order*

Some paragraphs describe details in the order that you would see them within a room, a building, or an outdoor setting.

Place order descriptions follow a regular pattern of direction in going from one place to another. The pattern may be from left to right or up to down. It may be near to far, east to west, or turning around in a circle.

When you read place order descriptions, it often helps to think of yourself as standing in one place and turning your head to see the different parts or walking from one part to the next in a regular way. Descriptions of places, settings, buildings, and groups of people usually follow place order.

Place Order Clue Words

Location words will help you know when space order is being used and how the description is moving through space: *near, far, in front, behind, above, below, under, over, beneath, next to, alongside, left, right, inside, outside.*

The following travel description of sights in southern Arizona uses the order of places that you will see as you go along the road.

> When you travel south from Tucson to the Mexican border town of Nogales you will see many reminders of the old West. Just outside Tucson you will find Old Tucson, built by Columbia Pictures in 1939. It is now open daily as a combination Western theme park and movie/TV studio. Nearby is the Arizona-Sonora Desert Museum, displaying the plants and wildlife of Arizona and northern Mexico. Traveling south you will come across an eighteenth-century Spanish mission. Called Mission San Xavier del Bac, it is still open for daily services. Further south are the ruins of the Tumacon Mission.

9b(3) *Noting Order of Importance*

Some paragraphs begin with details that the writer thinks least important and end with the most important. The importance of the details builds up as you go through this kind of paragraph. Order of importance is often used to present reasons in support of an idea and to describe several items or events one after another.

Order of Importance Clue Words

Words that judge importance help you know if order of importance is being used: *first, in the first place, to start, least important, next, more important, most important, major, greatest, most, ——— er, ——— est.*

The following discussion of cold starts with our ordinary ideas of cold weather and builds up to the very special kind of cold created by scientists. Only by going step by step can we come to see what serious cold really means. Notice how the word *coldest* three sentences from the end signals the most important part.

> How cold is cold? It all depends on who's talking. To us ordinary mortals nothing in the world may be so cold as falling through the ice on a frozen lake, or huddling on a windswept mountain hoping to be rescued in dead of winter. Some may even think they are freezing to death when plunging under an ice-cold shower just out of a warm bed. Indeed, we all know what cold means. Arctic explorers would laugh at such timid ideas. Down in the Antarctic, where scientists of many nations spend pitch-dark months living on a sheet of ice two miles thick, the temperature spends most of its time at 50 or 60 degrees below zero, often with hundred-mile winds and raging blizzards. This is the cold that is cold, to them. Space people have still another standard. . . . The coldest place in which a person can live and survive is some 400 degrees *hotter* than space itself. . . . The coldest place on earth — colder even than space — is inside a machine called a cryostat. Here, scientists and engineers in thousands of laboratories and factories in many parts of the world regularly *make* cold that turns the South Pole's worst into a balmy summer day. They are inching toward such cold that there is no temperature at all — down a frozen valley that leads to Absolute Zero, 459.65 degrees below our zero of a brisk winter's day.
>
> — *David O. Woodbury*

EXERCISES

1. Sequence Clue Words

1. In the example of *time order* (page 224), circle the words that help you see that paragraph details are arranged in time order.
2. In the example of *place order* (page 225), circle the words that help you see that paragraph details are arranged in place order.
3. In the example of *order of importance* (page 226), circle the words that help you see that paragraph details are arranged in order of importance.

2. Sequence

Look at the following details from the example of time order (page 224). Arrange the details in their proper time order by putting 1 in front of the first thing that happened, 2 in front of the second thing that happened, and so on.

7 ______ a. Mohammed advised the *imam* to drink the berries boiled in water.

3 ______ b. Kaldi ate the berries and danced.

8 ______ c. The drink was named *qahwah.*

4 ______ d. An *imam* passed by Kaldi.

1 ______ e. Goats were behaving strangely.

6 ______ f. The *imam* dozed during prayers.

2 ______ g. Kaldi saw the goats eating the berries.

5 ______ h. The *imam* brought the berries to his monastery.

3. Sequence

Reread the example of a paragraph of place order on page 225. Identify each place described in list *A* by writing the number of the correct answer from list *B* (page 228).

List A

4 a. the start of the trip

3 b. the place furthest south on the trip

6 c. nearest to Tucson

1 d. the third stop on the trip

2 e. the mission more north than the other

5 f. the last stop before the Mexican border

List B

1. Desert Museum
2. Mission San Xavier del Bac
3. Nogales
4. Tucson
5. Tumacon Mission
6. Old Tucson

4. Sequence

The following examples of cold all come from the example of order of importance on page 226. Using the numbers in front of each example, arrange them in order from least cold to most cold in the space below.

1. outer space
2. a frozen lake
3. inside a cryostat
4. the Antarctic (the south polar region)
5. a cold shower
6. absolute zero

least cold 5 2 4 1 3 6 most cold

5. Sequence

Read the following paragraph from a geology textbook describing the rock formations left behind when an ice glacier melts. Then answer each question.

All the rocky material dumped by a glacier after it melts is called *till*. Till is a mixed-up collection of many different sizes and shapes of pieces of rock. The rows and piles of till dumped at the edges of glaciers are called *moraines*. Till that was dumped along the sides of moving ice in a valley is called a *lateral moraine*. Lateral means on the side. A long row of till left where the front of the glacier stood for a long time is called *a terminal moraine*. Terminal means at the end.

— *Joseph H. Jackson and Edward D. Evans*

1. In the paragraph underline all the clue words that tell you what kind of order the details are placed in.
2. Match each term in list *A* with its definitions in list *B*.

List A

3 ______ a. moraine

4 ______ b. till

1 ______ c. terminal moraine

2 ______ d. lateral moraine

List B

1. till from the front end of the glacier
2. till from the sides of the glacier
3. till from the edge of the glacier
4. rocky material left by a glacier

b ______ 3. Which pattern most resembles the order of details followed in the paragraph?
   a. bottom to middle to top
   b. middle to edge to front
   c. inside to edge to outside
   d. past to present to future

6. Sequence

Read the following paragraph describing how different situations can cause stress. Then answer each question.

It is not just the big tragedies of life that cause stress. Happy events and small events can also increase your stress. Psychologists have, in fact, developed a scale to show how much stress can be caused by life situations. In this scale of a hundred points, Christmas rates at twelve points of stress and vacation rates at thirteen. And you thought holidays help you relax. More stress can be caused by achievements, such as starting or finishing school (twenty-three points), an outstanding personal victory (twenty-eight points), starting a new job (twenty-nine points), or switching careers (thirty-five points). Happy changes in personal relationships can be even more stressful, with gaining a new family member at thirty-nine points, pregnancy at forty, and marriage at fifty. The major tragedies, nonetheless, do cause the most stress, with personal injury at fifty-three, jail term at sixty-three, divorce at seventy-three, and death of a spouse at a hundred.

1. Underline the clue words in the paragraph that let you know how details are arranged. What kind of order do these clues suggest?

   order of importance

d 2. According to the paragraph, which kind of events cause the least stress?
   a. happy changes in personal relationships
   b. big tragedies
   c. achievements
   d. holidays

b 3. Which kind of events cause the most stress?
   a. happy changes in personal relationships
   b. big tragedies
   c. achievements
   d. holidays

b 4. What causes almost the same stress as pregnancy?
   a. marriage
   b. getting a new family member
   c. divorce
   d. finishing school

a 5. What causes almost the same stress as marriage?
   a. personal injury
   b. jail term
   c. outstanding personal victory
   d. changing careers

7. Sequence

Read the following paragraph from a travel pamphlet about Ohio. The passage describes the beauties of that state during the different seasons of the year. Then answer each question.

> Ohio is the show that never ends. Each season Ohio takes on a special beauty all its own. Spring is when Ohio's many gardens show off thousands of the earth's most beautiful creations. And sugar maples provide syrup just as they did for the Indians and settlers long ago. Ohio summers feature sunshine-filled skies. Build a sandcastle on any of Lake Erie's four islands or climb a sandstone cliff and picnic above it all. Ohio autumns are the time leaves flame with color. Follow the colorful blaze of fall foliage aboard a 1910 steam engine as it chugs along the Cuyahoga River. Ohio winters often dress forests in white. Wake to a crisp, alpine morning and then cross-country ski across fresh snow. Ohio is a place for all seasons and all reasons.

1. What special activity can you enjoy in each season?

   Summer **building sandcastles, climbing cliffs, picnicking**

   Winter **cross-country skiing**

   Spring **topping sugar maples, visiting gardens**

   Fall **taking a train ride**

2. What special feature does nature have in each season in Ohio?

   Summer **sunshine-filled skies**

   Winter **white forests**

   Spring **beautiful gardens**

   Fall **colored foliage**

3. Which season is described first? **spring**

   Next? **summer**

Next? fall

Finally? winter

8. Details

1. Of the three sample paragraphs on pages 228–231, which paragraph places details in time order?

   #7 on Ohio

2. Which paragraph places details in place order?

   #5 on till

3. Which paragraph places details in order of importance?

   #6 on stress

9. Details Arranged Through Combined Methods

The sequence of details in the following two paragraphs are arranged through a combination of methods. Read each paragraph and note the sequence. Then describe the sequence in the blanks. The first paragraph reveals how Harry Houdini did his most famous escape trick; the second shares some humorous memories about children and cars.

1. Harry Houdini's most famous escape was from a crate sunk in a river. He was handcuffed. The crate was nailed shut and tied in heavy ropes. Holes were drilled in it to make sure it sunk in the water. How did he do it? First and easiest, the handcuffs had a secret spring that opened them instantly. Next, Houdini had secretly taken a pair of nail cutters with him. As soon as his hands were free, he began cutting the nails. The moment the crate was under water, he pushed a few planks open, climbed out, and pushed the planks closed. After he and the crate were pulled out of the water, his assistants secretly removed the cut nails, and hammered in new nails. More important than the secret tricks were Houdini's skill and speed. He could work fast and control his breath for unusually long times. Most important, however, was his great courage. Even with the secret tricks and his great skill, the escape was dangerous. Many things could go wrong. Houdini had to keep a cool mind. Panic would have meant death.

In following Houdini's method, the paragraph uses time order, and it also uses place order in following his path out. However, overall, the paragraph follows order of importance in describing his special tricks and skills.

2. Do you remember traveling in a car when you were a child? All children share the same opinion about what seats are good and bad. Many family trips have been destroyed by sibling battles over who gets the place of honor. The middle back seat of the typical family car is universally known to be the pits. The hump in the middle of the floor presses your knees up to the chin and the adults on either side squash you. And your view is everywhere blocked unless you face backward with your knees on the seat. Anyway, that view lasts about a second until your mother yells "Sit right or you're gonna walk home." In the front middle seat at least you get a view through the windshield, but you had better keep your hands away from the driver and the controls, "unless you want your hands chopped off," as parents so delicately put it. The two side seats in the back are about as good as you are likely to get. Not only do you have a window to yourself, but if you get bored, you can always keep rolling the window up and down. Heaven, though, is the front side passenger seat: fantastic view, radio to play with (especially good for tormenting hated siblings by switching stations or by blasting hideous sounds), and a glove compartment to mess with. Unfortunately, only a major tantrum will get you control of that seat from adults who know a good thing when they see it.

The description follows place order, but the places also follow order of importance.

9c Sorting Out Major and Minor Details

As you find details and see how they are organized, you may find that your reading tells you much more than you thought — too much, in fact, to remember. The information in your reading may seem too detailed. Then it is time to sort out the most important details from the less important ones.

What makes a detail important? In general, a detail is important when it relates to the main idea of the reading. The detail may directly support or help explain that main idea. A *major*, or important, detail helps your basic understanding of the selection. A *minor*, or less important, detail simply helps fill out a picture already drawn. You can overlook a minor detail and still understand the reading. Minor details often help hold our attention and make the reading interesting, but we do not need to give them the attention we give to major details.

For example, in the selection about Jean Paul Getty on page 217, the fact that Getty once said "a billion dollars isn't worth what it used to be" is minor. The quotation helps make the story more amusing and makes Getty's wealth seem more impressive. But his wealth is clear from a major detail at the end — that at his death his fortune was between two and four billion dollars.

As you read the following paragraph from a business textbook, think about which details are more important than others for understanding the passage.

> Government also protects business firms in another way. Business has special techniques, inventions, and innovations that it may wish to protect. For instance, a business may invent a machine or a process that it wants to protect. Entrepreneurs sometimes get their start in a business by inventing something. A business that develops a new manufacturing technique would like to decide who can use that technique. The United States Patent Office will grant a *patent*, a legal "right" that prevents anyone else from making the same thing for seventeen years. Sometimes a business will decide to sell its patent to other businesses if the patent is particularly valuable. Other businesses are willing to pay for the use of the patented item or idea because they need it. They cannot just steal the idea without violating the law.
>
> — *Betty J. Brown and John E. Clow*

As you read the paragraph, you may have noticed the following important details:

Governments protect business firms.
Businesses may wish to protect techniques, inventions, and innovations.
A patent is a legal right that prevents anyone else from making the same thing for seventeen years.

If you understand these major details, you understand the main message of the paragraph. The other details are less important and only help develop these major details. We can see the minor details (items A, B, C, and D) supporting the major details, as shown in this outline:

I. Governments protect business firms.
II. Businesses may wish to protect techniques, inventions, and innovations.
   A. A business may invent a machine or process that it wants to protect.
   B. Entrepreneurs sometimes start in business by inventing something.
   C. A business would like to decide who can use its technique.
III. A patent is a legal right that prevents anyone else from making the same thing for seventeen years.
   A. The U.S. Patent Office grants patents.
   B. Sometimes a business will sell its patent.
   C. Other businesses will pay for the patented item or idea because they need it.
   D. Stealing the idea violates the law.

Here is how one student used underlining to separate the major details from the minor details in a textbook passage about the kinds of abnormal behaviors found in Americans. Before reading the passage, look at the information about "Separating Major Details and Minor Details" in the box on page 236.

> Perhaps the most thorough and comprehensive study ever conducted on the incidence of mental disorders in the U.S. adult population indicates that almost one adult in five (29.4 million) suffers from a mental disorder (*Archives*

Main idea: National Institute of Mental Health study shows one adult in five has a mental disorder.

of General Psychiatry, October 1984). The study, sponsored by the National Institute of Mental Health, is still in progress and will eventually include about 20,000 subjects. Some of the preliminary results are fascinating. For example, researchers found that men and women are equally likely to suffer from mental disorders but that they differ in the kinds of disorders they experience: Women are more likely to suffer anxieties, depression, and phobias. Men are more likely to exhibit substance abuse and antisocial personality.

With regard to incidence, anxiety disorders are the most common (8.3 percent or 13.1 million Americans), followed by drug and alcohol abuse (6.4 percent or 10 million Americans). Schizophrenia, often one of the most severe mental disturbances, afflicts 1 percent of the population, or about 1.4 million Americans.

In the National Institute study, an individual who is not in need of professional help is considered not to be afflicted by a mental disorder.

Separating Major Details and Minor Details

- State the main idea in your own words.
- Look for the information that directly supports that main idea.
- Look for signal words that emphasize information, such as *most important, the facts are, in support, finally, in fact, certainly,* and *necessarily*. Look for signal words that suggest minor details, such as *incidentally, less important, as an aside,* and *a minor point*.
- Underline the major details as you locate them.
- Look for punctuation such as parentheses or brackets, which often signal minor details.

By deciding on the main idea and writing it down, the student can spot the details that help explain the main idea. The main idea here is that according to an important National Institute of Mental Health study, one out of five adults suffers from mental disorder. The most important details, then, are those that show the results of the study. Men and women suffer equally but from different disorders. The kinds of disorders are important, as are the incidence, or frequency, of the disorders.

The student also passes over other things as not as important. Some of the details are interesting but not essential to understand the main idea. You can understand the piece without knowing the name of the journal that reported the study, *Archives of General Psychiatry*, or the date. Note how those details appear in parentheses. Other minor details reinforce or explain statements already made. The various references to numbers of people are minor because they only reinforce the percentage figures given in the sentences. The information about how severe schizophrenia is is minor here. The point being made is that, compared with other mental illnesses, schizophrenia afflicts only one percent of the population.

Keep in mind that not all details are equal in importance. Remember not to let minor details throw you off the track of the main idea. When you think about what you read, don't make a minor detail more important than it is.

EXERCISES

1. Major Details

Read the following paragraph about the invention of the potato chip. Then answer each question.

> Potato chips were originally called *Saratoga chips* after the site of their discovery. In the late 19th century a Native American named George Crumb worked as chef for Moon's Lake House in Saratoga Springs, New York, where a fashionable crowd convened to take the waters of the spa. A persnickety guest reportedly disliked the cut of his French fries one night, and kept sending the oversized potato strips back to the kitchen for a more refined look. Crumb, finally exasperated by the guest's unreasonable persistence, decided to cut the potatoes just as skinny as he could. He boiled the slices in fat

and presented them to the complaining diner, who was delighted and didn't think twice about the indecorous crunching and lip smacking and greasy fingers that accompanied their consumption. From this elegant dining room, the new and scarcely wholesome potatoes traveled throughout the nation, becoming one of the largest-selling snack foods in America.

— *Caroline Sutton*

a 1. What is the main idea of the paragraph?
   a. Potato chips were invented to satisfy a restaurant guest who liked his French fries thin.
   b. Potato chips have become the largest-selling snack food in the United States.
   c. Potato chips are made by cutting potatoes as thin as possible and then boiling them in oil.
   d. Potato chips should really be called *Sarotoga chips.*

2. Place a checkmark next to each major detail from the paragraph. (There are two.)

_____ a. The story took place in Moon's Lake House.

_____ b. Saratoga Springs has a spa.

√ c. A guest sent his oversized potatoes back to the kitchen.

_____ d. The chips made the customer's fingers greasy.

√ e. The customer found the chips delicious.

3. Place a checkmark next to each minor detail from the paragraph. (There are two.)

_____ a. The chef cut the potatoes as skinny as he could.

√ b. The chef was named George Crumb.

_____ c. The chef boiled the potato slices in fat.

√ d. The chef was a Native American.

2. Major Details and Minor Details

Read the following selection from a geography textbook describing Japanese sumo wrestling. This type of wrestling is different in many ways from the kind of wrestling we know in the United States. After you have read the selection, answer each question.

Wrestling, Japanese Style. According to legend, two princes wrestled for the Japanese throne over a thousand years ago. Although wrestling is no longer a way of deciding who will be emperor, thousands still crowd arenas throughout the country to watch *sumo* [soo-moh] — the oldest form of wrestling in Japan.

Many consider sumo the national sport. Every master wrestler has thousands of fans who eagerly follow his matches. Tickets for important tournaments are snatched up months in advance.

Not everyone can become a sumo wrestler. Those who are interested begin training in childhood. Many of these athletes weigh over three hundred pounds. They eat rich foods to fatten themselves and do special exercises to develop their muscles. When top wrestlers retire, they often spend their time helping younger men prepare for the sport.

Early sumo matches were part of the festivals held at Shinto shrines. Even today, before a match the two fighters purify themselves with water. They then sprinkle the ring with salt and say traditional prayers. Only after they have saluted each other by raising one leg high in the air and bringing it down with a mighty thud does the fight begin.

The crowd watches quietly until the two men spring out at each other. Then the first roars go up. The object of a match is to toss one's opponent out of the ring or to force his hands or knees to touch ground. Fans follow the fighting closely. Many can identify dozens of different holds and throws.

A match often ends within seconds. People carry on friendly arguments over who is really the best fighter while the next two wrestlers purify themselves for their match. Fans also take time for snacks. Some prefer traditional foods like tea and rice balls wrapped in seaweed. Others have sandwiches and soft drinks.

There are several major sumo tournaments every year. Each lasts for fifteen days. Those who cannot get seats watch on television. During the last days of a big tournament, practically everyone in the country follows the results.

— *Merwyn S. Garbarino and Rachel R. Sady*

b ______ 1. What is the main idea of the entire passage?
   a. Sumo wrestlers have special diets and training.
   b. Sumo wrestling has many special customs and traditions.
   c. Sumo wrestling started as a political contest and then became part of religious festivals.
   d. Sumo matches are quick, but the tournaments are long.

a ______ 2. What is the main idea of the third paragraph? Choose your answer from the choices for question 1.

3. In the selection are the following details major or minor? Write *major* or *minor* in the space following each detail.
   a. Many think sumo wrestling is the national sport.

      major ______

   b. Tickets are bought months in advance.

      minor ______

   c. Sumo wrestlers begin training in childhood.

      major ______

   d. Some sumo wrestlers weigh over three hundred pounds.

      minor ______

   e. Before a match fighters begin with a religious ceremony.

      major ______

   f. Fighters salute each other by raising one leg high in the air.

      minor ______

   g. A fighter tries to toss his opponent out of the ring.

      major ______

   h. Fans can identify dozens of holds and throws.

      minor ______

i. Fans eat snacks of tea and rice balls.

minor

j. Practically everyone in Japan follows the results of major tournaments.

minor

3. Major Details

Read the following textbook selection about tobacco use. Then answer each question.

The Tobacco Habit

The way tobacco is used has changed over the years. Pipes, cigars, chewing tobacco, cigarettes, and snuff have been in fashion at different times in history. The leaves of the tobacco plant are dried and crumbled. The crumbled tobacco is used in pipes, cigars, and cigarettes, which are smoked. *Snuff* is tobacco ground into a fine powder that is inhaled through the nostrils or held against the gums. *Chewing tobacco* is made of poor-quality leaves mixed with honey or molasses. It is chewed, and then the leaves and juices are spat out.

People have started to smoke for different reasons. Sometimes they are urged to do so by friends. Sometimes they wish to appear more grown up, at ease, or attractive. But the more a person smokes, the harder it is to stop.

Tobacco in History

Tobacco use was unknown to Europeans until Columbus reached America. The American Indians used tobacco in their religious ceremonies. They smoked it in pipes and chewed it. They also used snuff. Columbus returned to Europe with tobacco samples, but few people there used tobacco until 1580. In that year, Sir Walter Raleigh started a smoking fad in Europe. Raleigh, pictured in Figure 18.1, was a very popular person in Queen Elizabeth I's court. When he started smoking, many people copied him. Smoking soon spread to other European countries and to England's colonies in Africa and Asia.

Tobacco is one of the oldest industries in the United States. Tobacco's popularity in Europe helped the English colony in Jamestown, Virginia, survive. Jamestown was nearly aban-

FIGURE 18.1. While Sir Walter Raleigh was smoking a pipe of tobacco, his servant dashed him with water, thinking he was on fire.

doned in 1614. But tobacco crops that were sold to England soon brought prosperity.

Cigarettes became popular only after the cigarette manufacturing machine was invented in 1881. Growing public disgust at tobacco spitting also made people change to cigarettes. The cigarettes rolled out by the new machine were easy to keep lit up and came in handy packages. Cigarettes became more popular in the 1920's when large numbers of women began smoking. Until that time, it was not socially acceptable for women to smoke. The major increase of women smokers, however, began during World War II.

Smoking's popularity was at its height in 1964, when 42 percent of all adults in the United States smoked. In that year, the *Surgeon General's Report on Smoking and Health* linked smoking to heart disease, lung cancer, and other lung diseases. Since this 1964 report, the percentage of smokers over 17 years of age has declined to 33 percent today. In 1964, about one half of all men smoked whereas only 38 percent do so today. There has been a slight drop since 1964 in the percentage of women smokers to 28 percent today. Since 1965 each cigarette smoker, on average, has smoked fewer cigarettes or cigars. It is worth noting that well over one half the doctors, dentists, and pharmacists in the United States who once smoked have quit.

A setback to this trend is that a greater number of teenage girls are smoking today. About 13 percent of the girls between the ages of 12 and 19 smoke regularly. Only about 11 percent of the boys in the same age group smoke, but chewing tobacco and snuff have recently become more popular among them.

Tobacco in the United States is still a giant business that employs hundreds of thousands of people. The sale of tobacco products, 95 percent of them cigarettes, brings in billions of dollars a year. Tobacco sales supply the federal, state, and local governments with billions of dollars in taxes. The federal government gives the tobacco industry millions of dollars each year to control prices and to study how best to grow tobacco.

On the other hand, the government pays millions for scientists to study the dangers of smoking. It also spends large amounts of money for medical care and Social Security benefits for people with diseases caused by smoking. Private industry and people who pay for their own health insurance pay higher premiums because of illnesses caused by tobacco.

— *Bud Getchell, Rusty Pippin, and Jill Varnes*

1. Write in your own words the main idea of the entire selection.

   Using tobacco is a habit that has developed only gradually and peaked only in recent years.

2. In the first paragraph, what are the most important details?

   People have used tobacco differently in different times.

   It has been smoked, inhaled, and chewed.

3. What are the major details to know about the popularity of smoking in 1964?

   Smoking hit its peak in 1964 and has declined since then.

   Forty-two percent of all adults smoked in 1964.

   The Surgeon General's report in '64 linked smoking to diseases.

4. List the most important details about the tobacco business.

   Tobacco is a giant business earning billions of dollars. The federal government helps the tobacco industry, while it also pays the costs for diseases caused by tobacco.

5. List minor details about the history of tobacco in America.

   American Indians used tobacco in religious ceremonies. Jamestown survived because of tobacco. The cigarette-manufacturing machine was invented. It was not socially acceptable for women to smoke. Over half the doctors, dentists, and pharmacists who smoked have quit.

Unit Four

Interpreting What You Read

10

Interpreting Fact and Opinion

Understanding the ideas and details that a writer presents is an important part of reading. But it is not everything. You must also be able to interpret what you read.

You need to be able to interpret your reading so that you can know not only what the writer says but also what meanings you can take away from the reading. Interpretation involves deciding what you believe about your reading and what you need to think more about. Interpretation also involves finding the ideas and the conclusions that are suggested by the reading but that are not stated directly.

Not everything a writer writes is necessarily true. The writer gives both facts and opinions. The writer claims only that the facts are true. The opinions are merely what the writer thinks, not what everyone would necessarily agree with. For example, consider this statement by someone deciding which stereo system to buy:

> The 90-watt amplifier, dual cassette tape recorder, and 25-inch speakers make the Electromax A51 system the best audio buy around today.

Several facts appear in this sentence. The strength of the amplifier (90 watts), the size of the speakers (25 inches), and the cassette feature (dual) are facts. However, whether this system is the best buy is only a matter of opinion. Other people might prefer other audio systems.

Of course, it is not always easy to keep facts and opinions apart. Sometimes the writer presents as fact something that others would not agree with. Just try to get two people who were fighting to agree who threw the first punch! In that kind of situation, what one person believes is a fact to the other is just an opinion.

Sometimes the writer gets facts wrong. For years people wrongly said that Columbus discovered the Americas. People never stopped to think that Indians (now called Native Americans) had made the discovery long before. Even when correct facts are available, some writers do not always check their facts.

At other times the writer may mix facts and opinions together so closely that it is impossible to tell when facts end and when opinions begin. Philosophers argue about what a fact is and what an opinion is. Most people have some opinions that they believe represent true facts.

For most practical purposes, however, we can tell fact from opinion in our reading.

Facts are statements that tell what really happened or what really is the case. A fact is based on direct evidence. It is known by actual experience or observation.

Opinions are statements of belief, judgment, or feeling. Opinions show what someone thinks about a subject. Some opinions are, of course, based more on facts than others are. Such well-supported opinions are more reliable than others. Still, all opinions are just somebody's views and are not facts.

Look at the following statements about homeless people in the United States:

1. In 1985 the U.S. government gave $210 million to 3,650 volunteer organizations that help the homeless.
2. A private group believes that three million homeless people live in the United States today; a government consultant says that there are only 300,000.
3. It seems that the large number of homeless people is a major national problem that we must solve.

Sentence 1 is a statement of fact. Government records show the amount of money spent and the number of organizations receiving the money. Notice that the sentence gives no opinion about whether the money actually helped, only that it was given in order to help.

Sentence 2, even though it gives numbers, does not give us a fact about how many homeless people live in the United States. It gives only two separate opinions about the number. The words *believes* and *says* let us know that the numbers are only opinions. Of course, it is a fact that people disagree over the numbers. Here the author does not give any opinion but presents other people's opinions.

Sentence 3 is an example of the author's opinions. The opening phrase *It seems* lets us know that an opinion will follow. People also may disagree on what is *large,* what is *major,* whether there is a *national problem,* and whether we *must* do something. Some people may argue that there are far more people with homes than without them. Some people may say that the problem is only for the individuals involved and not for the nation. Finally, some people may say we *can* do something if we want to, but we have a choice. We can choose to work on other problems that we think more important. Words such as *large, major, problem,* and *must* all present individual judgments.

Opinion Clue Words

- Some words give an opinion by evaluating or making a judgment. Words such as *ugly, pretty, safe, dangerous, clever, stupid, well-dressed, sloppy, desirable,* and *hateful* always express someone's judgment.
- Some words clearly state that an opinion will follow. You know that an opinion is expressed when the writer says *I believe, I think, in my opinion, I feel,* and *I suggest.*
- Some words show that some doubt may exist about a statement. These words show that a statement is not always true or that other opinions are possible: *usually, often, sometimes, on occasion, probably, perhaps, likely, plausible, possible,* and *maybe.*

EXERCISES

1. Opinion Clue Words

In each statement of opinion, underline the clue words that let you know that you are reading an opinion and not a fact.

1. Being a cab driver <u>seems</u> a hard job.
2. You <u>probably</u> have to drive at least twelve hours a day to make a decent living.
3. Cab drivers look <u>to me</u> as if they are always in a rush.
4. <u>I bet</u> they often get into accidents.
5. I don't <u>think</u> I <u>would be</u> happy driving a cab.

2. Fact and Opinion

Write *F* before each statement of fact; write *O* before each statement of opinion. Then circle any words that help you recognize the opinion statement.

O 1. Some people who live in remote mountain regions claim to have lived to be 125 years old and older.

F 2. People have not been able to find birth certificates or other proof of these claims of long life.

F 3. One man from the Andes mountains, however, did have a birth record showing that he was born 134 years ago.

O 4. Researchers believe that the birth certificate belonged to the man's grandfather, who had the same name.

O 5. We would all like to live to be over a hundred years old.

O 6. Throughout most of history, the average human life span was probably only around thirty to forty years.

F 7. According to government statistics, the average life span in the United States today is seventy-two years.

3. Opinion

Read the following magazine story about how one movie star feels about the way radio, television, and movies encourage drug abuse. Then answer each question.

Paul Newman: "It's an Epidemic"

"Take a moment to think what our children's environment would be like if radio stations decided not to play records with pro-drug messages, if movie studios refused to distribute pictures with gratuitous drug scenes, and if television networks declined to air programs with casual and flippant remarks about drugs."

The speaker is Paul Newman. When he talks about drug abuse, it's from the perspective of a parent who has lost a child to what he calls "the insidious killer of our best and brightest."

Scott Newman, the actor's son by his first wife, Jacqueline Witte, died Nov. 20, 1978, at age 28, after mixing alcohol and Valium. . . .

To demonstrate his concern on the drug issue, Newman appeared at a Congressional hearing on March 20, when his daughter Susan testified during an inquiry into television's role in glamorizing substance abuse.

Newman, however, is uneasy about the government's shadow looming over Hollywood. "It's dangerous," he said. "It's something government should not be involved with. The fact they are getting involved is an admission that we can't police ourselves. It will be an evolving process, but I think we will because we have to. I think you can bring some pressure to bear on the major studios to avoid it when they can."

Asked if he supported an addition to the ratings system to warn of "drug favorable" films, he said: "I can live with that."

The Scott Newman Center was founded by the family four years ago. Among its goals are reshaping media's treatment of drugs and reaching youngsters before they become involved. It produces educational films, advises moviemakers and backs an awards program for TV writers, producers and directors who accurately depict substance abuse.

The center recently was affiliated with the University of Southern California, and Paul Newman donated $1.2 million for operating expenses and to endow an academic chair in the School of Pharmacy. "I think people look at drug abuse and think problems of this size are unmanageable," Newman said. "I don't buy that. This effort is worth it."

— Parade

1. Put a checkmark before each statement that accurately reflects Newman's opinions.

√ ______ a. Radio, television, and movies often carry pro-drug messages.

√ ______ b. Drugs hurt our young people.

______ c. The government should crack down on filmmakers.

√ ______ d. Young people are influenced by pro-drug messages.

√ e. The entertainment industry is not capable of policing itself.

√ f. The entertainment industry should police itself.

_____ g. The drug problem is too big to manage.

_____ h. Newman donated $1.2 million to fight drug abuse.

_____ i. A drug rating system will solve the problem.

2. Which statement represents a fact and which represents an opinion? Write *F* or *O* on the blank before each statement.

F a. Paul Newman's child died from substance abuse.

O b. Paul Newman has the viewpoint of someone who lost a child.

O c. The government's involvement shows that the entertainment industry has not been able to control its presentation of drugs.

F d. His family founded the Scott Newman Center.

O e. The center will be able to influence how the media portray drugs.

O f. A drug rating system is an acceptable action.

4. Fact and Opinion in a Textbook Selection

Read these paragraphs from an American history textbook. Then answer each question.

Nat Turner's Revolt Inspires Fear. In 1831 an insurrection in Virginia startled and terrified slave owners everywhere. This uprising was led by Nat Turner. Turner, a slave, had been taught to read by one of his owner's sons. When the white boys were sent to school and Turner was sent to work in the fields, however, he became deeply embittered. Encouraged by his mother, Turner grew up to be a preacher of considerable ability. He came to believe that he had a divine mission to deliver black people from bondage.

Turner was able to gather together a band of slaves and

organize a revolt. The uprising, first planned for the Fourth of July, was postponed when Turner fell ill. Turner and his band finally attacked a number of white homes on August 21, 1831. Before the end of the rebellion, about 160 people of both races had been killed. Turner and nineteen others were caught and hanged.

— *Henry F. Graff*

1. List at least three facts in this selection.

   Nat Turner led a slave uprising in Virginia in 1831.

   Turner, a slave, learned to read. About 160 people were killed.

2. List at least two opinions in the selection.

   The revolt startled and terrified slave owners. Turner was a preacher of considerable ability. Turner had a divine mission.

5. Fact and Opinion in an Advertisement

Advertisements often use strongly stated opinions to describe the products being advertised. Look at this advertisement, read the following advertising copy that appears in the ad, and answer each question.

> The Pilot Brougham rolling ball pen is like nothing you've ever written with. You'll experience smoothness and comfort that has never existed until now. And Brougham's advanced technology assures this unique writing performance will last for the life of the pen. Even through multiple carbons. At last, a pen that writes with a feeling . . . beyond smoothness. Only $1.19 ea.

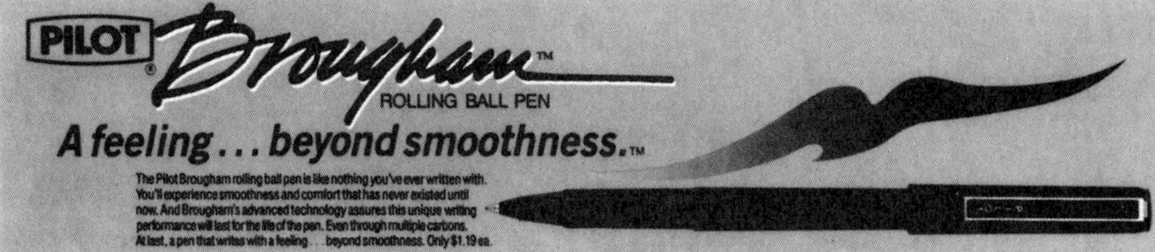

1. List as many facts as you can find stated in this advertisement.

   The pen is made by Pilot.

   It is called the Brougham Rolling Ball pen.

   It costs $1.19.

2. List at least five opinions stated in this advertisement.

   The pen offers a feeling beyond smoothness.

   The pen is like nothing you have used.

   The pen is comfortable to use.

   Such smoothness and comfort have never existed in a pen.

   The writing performance is unique.

3. According to the advertiser, what makes this pen better than others?

   smoothness and comfort

   Is the advantage of the pen supported by facts or opinions?

   opinions

11

Using Inference

Writers often tell you more than they say directly. They give you hints or clues that help you "read between the lines." Using these clues to gain a deeper understanding of your reading is called *inferring*. When you *infer*, you go beyond the surface details to see other meanings that the details suggest or imply.

Inference in some ways is like a guessing game but not a wild guessing game. You must look carefully at the facts and the details in the reading. You must add your own knowledge and experience to those details. Then you can judge what other things are likely to be true, even though they are not said directly. You cannot always be certain that the inferences that you make are absolutely right. But if you follow hunches based on evidence and reasonable judgments, you can be fairly sure about some things, even if they are only hinted at.

For example, a story begins this way:

> Suzanne looked down at the speedometer. Eighty-five. She tightened her grip on the steering wheel. Suddenly she heard a siren behind her.

You already know many things that haven't been said: Suzanne is in an automobile. She is driving it. She is going eighty-five miles an hour. She is breaking the law by going too fast. The siren is likely to be that of a police car pulling her over to give her a ticket.

How do you know these things? Because the facts stated have clear meanings that you know from living in this country. Speedometers are in cars. The driver is the one who usually looks at the speedometer and grips the steering wheel. The speed is usually given in miles per hour on cars in the United States. Speed limits generally are between fifty and sixty-five miles per hour. When people drive cars faster than the speed limit, the police often stop them by driving behind and turning on their sirens.

Writers rely on readers' being able to make inferences. It would be unnecessary and no doubt boring for the writer of Suzanne's story to spell out all these details, which every reader can easily infer. The writer can tell the story more quickly and forcefully by depending on the reader to fill out parts of the picture. The more that a writer can rely on a reader's inference skills, the more the writer can focus on the really important elements of the story. These elements make the story interesting or important.

Actually you use inference not only when you read but also when you participate in almost every aspect of life. You constantly use it, for example, to understand how other people are behaving. In this sense we are all like the great detective Sherlock Holmes, looking for clues to make inferences about people.

Let's say that you are sitting around the lunchroom with some friends, making your usual jokes and small talk. You make a perfectly ordinary comment about an incident in class involving someone who is not there. Suddenly Sam, who is sitting at the table, gets angry. "Why don't you get off her case. I don't have time for this," he shouts. Then he grabs his books and storms away.

Everyone at the table immediately infers that something is bothering Sam. How do your friends know that? They used their own background knowledge. When somebody gets angry we usually infer that there is a cause. But at the table the mood was pleasant, and there seemed no obvious cause for Sam's anger. Everybody at the table also infers that what is bothering Sam has something to do with your comment. It might be either the person that you were talking about or what you said, even though your remark at first seemed harmless enough. The people at the table can infer this because Sam got upset right after your remark. Further, he referred to your remark and to the person. You know from experience that often people seem to get angry over harmless remarks when those remarks reflect something on their minds.

You have to be careful, however, that your inferences do not go too far beyond the evidence you have available. If you make a guess on too little information, you are likely to be wrong. In the example, there is too little evidence to know exactly what is bothering Sam. People might start making guesses. Maybe Sam just started a friendship with the person you were talking about. Or maybe he is on edge about an exam coming up. Or maybe he is still angry about a similar remark you made about *him* two weeks ago. Each explanation is possible, but without more evidence there is no sure way of knowing. If one member of your group reports that Sam has been having a hard time asking the girl you were discussing for a date, then you might infer that that was really bothering him. But without that extra evidence, it is wiser to ask Sam "What's bothering you?" Otherwise we might guess incorrectly and do something inappropriate. Inferences must be based on valid and appropriate information, not just on vague suspicions and wild guesses.

You regularly use inference in looking at scenes, whether in photographs, movies, television programs, or real life. Inferences help you know what the scene is all about.

Look at the picture below. In a sentence, explain the point of the picture — that is, what you think the picture is all about.

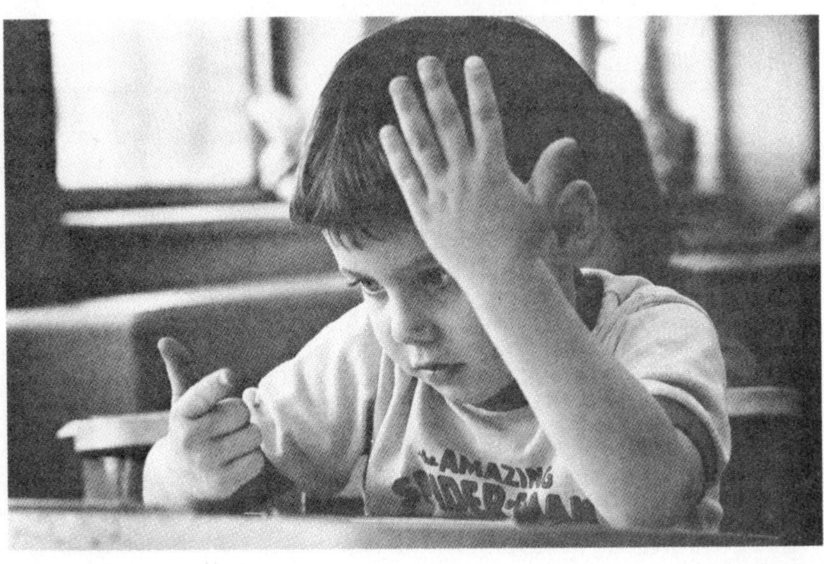

____

____

____

You probably said something like "A schoolboy is counting on his fingers." That description makes sense.

But think about how you came to your statement. How did you know the picture showed a boy rather than a girl? How did you know that the child was in school? How did you know that he was using his fingers for counting? These things are not shown directly. You came to all these conclusions by inferring from the details shown in the picture.

Write down some of the clues that helped you infer that the child was a boy.

____

____

Most likely the haircut and the Spiderman tee shirt together gave you the impression that the child was a boy. We often use clothing and hairstyle to judge people's sex.

What clues made you believe that the child was in school?

____

____

Was it that the child was sitting behind a desk? Or was it the hint of other desks and children in a straight row behind the child? Or was it the big windows?

What made you believe that the child was counting? Why did you not infer that the child was pointing with his right hand and waving with his left?

____

Most likely a combination of factors led to your inference. Other inferences about the age of the child, that the child is in a classroom, that the child is staring at his fingers and concentrating very hard all fit together in the inference that he is doing finger arithmetic.

The clues that we get from the picture help us figure out what is going on. We infer meanings from things that we actually see. Inference helps us complete the picture and fill in important information.

Look at this cartoon now and apply inference skills to answer each question.

b_______ 1. The woman wearing a hat is
a. Mr. Dithers' teacher.
b. Mr. Dithers' wife.
c. Mr. Dithers' secretary.
d. Mr. Dithers' mother.

a_______ 2. The cake had
a. many candles.
b. very large candles.
c. few candles.
d. no candles.

d_______ 3. The cake baked itself because
a. it was a no-bake cake.
b. the day was very hot.
c. the oven didn't work.
d. the candles made a lot of heat.

c_______ 4. Mr. Dithers is
a. a young man.
b. about twenty years old.
c. an old man.
d. dead.

To answer the questions you had to use inference skills. None of the information required to answer the questions is directly stated in the cartoon. But you can draw on your own background knowledge.

For question 1, how did you know to choose *b*, Mr. Dithers' wife? First you probably inferred that two women having lunch might be talking about their husbands. You also inferred that a wife might make a birthday cake for her husband. The other answers don't seem to be correct. Nothing in the cartoon suggests that the woman is either Mr. Dithers' teacher or his secretary. It's *possible* that either of these choices is correct, of course. But *b* seems much more likely than *a* or *c*. Choice *d* does not seem right: Mr. Dithers' mother would look much older than the woman in the hat.

For question 2, we must infer that the cake had many candles. Only *a* is correct. Few or no candles would not give off the necessary heat. And we know nothing about the size of the candles. Choices *b*, *c*, and *d* are incorrect.

For question 3, the cake baked itself, we infer, because of all the candles. Choice *d* is correct here; nothing in the cartoon suggests choice *a*, *b*, or *c*. (We never learn just why the candles are lit *before* the cake is baked. Usually we light candles for a cake that is already baked. Still, the absence of reality does not keep us from enjoying the cartoon.)

For question 4, we must infer that Mr. Dithers is an old man. We know from experience that the older we get, the more candles are placed on our birthday cakes. The custom, as you know, is that each year is represented by its own candle. A young man's cake would not have enough candles for it to bake itself. Twenty candles *might* bake a cake, but an old man's cake would have more candles and, as a result, would give off more heat. Mr. Dithers might be old enough for you to think him dead, but we don't bake birthday cakes for people in their graves. Only choice *c* is the correct inference; choices *a*, *b*, and *d* are incorrect.

Now read the following description. Inferences turn the plain facts into an amusing and surprising story.

The Last Wild West Stagecoach Robbery

It was pulled off by a woman in 1898. Pearl Hart and Joe Boot, her accomplice, robbed the Globe, Ariz., stage. Pearl Hart was 27 and working in an Arizona mining camp as a cook. She convinced Joe Boot that there was more money to be made robbing stages. As the Globe stage turned a bend, the two robbers were waiting, armed with rifles. The three passengers, a drummer, a dude, and a Chinese gentleman, were thrown to the floor and ordered to "shell out." The drummer gave $390, the dude $36, and the Chinese $5. The coach was then ordered on its way. The last stage holdup had netted $431. During their escape, Pearl and Joe became hopelessly lost and then were drenched in a tremendous storm. Three days later they were found (rather than caught) by the local sheriff. When the prisoners arrived in Florence, Pearl was asked, "Would you do it again?" She replied, "Damn right, pardner." Boot got 35 years, Pearl got only 5. She was the sole female prisoner in the Yuma Territorial Prison, and the governor was relieved when he released her after 2½ years. She was next heard of in 1903, when she was arrested at Deming, N.M., for conspiring to pull a train robbery, but she was released for lack of evidence. She was last seen in 1924, a small, innocent-looking 53-year-old woman, busy reminiscing — at the Pima County Jail.

— David Wallechinsky and Irving Wallace

c ______ 1. What can you infer about women and stagecoach robberies from this story?
   a. Women often robbed stagecoaches.
   b. Women never robbed stagecoaches.
   c. A woman robbing a stagecoach was surprising.

b ______ 2. These two robbers were
   a. experienced and skillful.
   b. inexperienced and unlucky.
   c. lucky and successful.

b ______ 3. Pearl Hart
   a. was ashamed of her criminal activity.
   b. liked the idea of being a robber.
   c. was talked into crime by evil friends.

You can infer that women stagecoach robbers were surprisingly rare. Several details in the paragraph and your own background knowledge of the Old West help you. Even though she was the brains of the operation, Pearl got the shorter sentence. This implies that the judge was not used to sentencing women criminals. She was the only female prisoner. And the governor was relieved to release her, as though he were unused to having female prisoners. The correct answer to question 1 is *c*.

You can infer that the two robbers were inexperienced because they got lost and did not hide very well. Being caught in the rain and being found by the sheriff also imply their bad luck. The correct answer to question 2 is *b*.

Finally, you can infer Pearl Hart's attitude toward being a

criminal from her talking Joe Boot into the crime, her tough words during the robbery and after it, her later criminal career, and her reminiscing. The correct answer to 3 is *b*.

Building Inference Skills

- Try to read beyond the words. Fill in details, information, and ideas based on the writer's suggestions and your own background knowledge.
- Ask yourself questions about your reading. In this piece you might have asked yourself what was special or surprising about the story or whether these stagecoach robbers were amateurs or experts. Questions help you put together the details of the piece to make inferences.
- If the writer describes a person, try to understand the person from how she moves, what she says, and what she looks like. You can infer things about someone's character from what the person does. Build a picture in your mind of what the person is like.
- If you have a hard time seeing how information fits together in a selection or what the selection's meaning is, try using inference skills. Sometimes a single inference can make sense of a whole picture. Imagine how pointless the picture of the schoolchild on page 257 would appear if you could not infer that he is doing finger arithmetic.
- If you cannot easily answer a question about what you have read, remember to use inference skills. Return to the reading looking for clues that will help you figure out the answer.
- Try to predict what might happen next. From a series of events you often can infer the outcome. Being able to predict outcomes is an important part of inference.
- Try to generalize about what you have read. When you *generalize,* you infer extended meanings. These meanings go beyond the particular information in the reading. You form principles, or "rules," based on what you've read. For example, from the picture on page 257, you might infer this general idea: *School children sometimes count on their fingers.* Based on the picture, the inference is valid.

EXERCISES

1. Inference from an Advertisement

Look carefully at the advertisement on page 264 and answer each question. To answer each question you must use inference.

c ______ 1. From the headline "Middle Management" you can infer that
   a. this is a job advertisement.
   b. producing and selling beef is a business that you should be concerned with.
   c. keeping your stomach under control is serious business.
   d. beef is a businessperson's food.

a ______ 2. According to the inference clues in this advertisement, dieting
   a. often means eating boring food.
   b. is very hard.
   c. is easy if you eat only tuna fish.
   d. can be made more fun through spices such as pepper and garlic.

d ______ 3. From which of the following can you infer that beef will help you stay thin?
   a. the picture of the tape measure
   b. the number of calories in a three-ounce serving
   c. the headline
   d. all of the above

b ______ 4. Beef
   a. is always healthy.
   b. can be a diet food.
   c. is a very good food.
   d. is not good for people who do not eat.

2. Inference from a Paragraph

Read the paragraph at the top of page 265 about how businesses show off how great they are in order to attract customers. As you read, think of what inferences you can make about the businesses and their claims. Then use your inference skills to answer each question.

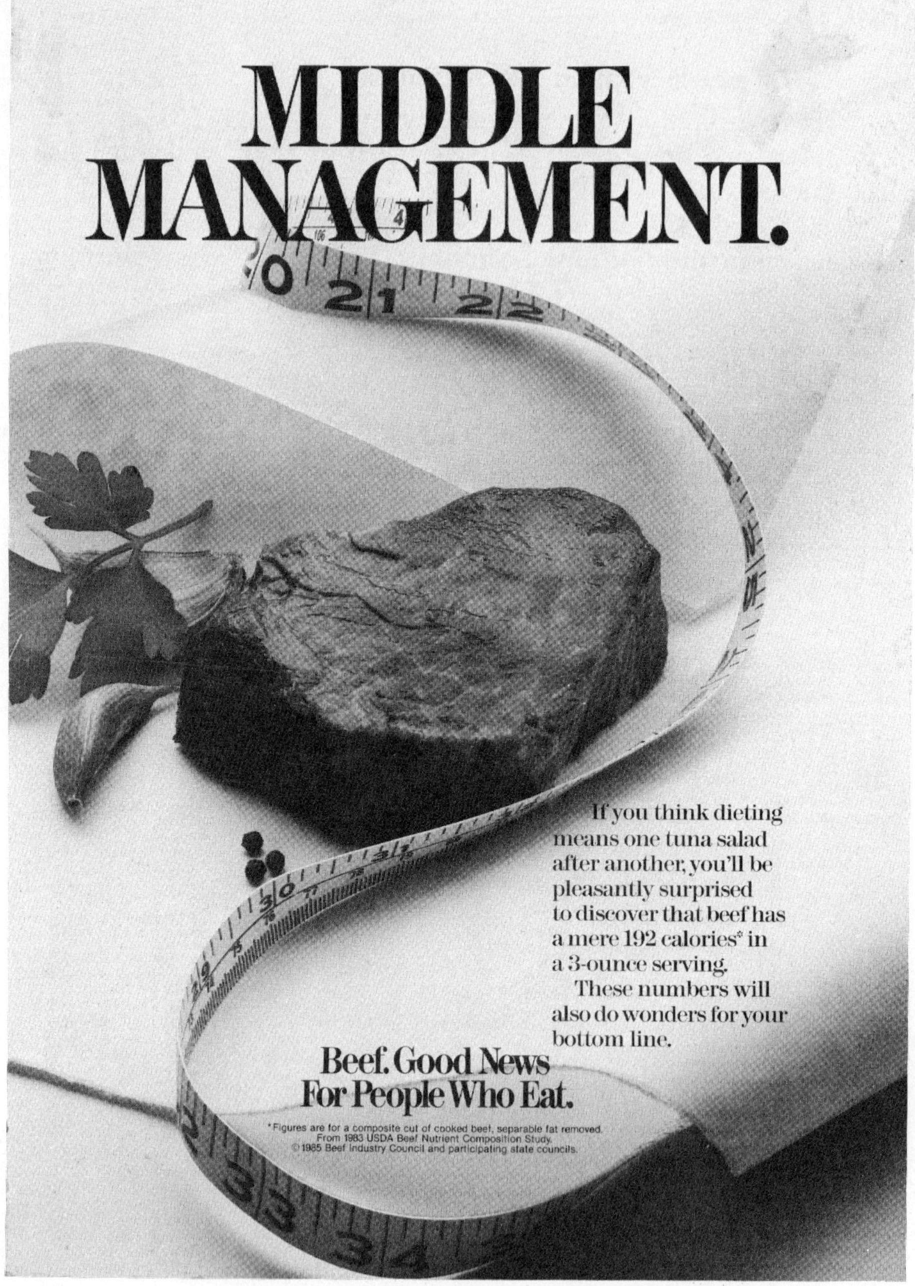
MIDDLE MANAGEMENT.
If you think dieting means one tuna salad after another, you'll be pleasantly surprised to discover that beef has a mere 192 calories* in a 3-ounce serving.
These numbers will also do wonders for your bottom line.
Beef. Good News For People Who Eat.
*Figures are for a composite cut of cooked beef, separable fat removed. From 1983 USDA Beef Nutrient Composition Study.
© 1985 Beef Industry Council and participating state councils.

There is an old story about a downtown city block which had five restaurants on it. The first restaurant boasted in a big sign in the window, "THE BEST RESTAURANT IN THE CITY." The next restaurant on the block had a bigger sign with bigger letters, "THE BEST IN THE STATE." The sign in the window of the third restaurant topped them both, "THE BEST RESTAURANT IN AMERICA." A fourth restaurant would not be beat, "THE WORLD'S BEST." Just at the end of the block a small, ordinary-looking lunch counter had a little sign with small letters, "the best restaurant on this block."

c ______ 1. The signs were put up by
   a. food critics from the newspapers.
   b. gourmets who have eaten at the restaurants.
   c. the restaurant owners.
   d. the same person in all five cases.

d ______ 2. The owners of the five restaurants
   a. were all telling the truth.
   b. have visited many other restaurants to compare.
   c. all own very good restaurants.
   d. will say anything to attract customers.

d ______ 3. The restaurant owner most likely to be telling the truth is
   a. the first.
   b. the second.
   c. the fourth.
   d. the last.

b ______ 4. The owner of the last restaurant
   a. is the best businessperson.
   b. wants to poke fun at the other restaurants.
   c. believes that his or her restaurant is not as good as the other restaurants.
   d. believes that the other restaurant owners are telling the truth.

3. Inference from a Paragraph

Read the following paragraph telling a story about how two kings compared how good the steel in their swords was. Then use your inference skills to answer each question.

Once during the Crusades in the Middle Ages, Richard the Lionhearted, king of England, boasted to the Moslem ruler Saladin that Richard's sword was of the best steel. The sword, made in England, could cut an iron rod in two. Richard, with a quick sword stroke, proved this. Saladin did the same. But then Saladin handed Richard a soft silk pillow and asked him to cut this in half with his sword. Richard tried but failed. His sword just made a quiet thud on soft pliable silk. Saladin then took his own sword which was made of steel from Damascus, Syria. With a single stroke he sliced neatly through the pillow.

b 1. The two kings
   a. were friends.
   b. were enemies at war.
   c. met to make a peace treaty.
   d. hated each other.

c 2. The two kings
   a. were modest.
   b. did not care what each other thought.
   c. liked proving that each was better than the other.
   d. made boasts with nothing to back them up.

d 3. Both kings were
   a. equally good kings.
   b. wrong about their swords.
   c. right about their swords.
   d. proud of their swords.

a 4. A sword that could cut through an iron rod is
   a. very strong.
   b. very sharp.
   c. better than a sword that can cut through silk.
   d. the best weapon.

b 5. Richard's sword could not cut through the silk pillow because
   a. it was not strong enough.
   b. it was not sharp enough.
   c. it was too heavy.
   d. swords cannot cut through soft things such as silk pillows.

d 6. The better sword belonged to
   a. both kings.
   b. neither king.
   c. Richard.
   d. Saladin.

d 7. Steel made in England
   a. made very poor swords.
   b. could hold a very sharp edge.
   c. was better for making swords than steel from Damascus.
   d. was not as good for making swords as steel from Damascus.

4. Inference Practice

Read the following story about how moviemakers showed the actor Christopher Reeve flying in the movie *Superman*. Then answer each inference question.

When Superman speeds across the heavens to save Lois Lane or fearlessly dives and swoops around the skyscrapers of Gotham or over the San Andreas Fault, kids really believe he's flying and many of the rest of us come close to believing, too. That's because the moviemakers put a lot of effort into not only getting Christopher Reeve airborne, but making the action of flying and all it entails really convincing, right down to the rippling of wind through his broad blue cape.

Getting actors and actresses off the ground by means of camouflaged wires is nothing new. But whereas in the past the flyer was suspended on only one wire and had little maneuvering ability as a result, a new system involves two wires, one from each hip. Superman wore a fiber-glass hip harness — or plastic underwear lined with fleece — and to this the wires were attached via ball-bearing swivel joints. High overhead the wires met a bar with a supporting system of cables and sheaves, operated by hydraulic rams. There, too, was a track along which the wires were moved, conveying Superman around the studio — with some near misses of the sets — landing our hero in a net. The wires were painted blue when Superman flew against a blue screen, and sometimes a completely new background was substituted so that no wires would be seen. A crane specially built for the effect was 250 feet high, and Reeve courageously veered around the studio, often at heights of 200 feet.

Despite Reeve's exceptional skill at this — something to consider when it is usually inanimate objects we see hurtling through the heavens in films these days — there was initially something not quite right about his flying. The cape wouldn't swirl properly and no wind machine was capable of making it do so. Les Bowie, responsible for matte painting in the film, came up with an unprecedented solution. He made a device, controlled by radio, that operated long rods and these in turn were attached by lines on Superman's cape. Somehow the various motions of the rods could make the cape billow and furl as naturally as clothes hung out to dry on a windy day.

— *Caroline Sutton*

1. Put a checkmark in front of each statement that can be inferred from the selection.

√_____ a. The scenes of Superman flying seem realistic to viewers.

______ b. The scenes of Superman flying represent real experience.

______ c. Only children watch movies about Superman.

______ d. Children are less likely to believe in the reality of movies than adults.

√_____ e. Many adults have seen *Superman*.

______ f. *Superman* was not a successful movie.

______ g. The scenes of Superman flying are usually comic.

√_____ h. The scenes of Superman flying are usually exciting.

b_____ 2. Actors and actresses
   a. have never appeared to be flying before.
   b. before did not have much control over where they flew.
   c. have appeared to fly just the way Christopher Reeve did.
   d. often refuse to fly by wires.

a_____ 3. Christopher Reeve needed to wear a hip harness
   a. to support his weight.

b. to make him look thin.
c. to control his direction.
d. as an added safety device.

c ______ 4. The ball-bearing swivel joints helped
a. the wires appear invisible.
b. hold the hip harness on the actor.
c. allow the actor to move more freely.
d. keep the actor safe.

c ______ 5. The flying scenes
a. were always safely under control.
b. were easy to film.
c. almost ended in some accidents.
d. were always very believable.

b ______ 6. Superman's cape
a. did not affect how the flying scenes looked.
b. had to swirl right to make the flying seem real.
c. was made to swirl by a wind machine in the final filming.
d. was made from special plastics.

c ______ 7. When you see the movie scenes,
a. you can see all of the machinery used.
b. you can see some of the machinery if you look carefully.
c. you cannot see any of the machinery.
d. you can usually figure out how it was done.

5. Inference from a Magazine Selection

Read the following selection from a magazine story about what National Football League referees do during the week. Then use inference to answer each question.

> Five days a week, Al Jury wears the tan uniform of the California Highway Patrol, pushing paper on felony cases involving drugs, drunks and manslaughter. On the seventh day, the 6-foot-1, 192-pounder slips on a striped shirt, tucks a yellow flag into the back pocket of his white pants, steps into the National Football League — and lays down the law.
>
> The football season opens Sunday. It's Jury's ninth year as an NFL official, his 17th as a highway patrolman. If the big

guys start throwing punches, he's both. "It's the same as being a police officer. You break it up," says Jury.

You won't find a butcher, a baker or a candlestick maker, but the NFL's 107 officials (15 crews of seven each, plus two swingmen) include a foot doctor, golf course director, motivational speaker, lawyer, longshoreman and bank boss, to name just a few occupations. They can tackle real-world jobs because, unlike other pro sports, these officials don't work four or five games a week — just one — and they had better get that one right.

— *Gary Mihoces*

d 1. From this passage, you can infer that
   a. being a football referee is a full-time job.
   b. being a referee of professional football pays a lot of money.
   c. football referees find their regular work boring.
   d. football referees hold other jobs during the week.

b 2. Refereeing a football game
   a. reminds all referees of their weekday work.
   b. reminds some referees of their weekday work.
   c. is the most important thing in the referee's life.
   d. is not important to the referees.

b 3. Referees for the National Football League
   a. all have athletic weekday jobs.
   b. include professional men.
   c. are made up of all kinds of people.
   d. all have college degrees.

6. Inference from a Newspaper Selection

Read the following selection from a newspaper story about the problems that Japanese schoolchildren have in learning to read. Then use inference to answer each question.

While all fifth-graders in this particular group are regarded as academic equals, some are less equal than others. Slightly more than half are found, through testing, to read below expectations. Seven percent have not even mastered third-grade texts.

A portrait of New York-area schoolchildren? So it might seem. But students described above are not fumbling their ABCs. Rather, they are struggling with intricate writing systems known as *kanji* and *hiragana,* for these are Japanese youngsters attending elementary classes.

In this era of global competition, Japanese students are often perceived as almost uniformly superior to their U.S. counterparts. But they, too, have their laggards. Young Taro and his classmates may well surpass Johnny in some subjects, notably mathematics. But when the Japanese youngsters are called upon to recite from a written language containing hundreds upon hundreds of characters, many are ill-equipped for the challenge. Even the brightest do not appear to move ahead as rapidly as the best American readers.

— *John Hildebrand*

c 1. We can safely infer that Japanese schoolchildren
   a. learn to read more easily than American students.
   b. do not work hard enough.
   c. have problems in learning to read.
   d. have as many problems in math as in reading.

b 2. The Japanese writing systems, we may infer,
   a. are simple.
   b. are more complicated than the English writing system.
   c. sharpen the minds of the bright students.
   d. are a lot like mathematics.

c 3. Which inference about writing systems can you properly make based on this selection?
   a. Writing systems are basically the same.
   b. Each language has only one writing system.
   c. Some writing systems create special problems for people who learn them.
   d. All writing systems are based on a few letters.

7. More Inference Practice

Read the following paragraph about the invention of the barometer. Then answer each question.

What would the weather forecast be without a map of highs and lows? How could the weatherman guarantee us a sunny weekend or predict a blizzard if it weren't for the barometer? This instrument is undoubtedly one of the meteorologist's most useful tools, but there's nothing magical or complex about it — its precursor was invented over 300 years ago.

In 1644 a protégé of Galileo's, Evangelista Torricelli, filled a glass tube with mercury and submerged one end in a basin of mercury, while keeping his finger over the other end. When he removed his finger, some of the mercury remained suspended in the tube rather than sinking to the bottom and slipping into the basin. The reason, according to Torricelli, was that "on the surface of the liquid in the basin presses a height of 50 miles of air." Atmospheric pressure was, in fact, keeping the mercury suspended in the tube and Torricelli watched its level change with different weather conditions.

"We live," remarked the inventor in a reflective mood, "submerged at the bottom of an ocean of elementary air."

— *Caroline Sutton*

d ______ 1. You can infer that in making tomorrow's weather forecast, the weatherman will
a. place a tube of mercury in a basin of mercury.
b. probably be wrong.
c. predict a blizzard.
d. use a barometer.

a ______ 2. When atmospheric pressure increases, you can predict that the mercury in Torricelli's tube will
a. go higher.
b. go lower.
c. remain the same.
d. reach a height of fifty miles.

d ______ 3. From Torricelli's experiment you can infer that the
a. air in the atmosphere weighs little.
b. air pressure remains the same all the time.
c. mercury mixes with the air to fill up the tube.
d. air in the atmosphere weighs enough to push up a mercury column.

b ______ 4. You also can infer that Torricelli's invention
a. was interesting but of little use.
b. was very helpful to weather forecasting.
c. was not clearly thought out.
d. made weather forecasting an exact certainty.

a ______ 5. From this selection you can infer that, in general,
a. a change in the weather brings a change in atmospheric pressure.
b. mercury will rise up a tube.

c. atmospheric pressure is unpredictable.
d. weather forecasting methods are complex.

8. Inference from a Textbook Selection

Read the following textbook description of how sound is made. Use inference to answer each question.

> Sound is made when the particles that make up a gas (such as air), a liquid (such as water), or a solid (such as iron or wood) move rapidly back and forth. This back-and-forth motion is called *vibration*. When an object vibrates in air, the object pushes air outward from itself in a series of air-waves. When these waves strike our ears, we hear a sound. For example, when a gong is struck, the gong vibrates. The metal shell of the gong moves first in one direction, then in the opposite direction. When any portion of the shell moves in one direction, it squeezes together air particles in its path as it shoves them outward. As the same portion of the shell moves in the opposite direction, the air particles behind it are spaced out. (Of course, when the air on one side of the vibration portion is being squeezed together, the air on the other side is being spaced out.) The alternate squeezing and thinning out of air particles produces sound waves.
>
> — *Martin C. Keen*

1. If you stop the gong from vibrating, what can you infer will happen?

   The sound will stop.

2. Based on the selection, if you cause a stick held in the air to move back and forth rapidly, what can you infer will happen?

   The stick will create sound waves in the air.

3. If you are on a planet with no air and a gong vibrates next to you, what do you think you will hear?

   nothing

9. More Inference Practice

Read the following textbook selection about the different peoples of the world. This selection deals with the values learned by Bedouin children. The Bedouin people live in the deserts of Arabia and Northern Africa. Then answer each question.

Loyalty and Honor. The Bedouin people think most highly of people who show loyalty. To them loyalty does not mean that one is devoted to a country, a place, or a leader. Loyalty means being faithful to one's family and tribe.

The Bedouin take pride in their ancestors. They do not admire a hero from an ordinary or poor family as much as one who comes from an honored family. They particularly respect those who have inherited a good name and then have passed it on to their children.

A man's position among the black-tent people depends upon his ancestors, relatives, and fellow tribesmen. If they are honored, he is also honored. If they are disgraced, he too is disgraced. Therefore one carefully guards the honor of his family, his lineage, and his tribe.

A man can protect his family's honor by being brave and generous and by giving protection to those who ask for it. He also guards it by carefully watching the women of his family.

A Bedouin woman cannot bring honor to her family, but she can bring disgrace. Even if a woman only looks as if she has done wrong, she may be killed. The honor of her family depends upon her virtue.

— *Merwyn S. Garbarino and Rachel R. Sady*

c ______ 1. Based on this passage, you can infer that a Bedouin man will feel disgraced if he
   a. does not succeed at business.
   b. needs to ask for help from his brothers.
   c. does nothing when a member of his family is insulted.
   d. does not help a stranger who asks for assistance.

a ______ 2. From this passage you can predict that if a Bedouin woman betrays her husband with another man, the
   a. woman will be punished.
   b. other man will be punished.
   c. husband will ask for a divorce.
   d. woman will be forgiven.

b ______ 3. From this passage you can infer that the Bedouin people
  a. respect people who leave their families to seek success on their own.
  b. respect people who value their families above all else.
  c. blame government officials who use their power to get special favors for their families.
  d. are self-centered.

d ______ 4. You can infer that Bedouin women are
  a. treated as the equals of men.
  b. always listened to carefully when they tell their side of a story.
  c. respected for the many things they do.
  d. not respected as much as men.

b ______ 5. You can infer from this passage that the Bedouins
  a. are a peaceful people.
  b. center their lives around their families.
  c. are not concerned with status and honor.
  d. are quick to recognize individual excellence.

Unit Five

Writing to Read

12

Underlining, Listing, and Summarizing

Most of reading goes on inside your head. Your eyes see dark spots on paper, and your brain makes meaning out of those spots and remembers that meaning. That is a lot of activity to keep straight inside your head. You often can get and remember more meaning from reading if you do some of the work outside your head.

If you mark down the most important parts of your reading in one way or another, you can see more easily how these parts fit together into a total meaning. When you write down the main points of a reading selection, you also can refresh your memory easily about what you have read. Finally, the simple act of marking something down impresses that idea on your mind. To write something often means to know it.

There are many ways to mark down directly the ideas from your reading. Most involve writing. Through your writing, the ideas you get from reading turn into words that you yourself have worked with.

This chapter discusses three ways of writing to read. The first, underlining, requires you to mark the main points of meaning in a selection. The second, listing, requires you to put down these points in your own writing. And the last, summarizing, requires you to put the ideas together by writing your own statement about the selection. Underlining is a bit active. Listing is more active. Summarizing is most active and thus is the best method for helping you understand and remember meaning. The skills you learn in underlining and listing will help you summarize.

12a Underlining

By underlining main ideas and major details when you read, you actively mark out what you think is most important in a passage. And, later, if you ever need to reread or look over the passage, the underlining will draw your eye to the most important parts.

Underlining

- Underline only in books that belong to you. Do not underline in library books, borrowed books, or books belonging to your college. Underlining is a personal process. Your underlining may interfere with other people's use of a book.
- Mark the main ideas and the major details differently. Underline the main ideas with a double line and the major details with a single line. Or use two different colors of highlighter pens.
- Find main idea sentences by following the suggestions on pages 163–214. Underline the sentences (or parts of sentences) that state the main idea of a paragraph. If the main ideas are only implied, write your own main idea sentence in the margin.
- Find major details by following the suggestions on pages 234–244. Underline these major details.
- Use circles, brackets, asterisks, numbers, or any other symbol to mark parts that are especially interesting or important to you. If you note ideas in a sequence, number them 1, 2, 3, 4, and so on.
- Write notes or comments to yourself in the margins. The margins are good places to put down your own thoughts as you read. Notes in the margin can help you connect ideas from different parts of the reading. Notes also can help you connect your reading to other things that you have read, that your teacher has said, or that you have experienced.

Look at the following example of a student's underlining of a selection from a book about how to drive a car. This selection describes everything you must do even before you turn the car key. Notice how the student's underlining and notes help organize the many details so that the overall meaning can be seen easily.

Predriving Checks

Before entering Before getting into the car, make sure that nothing is in its path. Clear the windows, if necessary. Enter your car from the curb side. If you must enter the car from the street side, *Entering* approach the door from the front of the car. From this position, you can see and avoid approaching traffic. When it is safe to do so, open the door and get into the car. Close and lock the door quickly.

Clearing Once inside the car you can put the key in the ignition while you make the remaining predriving checks. Clear all objects from the front and rear window ledges. These items can block your view and also become hazards if they slide off during a sudden stop. Be sure all windows are clean.

Seating Seat yourself comfortably with your back against the seat and your arms and legs slightly bent. Rest your left foot on the floor beside the clutch or brake pedal. Rest the heel of your right foot on the floor and the ball of your foot on the gas pedal. Grasp the steering wheel with both hands. To position your hands properly, think of the steering wheel as a clock. Place your left hand between the 9 and 10 o'clock positions. Place your right hand between the 2 and 3 o'clock positions. Move the seat forward or backward until you are comfortable and can reach all the controls. Make sure you can see over the steering wheel. If necessary, use a cushion. *Adjust* Adjust the head restraint so that it is directly behind the middle of the back of your head.

Be sure you can hold the wheel with both hands in the correct position. Then adjust the mirrors properly.

Don't forget!

Once you are properly seated, fasten your safety belt and make sure that all passengers have fastened theirs. Next, check the mirrors. Adjust the inside mirror so that you can see out of the entire rear window. Adjust the outside mirror so that you can see the area to the left of your car and only a small part of the side of your car.

— *Duane R. Johnson and Donn W. Maryott*

EXERCISES

1. Underlining

1. Read the selection about asbestos on pages 219–220. Underline the important information in the passage.
2. Review Chapter 10 on pages 247–254 of this textbook by underlining.

2. Underlining

1. Underline a chapter in a textbook assigned in another course. Underline and make other marks to highlight important information.
2. Underline the following selection from a psychology textbook. This selection deals with weight-control problems.

Problems with Weight Control

Weight is an aspect of appearance that may be particularly likely to become a source of concern during the adolescent years. Before children enter junior high school, being overweight may not cause too much anguish, partly because younger children do not treat appearance as an especially important characteristic and partly because of egocentric thinking. During the secondary school years, however, appearance *does* become important and adolescents become very much concerned about what others think of them. Weight control is much more of a problem for females than males. Girls are more likely than boys to be placid and inactive early in life (due to genetic as well as environmental causes). As a consequence, female infants are more likely to be fat, and (as noted earlier) early tendencies toward fatness are likely to be perpetuated. During the preschool and elementary school years, the typical girl is more likely than the typical boy to engage in sedentary as opposed to athletic activities. Thus, a habit of overeating coupled with lack of exercise is likely to cause girls to become overweight, but the condition might not be reacted to as a problem until after puberty. Once fatness *is* perceived as a problem, the adolescent girl may feel that she has less control over the condition than boys the same age. An overweight high school boy, for example, can take the initiative (because of social traditions) to ask a girl for a date. By contrast, an overweight adolescent girl who is unattractive to males because she is fat, may feel that she can do nothing about the situation. Consequently, she may develop feelings of resignation, fatalism, and self-pity. Such a reaction may lead to the establishment of a vicious circle. An overweight adolescent girl who is rejected by males (and perhaps females as well) may feel humiliated and isolated to the point that she suffers severe adjustment problems. Her own "solution" to these problems may be to turn to eating as "therapy," which perpetuates, or even intensifies, the condition.

The number of books and articles in magazines and newspapers about diets and dieting, together with the number of advertisements for diet centers and plans, attests to the fact that many overweight females are concerned about their condition and want to do something about it. If a series of "miracle" diets all turn out to be ineffective or if a diet program seems to be too difficult to maintain, the overweight girl may develop conditions that are harmful physically as well as psychologically.

Bulimia

One reaction to concern about fatness is called *bulimia*. This condition is characterized by eating binges that may become so extreme that the young woman feels she cannot stop. The binge may come to an end when the voracious eater experiences abdominal pain, which she may attempt to relieve by self-induced vomiting. The woman with bulimia may eat normally for a few days or weeks, only to succumb to the urge to embark on another eating binge. In quite a few cases, the female who has developed bulimia may become so uncomfortable after an eating orgy that she makes a resolution to go to the opposite

— ***Bulimia: insatiable appetite during eating binges***

extreme. This sometimes leads to a situation where the cure is worse than the disease.

Anorexia Nervosa

Some young women who conclude that they are overweight, either because of bulimia or for a variety of other reasons, make a firm resolution to go on a diet. Once they begin to restrict their intake of food, however, they seem unable to stop. If the dieting becomes so extreme that the young woman becomes abnormally thin, she may be said to be suffering from *anorexia nervosa.* (*An* is the Greek word for without, *orexis* means longing, so *anorexia* indicates that someone is without a longing for food.) Some anorexics become so preoccupied with not eating that they die, but most maintain their weight at far below average levels. An interesting aspect of anorexia is that even though others see the underweight young woman as unattractively emaciated in appearance, she perceives herself as either just the right weight or perhaps a bit on the fat side. Another common trait of anorexics is that they become preoccupied with food preparation. They collect recipes, avidly read cookbooks, and prepare gourmet meals — for others to eat.

— ***Anorexia nervosa: abnormal preoccupation with not eating***

A number of explanations have been proposed to account for anorexia. One hypothesis is that growing up seems so threatening to some high school age females that they try to make themselves appear like little girls by, in effect, "shrinking" themselves (Bruch, 1973). Girls who fear growing up are often dependent and compliant and they may fear that their parents will withdraw support if it becomes obvious that they are mature. In an effort to "resist" the physiological changes that occur at the time of puberty, the girl may reduce food intake so that maturation will

— ***Anorexia may be due to a desire to resist growing up***

not seem so apparent (Levenkron, 1978). (If a postpubertal girl reduces food intake beyond a certain point, menstruation ceases.) If the parents of an anorexic female express concern about her condition, they may unwittingly reinforce feelings of dependency, as well as the girl's conviction that not eating is a desirable form of behavior.

Because relationships with parents are often a key factor in the treatment of anorexic high school girls, therapy appears to be most effective when the entire family is involved (Minuchin et al., 1978). In extreme cases, high school girls, as well as older females who no longer have contact with their parents, may need to be hospitalized for physical, as well as psychotherapeutic care.

12b Listing

When you read, you can list the ideas and the major details. By writing the ideas and the details on a sheet of paper, you are an even more active reader than you were when you simply underlined. You pay special attention to ideas and details and check out whether you understand the meaning fully. Also, when you organize the list later on, you can organize the reading in your own mind.

The wording for the list may come from the original or may be your own rephrasing. You can copy whole sentences and phrases, or you can shorten them, as long as they keep the main point. Choosing your own phrasing makes you think even more actively about the meaning.

Making a list is like taking notes or writing an informal outline. When you are done, you have your own statement of what is important in the reading.

Look at the following student's list of ideas and information made from the selection on what a car driver must do before turning on the motor (see pages 281–282). But first read the information about "Listing Ideas and Information" in the box on page 286.

Listing Ideas and Information

- Find the main ideas by following the suggestions on pages 163–214. Write these main ideas on notebook paper, starting at the left margin of the paper. You may copy the entire main idea sentence as it appears in the reading, shorten it, or put the idea in your own words. Or, you may jot down a few key phrases as long as they capture the main idea.
- Find the major details by following the suggestions on pages 234–244. List these details beneath the main ideas that they support. List each detail separately. Indent the details a bit so that you can tell the details from the main ideas. Again, you need not copy whole sentences. Phrases will do. Use either your own wording or the wording of the original as long as you capture the meaning.

Predriving Checks
outside, check road and windows are clear
get in car safely, from curb if possible
clear ledges and windows
sit comfortably, place hands and feet
adjust seat, safety belt, mirrors

In this list the student includes all the main things that must be done but leaves out all the specific details, such as exactly where the hands should be placed on the wheel.

EXERCISES

1. Ideas and Information

1. List the major ideas and details from the selection about Jean Paul Getty on page 217.

Jean Paul Getty made most of his money on his own.

He made his money on oil dealings.

He started business in Oklahoma, but he went on to deal around the world.

He was the richest man in the world, worth between two and four billion dollars.

2. Review Chapter 11 on inference (pages 255–275) by listing the important information.

Inference helps you read between the lines by using hints and clues.

Inferences cannot be certain, but if we are careful we can be fairly sure of what they suggest.

Writers rely on inference.

We use inference through all aspects of life, such as in figuring out what people are feeling.

2. Ideas and Information from Textbooks

1. Study a chapter for a textbook assigned in another course by listing the important ideas and information. Use a separate sheet of paper.
2. List the important ideas and information from the textbook selection on weight-control problems on pages 282–285. Use a separate sheet of paper.
3. Read the following selection from a biology textbook. This passage describes how cells combine to make complex life forms. On the blanks provided at the end, list the important ideas and information that you find in the selection.

Organisms Have Different Levels of Organization

How would you describe a large city? You could list all the buildings in the city, or tell the name and location of the city, or describe the businesses and people there. But that is a lot to consider all at once. It would be easier to look at different parts of the city, one at a time.

Many of the people in a city are members of small groups called families. Several families live on each block. All the blocks in one area make up a neighborhood. All the neighborhoods, with all the different people in them, make up the city. This way of looking at the city takes into account the way it is organized at different levels. Each higher, larger level contains the parts in the smaller level before it.

In studying living organisms, there is a lot to look at too. You can examine organisms by their *levels of organization,* just as you can with a city. Looking at levels of organization helps you understand how an organism works.

The cell is one level of organization in organisms, just as people are one level of organization in a city. You have seen many different kinds of cells. Each specialized cell has a particular function in the organism.

Groups of specialized cells work together in many-celled organisms. A group of specialized cells make up a structure called tissue. A *tissue* is a group of cells that are alike in appearance and function. It is the next level of organization after the cell. Each tissue has a particular function in the body. There are several kinds of tissue in many organisms.

For example, your stomach contains muscle tissue that helps break down food. Your stomach also contains a lining tissue that protects the stomach wall, and tissues that produce digestive juices. The cells of these different tissues have different functions and appearance.

Different tissues that work together make up an *organ,* the next level of organization. Each organ has a specific function in the body. Your stomach, with its three types of tissue, is an organ. It breaks down food. Your lungs, heart, and blood vessels are all organs with different functions. In the lungs, oxygen enters the blood and carbon dioxide leaves the blood. The heart pumps blood to all parts of the body. The blood moves through the blood vessels.

A group of organs that work together is called an *organ system,* the next level of organization. Each system has a function. The heart, blood, and blood vessels make up the circulatory system, which moves materials through the body. The organs that move and digest food make up the digestive system.

All the organ systems together make up the living organism, the next level of organization. The organism is like the city described at the beginning of this section. All the systems together carry out all the basic life activities of the organism. In Unit Two you will learn about the different systems in your body.

The same levels of organization apply to plants as well as to animals. Cells that carry on photosynthesis make up leaf tissue. This leaf tissue, along with tubes that carry water and food, and a skinlike tissue that covers the leaf, make up an organ — the leaf. The organs of a tree include the leaves, stems, and roots. Food is made in the leaves. The stem supports the leaves. Water and food move through the stem. The roots anchor the tree in the ground. Water and other materials move out of the soil into the roots. One system in a tree is the root system. The stems and leaves make up another system above ground.

You can see that a many-celled organism, such as a human, snake, or tree, may be oganized at many levels. Cells with the same appearance and function make up a tissue. Tissues that work together make up an organ. Organs working together make up an organ system. All the organ systems together make up a living organism.

James E. McLaren, John H. Stasik, and Dale F. Levering

Organisms are structured by levels of organization. Specialized cells working together form a tissue. Tissues working together make up an organ. A group of organs working together is an organ system.

12c Summarizing

In summarizing, you combine all the main ideas and the major details of a reading passage in a new, shorter statement. This statement fits together all the important parts into a connected whole.

When doing a summary, you think about meaning even more actively than you did with listing. As with listing, you must think about what is important and how to phrase each idea briefly. But you also must think about how the parts fit together, and you must show that connection through the way you write the summary.

The summary should be about a quarter or a third as long as the original. To make a short summary, you have to think carefully about what is really important in the passage and what is not. Underlining or listing main ideas and major information will help you decide what to include in your summary. Crossing out minor information in the original also can help you decide what not to include.

Once you decide what information to include, you must put together the ideas and the information in readable sentences. You must show the connection between ideas and facts. The words for the summary can be either your own words or words from the original reading. Usually, in fact, the wording of a summary is a mixture of the two. More important, the wording must be brief. State the main points and leave everything else out. The summary, however, must be written in complete sentences that fit together smoothly. Unlike a list, which can include broken phrases, a summary must be a readable piece of writing.

Writing a Summary

- Read and make sure that you understand the passage that you wish to summarize. Check in a dictionary the meaning of all words that you feel uncertain about.
- Choose the main ideas and the major details of the reading selection by either underlining or listing.
- Make the main idea of the selection the most important sentence of the summary. This will usually be the first sentence of the summary.
- Rewrite the information that you underlined into sentences that show the connections among facts and ideas. You may combine several facts or facts and ideas in a single sentence as long as the ideas do not get confused.
- Omit extra words in your summary and emphasize the important words.
- Make sure that you present the ideas and the information in an organized way that follows the meaning of the original. Don't jump suddenly from one point to the next. Use connecting words such as *first, second, on the other hand, because,* and *although* to show how the different statements fit together. Use sentences that bring together related ideas, facts, or examples.

The following sample summary is based on the same selection on predriving checks that you read as an example of underlining on pages 281–282 and listing on page 286. Notice how the summary uses the ideas, information, and even words picked out by underlining and listing. But the summary then combines these things into readable sentences that fit together as a single unit.

> Before getting into a car, make sure the car's path and windows are clear. Then enter the car safely, from the curb side if possible. On the inside make sure no objects on the ledges can slide around or block your vision. Then sit comfortably, with feet on the pedals and hands on the steering wheel. You can then adjust the seat, the seat belt, and the mirrors to fit your position.

In order to understand more fully how to write a summary, examine the process by which one student summarized a passage from a geology textbook. First, the student read the passage through for overall understanding. She had a pencil in hand to circle any words she needed to look up and to underline parts she thought were important. As you read the passage, notice what parts she marked.

What Causes Earthquakes?

People have tried to explain the cause of earthquakes since earliest times. Some people thought that quakes were sent from heaven to punish the wicked. Others believed that the earth rested on the backs of animals (Figure 16.1). When these creatures moved the earth would tremble, causing earthquakes.

We now have more scientific explanations of the causes of these destructive earth tremors. Earthquakes are evidence that some process is at work below the surface of the earth. Large bodies of magma may be in motion. These and other internal movements can result in a sudden release of energy by breaking the overlying, brittle rocks.

During earthquakes, rocks beneath the surface are clearly bent and broken. In other cases deformation takes place slowly and without recognizable earthquake shocks. For example, in a drill hole in the Great Valley of California, earth movements have been measured for years. The rocks here are moving at a rate of about one meter per century.

Another example of slow earth movements is at a winery in

> Hollister, California. By chance it was built on a fault associated with the San Andreas Fault Zone. Over the years there have been slow, steady movements without accompanying earthquakes. The winery building, originally a rectangle, has been pulled into a diamond shape (Figure 16.2). The land at this particular location moves about one centimeter a year.
>
> In some places pressure slowly builds up until the rocks break and quickly snap back into position. The faulting releases energy that may have built up in the rocks for hundreds or thousands of years. This sudden burst of energy causes vibrations that travel through the rocks. These vibrations are an earthquake.
>
> Most earthquakes are so small that they can be detected only by sensitive instruments. But when violent earthquakes occur in inhabited areas, they can cause great destruction and human misery.
>
> In large earthquakes most of the stored energy is released in the first movement along the fault surface. However, energy may continue to trickle off in *aftershocks.* These shocks are much less severe than the main shock and may continue for months after the initial earthquake.
>
> — *American Geological Institute*

The student looked up the words *magma* and *fault* in the glossary at the back of the textbook. (If there had been no glossary, she could have used a dictionary.) She then looked over all the parts she had underlined as important and made sure that she understood what the whole passage was about.

She noticed that the entire passage answered the question of the title, "What Causes Earthquakes?" She then realized that the main idea of the passage would be the part that most directly answered the question. She found two related main idea sentences: "Earthquakes are evidence that some process is at work below the surface of the earth. . . . These and other internal movements can result in a sudden release of energy by breaking the overlying, brittle rocks." She combined the opening question and these two sentences into a single main idea sentence. She then used it to start her summary: "Earthquakes occur when internal movements of the earth suddenly release energy by breaking the overlying brittle rocks on the earth's surface."

The passage was mostly about the way scientists explain earthquakes today. The student felt that all the old explanations in the first paragraph were minor and should be left out.

From the rest of the passage she kept the major details of the explanation and eliminated most details of the examples.

Throughout, she combined sentences and eliminated extra words to bring out the main ideas in as few words as possible. Here is her final summary:

> Earthquakes are caused when internal movements of the earth suddenly release energy by breaking the overlying brittle rocks on the earth's surface. During earthquakes, rocks are clearly bent and broken. Elsewhere, rocks may be slowly deformed over many years. Then the pressure may build up until the rocks break and snap back into position. This break releases the built up energy in the rocks and causes vibrations to travel through the rocks. Most earthquakes are so small that they can be barely detected, but large violent earthquakes can destroy inhabited areas. In large earthquakes, smaller aftershocks may follow after the first large movement of the rocks.

EXERCISES

1. Summarizing Paragraphs

Summarize each paragraph in a single sentence or two. Use the blanks following each selection. **Answers will vary.**

> On June 4, 1896, the editor of the Binghamton, New York, *Republican* offered what most of his readers must have regarded as a rather startling prediction. The airplane, he remarked, would likely be the work of bicycle makers. "The flying machine will not be the same shape, or at all in the style of the numerous kinds of cycles," he admitted, "but the study to produce a light, swift machine is likely to lead to the evolution in which wings will play a conspicuous part." The editor's judgment was confirmed seven and a half years later. On December 17, 1903, Wilbur and Orville Wright made four flights over an isolated stretch of dune a few miles south of Kitty Hawk, North Carolina. Two bicycle makers had launched the air age.
>
> — *Tom Crouch*

Bicycle makers had special knowledge that helped

them build airplanes.

I'm the last man in America who can't cook. This is not to say I don't cook. I live alone and cook for myself — if cooking is the term for putting bologna between two slices of bread. I can also cook a hamburger, or anything that's willing to pretend it's a hamburger, such as a pork chop or those slices of bologna. I can cook anything that's flat and needs to be flipped only once. (Incidentally, you can get chicken to cook exactly like a hamburger if you beat it with a hammer first.)

— *P. J. O'Rourke*

I cannot cook, although I do make easy things for myself

that you wouldn't exactly call cooking.

When compact discs were first introduced, their manufacturers fretted about how they would play in the record stores. What if consumers refused to abandon their precious album collections for the new technology? Now the question isn't whether CD's will last; it's whether *vinyl* will survive. Although long-playing albums still outsell CD's 3 to 1, the surging demand for compact discs has already begun to drive some LP's out of the stores. "No one thought it would happen so fast," says Larry Rosen, copresident of GRP Records Inc. "The end of vinyl may happen sometime in the next five years."

— *Penelope Wang*

CD's are driving vinyl records off the market.

2. Summarizing Short Selections

Summarize each short selection from a magazine article. Use the blanks provided after each selection.

The family TV set is no longer just that big box at one end of the living room. More and more, TV sets are designed to be part of a "home-entertainment system," wired in with a VCR, a hi-fi, and perhaps a computer.

TV sets can now hold their own with other audio and video

gear primarily because stereo and high-fidelity sound are becoming commonplace, in broadcasts as well as in prerecorded tapes. That's a welcome and long-overdue development. Of course, you can still park the set at one end of the living room and never mind the home-entertainment system. But to take full advantage of a TV set's capabilities, you may soon be connecting it to one or two other components.

— Consumer Reports

Student responses will vary.

The East Texas town of Longview may have only about 63,000 residents, but to Clara McLaughlin, the population is a big deal. She discovered just how important it was six years go, when she was in the market for a television station and found that Longview was one of the largest cities in the country without one.

Obtaining the station was a lofty goal. The competitive and lucrative world of TV broadcasting has long been the domain of white men, and few black men and no black woman had ever owned a station. To make things more complicated, Mrs. McLaughlin was faced with building the facility from the ground up, and she had no experience in the industry.

A woman who has always loved a challenge, she went ahead with her plans anyway. Now chairman and chief executive officer of the East Texas Television Network, she not only has CBS affiliate KLMG-TV on the air in Longview, but has acquired three more stations in the smaller Texas towns of Paris, Nacogdoches and Denison. She hopes to have the three operating by spring.

— *Marilyn Marshall*

Student responses will vary.

America is a relentlessly heterosexual society, but when it comes to friendship, each sex prefers its own kind. We all know — or think we know — what same-sex friendships are usually like. Men are fun-loving and loyal to each other while women are intense and intimate. Men compete while women comfort. Men have a greater variety of friends, while women's friendships are richer, deeper and more meaningful.

What may not be so obvious are the payoffs and consequences of these friendship styles. Are men worse off because they develop a wide network of rather superficial relationships? Are women profiting from their devotion to family and friends? To both questions the answer must be, not necessarily. In truth, both sexes would benefit if they studied, and in some ways emulated, the other.

— *Letty Cottin Pogrebin*

Student responses will vary.

3. Summarizing a Textbook Selection

Summarize the following excerpt from a chapter in a history textbook. The selection deals with an ancient tribe of people in the Southwest. Use the blanks after the excerpt.

Many Cultures Arise North of Mexico

Hundreds of different cultures and languages developed among the Indians who settled the North American continent north of Mexico. These different peoples are often grouped by geographical regions where people had similar ways of life (map, page 305). As in Mesoamerica, archeologists have found evidence that several distinctive cultures emerged as early as 1000 B.C. Some were influenced by the Mesoamerican civilization to the south. Trade, agriculture, and arts flourished, and different forms of political organization developed.

The Anasazi Build Cities in Cliffs and Canyons. By the first century A.D., a people known as the Anasazi (ah-nah-SAH-zee) had created a farming culture in the dry lands of the Southwest — present-day Arizona, New Mexico, Colorado, and Utah. The name Anasazi was given them by the Navajo Indians, who much later discovered the ruins of their huge, many storied homes. In the Navajo language *Anasazi* means "strange ancient ones."

The early Anasazi probably learned farming techniques about 1500 B.C. from the peoples of Mesoamerica. Corn, beans, and squash became their staple foods.

The Anasazi at first lived in dugout houses roofed with logs. About A.D. 700, as the population increased, they began to build houses of stone or sun-baked clay called adobe (uh-DOH-bee). Communities grew more crowded, and society became more complex. Houses were built close together and on top of each other. Hundreds of people in the community worked together to build huge "apartment houses," which were several stories high and had many rooms (picture, page 306). People hauled logs long distances to make the framework and roof; they cut blocks of sandstone for the walls. The Spaniards who arrived several hundred years later called these huge buildings *pueblos* (PWEB-lohz), which means "towns" in Spanish.[1]

Many pueblos were built in canyons or high on steep cliffs. One of the largest, Pueblo Bonito (in present-day New Mexico), took more than a hundred years to build and was completed about A.D. 1085. It had 650 rooms and could house well over a thousand people. Nearby pueblos in the same canyon were almost as large. Every great pueblo had a central room or *kiva* (KEE-vah) used for community ceremonies and religious rituals. Colorful murals decorated the walls of the kiva.

As farmers in a dry land, the Anasazi were dependent on natural forces, and these were the center of their religion. The

[1]This term is now used both for the buildings and for the present-day Indians, such as the Zuñi and Hopi, who are the Anasazi's descendants.

Anasazi devised a kind of "sun clock" to track the seasons and the cycles of the sun. Men oversaw the rituals that people hoped would bring good hunting, enough rain, and successful crops. Women in Anasazi society owned all the houses and property and headed family clans.

The Anasazi culture stretched over a huge area in the Southwest. Networks of wide roads linked central pueblos with outlying villages and other centers. The people traded with Mexican Indians for copper and feathers and with Indians of the Great Plains for buffalo meat. Their only farm animals were turkeys, but they kept dogs as pets.

About 1150, a very long drought struck the central area of Anasazi culture. Gradually all the great pueblos were abandoned. The Anasazi moved away to join neighboring groups, and the first great culture of the Southwest vanished.

The Hopewell People Carry on Widespread Trade. About the fifth or fourth century B.C., a highly organized farming society developed in the Ohio River valley. Living in villages along the river, these people became known as "Mound Builders" because of the large earthen mounds they constructed. Some of these structures were burial mounds, and others were ceremonial mounds in the shape of animals such as snakes, turtles, or birds. The Mound Builders traded widely along the rivers and lakes, acquiring copper from the northern Great Lakes region, seashells from the Gulf of Mexico, and mica (a shiny mineral) from people to the east. Their artists worked with wood, stone, and copper to make ornaments and household objects (picture, page 306). The Mound Builders' way of life, called the "Hopewell culture,"[2] spread over the central part of the continent from what is now Wisconsin to the Gulf Coast and as far west as present-day Kansas. The Hopewell way of life lasted for about a thousand years, until A.D. 400 or 500.

The Mississippian Culture Borrows from Mesoamerica. Both ideas and goods were exchanged in the trade among the Indian peoples of the Americas. By about A.D. 1200, people along the lower Mississippi River had built the most advanced culture north of Mexico. Their culture, which archeologists call the Mississippian, was influenced by ideas from Mesoamerica. Mississippian society was divided into

---

[2] The culture was named for a farmer in southern Ohio, on whose land archeologists discovered mounds and objects from this culture.

strict classes under a ruler known as the Great Sun. In the center of the walled villages stood steep-sided earth pyramids with wooden temples on the flat summits. High-ranking nobles built their homes on smaller mounds, and other mounds were used for burials. Religion included the Mesoamerican idea of a feathered serpent god.

Student responses will vary.

4. Summarizing More Textbook Selections

1. Summarize the passage about Japanese wrestling on page 239. Use a separate sheet of paper.
2. Study Chapter 7 of this textbook (pages 137–159) by summarizing it. Use a separate sheet of paper.
3. Summarize the passage from a biology textbook (pages 287–289). Use a separate sheet of paper.

13

Keeping a Reading Journal

It is one thing to understand the words that a writer has written. It is another to feel that the words are important to you. Skillful reading is not just understanding the words. It also is connecting your life with the words, so that the words become part of you. Skillful reading is discovering personal meanings for yourself — by making the words part of your thinking, your experience, and your life. Simply stop for a minute to think about how what you are reading relates to what you have already experienced, what you know, and what you feel.

A good way to take that extra moment is to write about your reading. Keep a notebook, or a journal, just for your personal thoughts about your reading. Every time that you read something, take an extra five minutes to write down a few ideas about your reading.

What kinds of things can you write about in this journal?

It's best to keep a number of questions in mind (see the box on page 301). When you write a journal entry, you should try to follow up on your thoughts. Don't worry about grammar or spelling. For every statement that you make, ask yourself why you believe that or what experiences or feelings lie behind your statement. If one idea leads to another, continue writing about the new idea. The more you put your thoughts on paper, the more you will see how the reading connects with things that are important to you.

Before you read what one student wrote in her journal in response to the selection about children's favorite seats in the family car (page 233), read the "Questions to Answer in Your Reading Journal" in the box on page 301.

> I grew up a city kid, and the only car seats we got to sit in were in abandoned wrecks. The great thing though was not cars, but subway cars. Me and my brothers, we would run

right up to the front of the first car in the train. We would push our noses against the window in the front door. Then we would watch the signal lights flash by us as we speeded through the dark tunnels. It was like outer space. And the subway noise was so loud we couldn't hear anyone. Just like going through space. I guess kids everywhere find their special places.

Questions to Answer in Your Reading Journal

- How do you feel about the subject of the reading? Are your feelings similar to the writer's?
- Which parts of the reading seemed exciting? dull? funny? depressing? outrageous? Why did you feel that way?
- Do you feel sympathy with any of the people described in the reading?
- What experiences have you had that are similar to the events described in the reading?
- What people do you know who are similar to the people described in the reading?
- What places or situations or problems resemble those that you know?
- How do your opinions about the subject compare with the writer's? With which statement do you particularly agree or disagree?
- What is the writer trying to say?
- How important to you are your beliefs on this subject?
- Has the writer changed your mind or made you start thinking about a new point of view? How?
- How convincing are the ideas and the arguments that the writer presents?
- How might some people disagree with the writer?
- As you were reading, what ideas went through your mind?
- Did the reading remind you of other thoughts that you have been having? Which thoughts?
- How does the reading connect with any subject that you have been thinking about?
- Did you have any new thoughts after doing the reading? What were those thoughts?

When reading the selection on Japanese schoolchildren (pages 270–271), another student wrote this journal entry:

> I was surprised to read about struggling Japanese schoolchildren. Everything I've ever heard about education in Japan says that Japan's children are wonder kids. They always seem to be studying hard and achieving very high. I suppose that their written language is much harder than English so I can understand kids who have trouble. But I wonder what other school subjects they have trouble with? I wonder if quicker and slower learners are found in the same proportion there as here. And is it possible that "the grass is always greener"? Maybe our own problems with education make us see everybody else's as not too important.

In both these cases, students got a better understanding of their original reading by looking at their own feelings and thoughts as they were set in motion by the reading. When the first student remembered her own special travel place, she felt a little closer to the experience described in the reading. When the second student weighed the points she learned, she developed new insights into the topic.

EXERCISES

1. A Reading Journal

Begin a reading journal. Every time you have a reading assignment (or whenever your teacher suggests), write fifty to one hundred words describing your feelings and thoughts about the reading. This will be particularly useful as you read the selection in the second half of this textbook.

2. Personal Thoughts

Reread the selection about Paul Newman's opinions on drugs and the entertainment industry (pages 250–251). Do you agree or disagree with him? Write a paragraph describing your own thoughts on the subject.

3. Personal Experiences

Read the following comic piece about how children eat. Does this passage remind you of anything that you used to do as a child or that you have seen young children do? On a separate sheet of paper, write a paragraph describing your experiences with how kids eat. You may want to discuss whether these experiences fit the ways of eating described in the article.

How to Eat Like a Child

Peas: Mash and flatten into thin sheet on plate. Press the back of the fork into the peas. Hold fork vertically, prongs up, and lick off peas.
Animal Crackers: Eat each in this order — legs, head, body.
Sandwich: Leave the crusts. If your mother says you have to eat them because that's the best part, stuff the crusts into your pants pocket or between the cushions of the couch.
Spaghetti: Wind too many strands on the fork and make sure at least two strands dangle down. Open your mouth wide and stuff in spaghetti; suck noisily to inhale the dangling strands. Clean plate, ask for seconds, and eat only half. When carrying your plate to the kitchen, hold it tilted so that the remaining spaghetti slides off and onto the floor.
Ice-cream Cone: Ask for a double scoop. Knock the top scoop off while walking out the door of the ice-cream parlor. Cry. Lick the remaining scoop slowly so that ice cream melts down the outside of the cone and over your hand. Stop licking when the ice cream is even with the top of the cone. Be sure it is absolutely even. Eat a hole in the bottom of the cone and suck the rest of the ice cream out the bottom. When only the cone remains with ice cream coating the inside, leave on car dashboard.
Spinach: Divide into little piles. Rearrange into new piles. After five or six maneuvers, sit back and say you are full.

— Judith Viorst

Reading Selections

Introduction

These selections will help you to practice the reading skills you've learned so far. The questions for each selection check your understanding of what you have read. In some cases you will be able to answer the questions without returning to the selection; in other cases you will want to return quickly to specific passages before you choose an answer. Returning to the selection to check *every* answer will slow you down and make your reading a chore. Try to remember as much as you can when you read each piece. On the other hand, when you are not certain about something, it's best to check back before writing an answer.

You'll notice that numbers and letters in parentheses appear at the end of each question. These refer to the chapter and section in the first part of the book where the skill you need for answering the question is explained. If you are still stumped after you've checked the selection again, turn to the appropriate section of the handbook and review your skills.

Two approaches help you learn the new words in each selection. Key words are listed with their definitions in a section called "Word Highlights" right before the selection. When a difficult word appears in the selection, you can look it up easily. In addition, a vocabulary exercise appears at the end of the questions on each piece. The vocabulary exercises ask questions about the uses and meanings of new words. You will want to add the new words to your reading, writing, and speaking vocabularies as soon as possible. That means writing the words down, using them in sentences, and following the other guidelines given in Chapter 1. You should also keep a list of other words you don't know in each selection. Check their meanings and learn them, too.

The writing assignments provided for each selection will help you think critically about what you have read. Use a separate sheet of paper for these assignments. You may have to summarize important points in the reading, compare experiences presented in the reading with your own experiences, or express your opinion about a point raised in the reading.

The works chosen for this section will teach you, amuse you, and make you think. You'll find articles, essays, and sections of books, newspapers, and magazines. In short, the anthology provides a varied program of reading similar to that required of today's college student.

1

Two Worlds

Jim Yoshida (with Bill Hosokawa)

What happens when a Japanese teenager's desire to play football for his Seattle high school team conflicts with his father and mother's values? Read about how Jim Yoshida at first challenged and then successfully overcame his parents' objections.

Getting Started

Make a list of everything that comes to your mind about *playing football.* **(5a)**

Word Highlights

scrimmage practice game between teams
rationalize to develop self-satisfying but not really correct reasons to do something
interference something that gets in the way of something else
varsity the principal team representing a school in sports competition
transgression bad deed; lie
deceive mislead on purpose
absorb soak up
impact collision
exhilaration excitement
intermediate going between two extremes

When I was fifteen years old and a freshman in a Seattle high school, I stood 5 feet 7 inches tall and weighed 168 pounds. Many of my friends signed up to try out for the freshman football team. I couldn't because I had to go to Japanese school.

Still, I figured it wouldn't hurt to watch football practice for a little while. I sat on the sidelines, glancing at my watch frequently to make sure I would leave in time to get to Japanese school. On the third day of practice, the freshmen engaged in a scrimmage, and I couldn't tear myself away. I had played some sandlot football, and I figured I could do just as well as the freshmen in uniform. Before I knew it, it was too late to get to Japanese school on time. It didn't take me long to rationalize that being absent was only a little worse than being tardy. I decided that I might just as well watch football practice for the remainder of the day. Before long, nothing seemed to be more important than playing football with the freshman team. I approached the coach and told him I wanted to try out.

Coach Heaman looked at my stocky frame. "What's your name?" he asked.

"Jim Yoshida," I replied.

He reached into a pocket and pulled out a form. "You have to get your parents' permission," he said. "Take this home and get it signed. Come down to the locker room after school tomorrow and check out a uniform."

My heart sank. Here I was being invited to try out for the team, and parental permission — an impossible obstacle — blocked the way.

Full of apprehension, I went home at the normal time. Apparently Mom was unaware of my absence from Japanese school, and if my sister Betty had noticed, she hadn't said anything. I knew that Mom could sense when I had something on my mind. Besides, I wanted to talk to her before Dad came home, so I came straight to the point.

"Mom," I ventured, "I want to try out for the football team at school."

After hesitating a moment she replied, "What if you were injured playing football? Besides, what would you do about Japanese school? I think you had better forget about football."

I knew it was useless to try to change her mind and even more useless to talk to Dad.

Next day during a study period, I gave myself permission to play football. My hands were clammy when I gave the slip to Coach Heaman. I was sure he could hear the pounding of my heart and see the look of guilt that I knew was written on my face. He failed to notice, however, and routinely filed the permission form and issued me an ancient, hand-me-down uniform and a pair of ill-fitting shoes.

I made the team as a running guard. This meant I pulled out of the line and ran interference for the ballcarrier. If I did what I was supposed to do and threw a good block, the ballcarrier had a chance of making a good gain.

At the end of the freshman season, I was one of several freshman players invited to suit up with the varsity. In the season finale, the varsity coach let me play half the game.

Meanwhile, for some reason I have never understood, my absence from Japanese school went unnoticed until Betty brought home her Japanese-school report card right after the football season ended. Mom and Dad grinned as they examined her record. I knew what was coming next; Dad turned to me and asked to see my report card.

"Sir," I said, "I don't have one."

His eyebrows shot up. "Why not? Did you lose it?"

"No, sir, I haven't been attending Japanese school."

He fixed me with a stare that bored right through me. We were at the dinner table, and all of us had hot boiled rice to eat with cooked meat and vegetables. Steam rose from the bowl in front of my father, and I could see his temper rising too.

"Explain yourself," Dad ordered.

So I told him the whole story, including the way I had signed the form, and his frown grew darker and darker. Mom averted a very explosive situation by suggesting that the dinner table was not the place for a scolding. She suggested we finish our dinner and then talk about the problem.

Sometime during the meal, Dad must have seen the humor of my transgression. Perhaps he remembered pranks he had pulled as a boy. I was relieved to see his anger had given way to simply a serious mood when finally the dishes were cleared away.

First he lectured me about how wrong it was to deceive one's parents, and I had to agree with him. Eventually he got around to football. "I can understand why you would want to play the game," he said. "You should, however, take an interest in a Japanese sport like judo."

Judo is like wrestling, a sport in which a smaller and weaker person learns to use an opponent's strength to defeat the opponent. I didn't have much enthusiasm for judo.

Dad was saying, "Judo will give you the discipline you need. You must learn to grow tougher physically, mentally, and morally."

Then I saw a way that I might be able to play football next season. I apologized for what I had done. I *was* truly sorry. I agreed to go back to Japanese school and try my best to make up for what I had missed. I said I would go to judo class — if I could play football again next year.

The smile that had started to take shape on Dad's face vanished. Then he said, "All right, play football if it's that important to you, but remember there are things that are important to me too. So go to Japanese school and try to learn a little about the language; and go to judo classes and learn a little about discipline." We shook hands.

Several nights later, when I came home from Japanese school, Dad introduced me to a man who was about ten years older than I. His name was Kenny Kuniyuki; he was an instructor at a judo school. Dad told me Kenny would be my judo teacher. I liked Kenny immediately. We had dinner together, and then he drove me to the judo school.

For the next three weeks, every Monday, Wednesday, and Friday, I went to the school and learned to fall. Falling without hurting yourself is an art in itself. Gradually I learned to roll to absorb the impact as I hit the mat and to break the momentum with my arms and legs and shoulders before I crashed to the floor. Then Kenny began on the holds and throws. From seven to nine-thirty I would practice throwing and being thrown with the other students. After everyone else had left, Kenny had me stay and practice with him.

I must admit that I thought about quitting, especially on mornings after a particularly strenuous workout. I knew, though, that if I dropped judo, I could forget about playing football.

Approximately six months after I began judo lessons, everything began to fall into place. I was tough physically; I had learned, finally, to take the hardest falls without hurting myself; and I was able to coordinate my skill with my strength. I found a new exhilaration and excitement in judo. Judo was as much fun as football!

Soon I was good enough to skip over all the intermediate steps — yellow, green, brown, and purple — and get a black belt. It usually takes a student three or four years of hard work to win black-belt rating. I had done it in a fraction of that time. Mom and Dad beamed approval.

Dad raised no objection when I turned out for football in the fall of my sophomore year. I had kept my end of the bargain, and he kept his. I made the team as a running guard and was lucky enough to be an all-city selection even though we didn't win a single game. I still continued practicing my judo after the daily football workouts.

When I returned to school for my junior year, I had 190 muscular pounds on my 5-foot-9½-inch frame. The judo training had given me a better sense of balance, which helped me as a football player. I had no trouble making the team, and at the end of the season, I was again named all-city.

By the time my senior year rolled around, both my parents had become ardent football fans, and they came to watch me play. My new coach shifted me to fullback. I guess the move was a success because even though we still didn't win a game, we scored a touchdown — the first in three years. I was the one who carried the ball over the line! As I picked myself up after scoring, I saw Dad standing just outside the end zone with a big grin on his face. I think the sight of that grin made me the happiest of all! ❑

EXERCISES

Understanding

b_____ 1. The two worlds in the title refer to the topic of this selection. What are the two worlds? **(8b)**
   a. childhood and adulthood
   b. American values and Japanese values
   c. schoolroom and schoolyard
   d. parent and child

c_____ 2. Which of the following is the main idea of this selection? **(8d)**
   a. Parents make unfair demands on their children.
   b. Choosing football over judo causes problems in a Japanese household.
   c. It is possible to succeed in two cultures even when they make competing demands.
   d. Honor your father and mother.

b
____ 3. The obstacle that Jim saw to playing football was **(9a)**
a. the coach.
b. the parent permission form.
c. his low weight and small frame.
d. his poor playing.

a
____ 4. When he told his mother of his plans to play football, she advised him to **(9a)**
a. forget about it.
b. talk to his father.
c. build up his body first.
d. play for the team at the Japanese school.

a
____ 5. When Jim tells his father the whole story about playing football, his father **(9a)**
a. tells him to take up judo.
b. insists that he give up football.
c. tells him to get an "A" average before he can play the sport.
d. scolds Jim's mother for allowing their son to play such a dangerous sport.

d
____ 6. Kenny Kuniyuki is Jim's **(9a)**
a. football coach.
b. Japanese teacher.
c. English teacher.
d. judo instructor.

7. Write *major* after each major detail and *minor* after each minor detail from the selection. **(9c)**

a. Jim Yoshida went to Seattle High School. minor

b. Coach Heaman was the one who took the permission slip. minor

c. Jim was invited to suit up with the varsity team. major

d. The intermediate steps in judo are yellow, green, brown, and purple belts. minor

e. Jim became as good at judo as he was at football.

major

f. Jim's father allowed him to play football if Jim also would learn Japanese and take judo lessons. **major**

8. Arrange the following details in the proper sequence. Put a 1 after the first detail, a 2 after the second detail, and so on. **(9b)**

Jim becomes an all-city football team selection. **9**

Jim's dad grinned at Jim's scoring a touchdown. **10**

Coach Heaman asks Jim his name. **2**

Jim's absence at Japanese school goes unnoticed. **3**

Jim agrees to go back to Japanese school. **6**

Jim makes the team as running guard. **4**

Jim's father introduces him to Kenny Kuniyuki. **7**

Jim coordinates his skill with his strength. **8**

Jim's mother averts an explosive situation. **5**

Jim's friends signed up to try out for the freshman football team. **1**

Interpreting

1. Write *F* after each statement that is a fact and *O* after each statement that is an opinion. **(10)**
   a. Jim stood 5 feet 7 inches tall and weighed 168 pounds.

   F

   b. Being absent was only a little worse than being tardy.

   O

c. Nothing seemed more important than playing with the freshman team. **O**

d. Jim ran interference for the ball carrier. **F**

e. Judo was as much fun as football. **O**

d 2. From the sentence "I gave myself permission to play," we are to infer that Jim **(11)**
   a. got his father to agree to let Jim sign his father's name.
   b. talked to himself.
   c. spoke with the coach for special treatment.
   d. forged his father's signature on the form.

a 3. We can infer that Jim gained 30 pounds from his freshman to his junior year because **(11)**
   a. football and judo both helped build up his body.
   b. he was unhappy and snacked out of frustration.
   c. he ate too much boiled rice, cooked meat, and vegetables.
   d. he did not get enough exercise.

a 4. We may infer that if Jim had another opportunity to deceive his parents, he would **(11)**
   a. not deceive them again.
   b. deceive them another time.
   c. discuss it with Kenny Kuniyuki first.
   d. only tell a little white lie.

b 5. We may infer that one reason Jim's father wanted his son to take up judo was that **(11)**
   a. football is too dangerous.
   b. he wanted his son to stay in touch with his Japanese background.
   c. he wanted his son to defend himself against the football players who disliked Jim.
   d. it is a very easy sport to learn.

d 6. We may infer that Jim and his father shook hands because **(11)**
   a. they wanted to avert a fight.
   b. it's a Japanese custom.

c. they were saying good-bye.
d. they were sealing an agreement.

a ______ 7. If Jim were to go to college and wanted to play football, his parents would **(11)**
a. encourage him.
b. discourage him.
c. neither encourage nor discourage him.
d. forbid him from joining the team.

Vocabulary

Determine the meaning of each word in the list below by using word-part clues — prefixes, suffixes, roots, and compound words. Use a dictionary only if you have to. Then write each word in the blank spaces beside the correct definition. The letters that fall in the circles will spell an important word in the selection. **(1d)**

ball-carrier	sandlot
hand-me-down	unnoticed
ill-fitting	useless
parental	workout

1. i l l - (f) i t t i n g — 1. too big or too small
2. u n n (o) t i c e d — 2. not seen
3. w o r k (o) u t — 3. exercise session
4. s a n d l o (t) — 4. open field where amateur games are played
5. (b) a l l - c a r r i e r — 5. someone who is supposed to gain yards in a game
6. h (a) n d - m e - d o w n — 6. an object, usually clothing, passed on from one person to another
7. u s e (l) e s s — 7. not of any value
8. p a r e n t a (l) — 8. having to do with a mother or father

WRITING PRACTICE

1. Summarize the major events in the selection from the conversation at dinner to the end of the story. **(12c)**
2. Write a letter to Jim Yoshida telling him why you think it is important (or unimportant) for him to keep up his ties with his Japanese background.

2

How to Behave at School

Judith Viorst

People are always telling children to behave. The advice that Judith Viorst gives here is unusual but funny. It should also be familiar. As you read, see whether the advice reminds you of anything.

Getting Started

Before reading this selection, make two lists. In the first list, write the rules that told you how you were supposed to behave in school. In the second list, write how you actually behaved in school. **(5)**

Word Highlights

align put in a straight line
inconspicuous hard to find
nonchalant seeming relaxed

Ma, I don't feel good. Maybe I shouldn't get up today. I feel sorta blah. I don't know — I just feel yucky all over. Ma? Ma, would you feel my forehead? I don't? Are you sure? Are you positive? OK, I'll get up. I'll get up, but you'll see — I'll probably just get to school and have to turn around and come home again.

Arrive at school late. Explain that you are tardy because you couldn't find your shoe.

As soon as the teacher turns to write on the blackboard, open your desk, pull out *Mad* magazine, and put it inside the language arts workbook. Read *Mad* magazine while it looks as if you are reading language arts.

Chew a pencil, tear off the corner of a piece of paper, and write: "You are a dodo. Pass it on." Gripping the pencil between your teeth like a pirate with a knife in his mouth, fold note in half, quarters, eighths. Use your ear as a pencil holder as you drop the note on the floor and pass it with your foot to your friend across the aisle. Then, pretending to play the drums, tap your desk with a pencil, and when it's time to hit the cymbals, tap the head of the kid in front. If he turns around and says, "Cut it out," say, "Cut *what* out?" As soon as he faces front again, kick him and say, "Sorry, I didn't mean to." Click your pen.

Deny that you are chewing gum and stick it on the roof of your mouth.

Whisper. Stop when the teacher asks if you'd prefer to spend class in the hall. Ask to change your seat.

Pretend that your pencils are ships; steer them around your desk and make them collide. Look at the clock.

When the teacher asks for a volunteer to take names while she is out of the classroom, raise your hand, shake it frantically, stretch so that your body is nearly a horizontal line between your desk and the teacher, and call out, "Me, me, me, me, me, me, me." You do not get chosen.

What to Do While the Teacher Is Out of the Classroom: Hold your nose and say in a high-pitched voice, "Now class, behave." Run to the front of the room and draw your fingernails down the blackboard. Return to your seat like Groucho Marx, hunched over, looking both ways, wiggling eyebrows, and chomping on a pencil as if it were a cigar. Get your name taken.

Get it erased by threatening to get the name-taker at recess.

Sail a paper airplane and when it lands, raise your hands, clasp them above one shoulder, then the other: You are the champ. Get your name taken.

Throw an eraser.

When a kid shoots a spitball and doesn't get his name taken, say, "How come you took my name and not his?" Get his name taken while he tells you to shut up, calls you by your last name only, and says, "Mind your own beeswax." Burp.

Smell something funny. Shriek, "Someone laid one, someone laid one, silent-but-deadly, smell-y, whew, P.U., major fart alert, major fart alert, major fart alert." Wave hand in front of face. Crack up. Pound desk. Hold nose while each kid in the class also holds his nose and insists that it was another kid.

Yell, "She's coming," and fall out of your chair just as the teacher returns.

Ask to get something from your coat in the cloakroom.

Ask to sharpen your pencil.

Tell the teacher, for the second time this week, that you do not have your homework because the dog ate it. She will say that if this kind of behavior continues, she will have to note it on your permanent record card.

Look at the clock.

Ask to get a drink of water.

How to Act If You Do Not Want to Be Called On

- Make yourself invisible. Align head and shoulders with those of a student directly between the teacher and you. If the teacher moves, adjust alignment.
- Make yourself inconspicuous. To accomplish this, assume a casual pose. Concentrate on fitting the top of the pen into the bottom; perhaps even hum to yourself. Or engage in nonchalant play with a pencil: Hold it upright, point against paper, and slide fingers from eraser to tip. Turn pencil over; slide from tip to eraser. Turn and slide. Turn and slide.
- If the teacher calls on you anyway, do not respond immediately in the hope that a kid with the answer will just yell it out. If no one rescues you and the question calls for a yes or no response, pick one. Otherwise, give a joke answer. The class will laugh. The teacher will say that it won't be so funny when you get your report card. ❑

EXERCISES

Understanding

a ______ 1. The topic of this selection is **(8b)**
   a. children's school behavior.
   b. teachers of children.
   c. behavior.
   d. getting called on in school.

2. Write the main idea of the selection in your own words. **(8d)**

Student responses will vary.

Children like to fool around and avoid work at school.

b ______ 3. The details in this selection are arranged mostly according to **(9b)**
 a. how funny they are.
 b. time.
 c. importance.
 d. space.

d ______ 4. The behavior described in this selection includes all of the following except **(9a)**
 a. throwing paper airplanes.
 b. passing notes.
 c. making noise.
 d. calling the teacher names.

b ______ 5. The selection advises you to use your pencil for all of the following except **(9a)**
 a. chewing.
 b. writing school work.
 c. tapping your desk.
 d. playing ships.

d ______ 6. According to the reading, you can avoid having your name reported to the teacher by **(9a)**
 a. behaving properly.
 b. volunteering to be the name-taker.
 c. winning a bet with the name-taker.
 d. threatening the name-taker.

c ______ 7. According to the advice given here, you should remain quiet only when **(9a)**
 a. the teacher leaves the room.
 b. the teacher asks for volunteers.
 c. the teacher asks questions.
 d. other children do something wrong.

Interpreting

a 1. You can infer that the first paragraph in the selection takes place **(11)**
   a. before school.
   b. after school.
   c. during morning classes.
   d. during lunch period.

c 2. You can infer that the mother **(11)**
   a. believes her child is telling the truth.
   b. does not care about getting her child to go to school.
   c. thinks her child is faking illness to get out of going to school.
   d. has checked with the doctor to make sure that her child is not really ill.

c 3. You can infer that other children in the class **(11)**
   a. all behave better than the child described.
   b. all behave worse than the child described.
   c. behave in ways that are similar to how the child described behaves.
   d. tell their mothers about the bad child in their class.

d 4. You can infer that the teacher does not choose this child to take names because she **(11)**
   a. has a favorite.
   b. does not like this child.
   c. has more important things for the child to do.
   d. does not trust this child to be responsible.

a 5. "How to Act When You Do Not Wish to Be Called On" is for **(11)**
   a. when you do not know the answers to the questions.
   b. when you wish to make the teacher laugh.
   c. good students.
   d. college classes.

a 6. You can predict that by the end of the day the teacher of this class will feel **(11)**
   a. exhausted.
   b. proud.
   c. happy.
   d. like laughing.

c
______ 7. If a child really follows the advice given here, you can infer that the child will **(11)**
a. learn a lot.
b. make a lot of friends.
c. not learn much.
d. be thrown out of school.

a
______ 8. You can infer that the child described here **(11)**
a. gets into lots of mischief.
b. loves school.
c. hates everything about school.
d. is a good student.

c
______ 9. You can infer that the selection **(11)**
a. offers serious advice.
b. is totally confused.
c. exaggerates real behavior.
d. makes up totally unbelievable details.

d
______ 10. From this selection, you can say, in general, that children **(11)**
a. like to please teachers.
b. always get into trouble.
c. are more imaginative than teachers.
d. often have their own ideas about what to do in class.

Vocabulary

Complete each sentence by filling in the blank with one of the following words. **(2)**

volunteer	cymbals
frantically	tardy
horizontal	concentrate
collide	engage

1. I promised to come on time and never be ___tardy___ again.
2. The student began to ___concentrate___ on the half-finished exam.
3. The teacher searched ___frantically___ for the grade book that the students had hidden.

4. The two boys began to **engage** in an imaginative battle of insults.

5. The girl decided not to **volunteer** to carry the message to the office because she did not want to miss the fun.

6. Make a **horizontal** line on the paper.

7. The two halves of the tin pencil box made a wonderful pair of **cymbals**.

8. The children running down the hall began to **collide** with each other.

WRITING PRACTICE

1. List the five things that the article suggests you do when the teacher is calling on students for answers. **(12b)**
2. Write a comic set of rules or advice on "How to Act on a Date" or on "How to Behave at a Job Interview."

3

Pedro

Jovita Gonzalez

Here is the story of a proud Mexican traveler who left the land of his youth. He learns something about himself in Houston, Texas. What happens to Pedro in the big city?

Getting Started

Before you read, do brainstorming **(5c)** on *travelers, travel, trips.* That is, raise questions about any or all of those items. Use a separate sheet of paper to write your questions on.

When you read, see how many of your questions the story "Pedro" addresses.

Word Highlights

renowned well known everywhere
superiority being better than others
vaquero cowboy
auditors here, the word means "listeners"
el Tren Volador Spanish for "the Flying Train"
envy wanting to have what someone else has; jealousy
mellow soft and full
rank strong in odor
corral a pen for cows and horses
jerky beef prepared by smoking or drying in the sun

Pedro was a wonderful person among all the people of the ranch. Besides being the most renowned hunter, he had seen the world, and conscious of his superiority, he strutted among the vaqueros and other ranch hands like an only rooster in a small barnyard. Besides, he spoke English, which he had learned on one of his trips up North. Yes, Pedro was a traveled man; he had been as far away as Sugar Land and had worked in the sugar-cane plantations. Many strange things he had seen in his travels. He had seen how the convicts were worked on the plantations and how they were whipped for the least offense. Yes, he, Pedro, had seen that with his own eyes.

He did not stay in the Sugar Land country long; the dampness was making him have chills. So he hired himself as a section hand. His auditors should have seen that big black monster, *el Tren Volador.*[1] It roared and whistled and belched fire and smoke as it flew over the land. He would have liked being a section hand on the railroads had it not been for the food — cornbread and salt pork.

He had been told that if he ate salt pork, he would soon learn to speak English. Bah! What a lie! He had eaten it three times a day and had only learned to say "yes." But being anxious to see a city, he came to Houston. As he walked through the downtown streets one Saturday evening, he saw some beautiful American ladies singing at a corner. What attracted his attention was that they played the guitar. And that made him homesick for the ranch. He stopped to listen, and the beautiful ladies talked to him and patted him on the back. They took him with them that night and let him sleep in a room above the garage. He could not understand them, but they were very kind and taught him to play the drum, and every evening the ladies, after putting on a funny hat, took the guitars and he the drum, and they went to town. They sang beautifully, and he beat the drum in a way that must have caused the envy of the passers-by, and when he passed a plate, many people put money in it. During the winter he learned English. But with the coming of spring he got homesick for the *mesquitales,* the fragrant smell of the *huisache,* the lowing of the cattle at sundown, and above all, for the mellow, rank smell of the corral. What would he not give for a good cup of black, strong ranch coffee, and a piece of jerky broiled over the fire! And so one night, with his belongings wrapped up in a blanket, he left south by west for the land of his youth. And here he was again, a man who had seen the world but who was happy to be at home. ❑

---

[1]Spanish for "the Flying Train."

EXERCISES

Understanding

b
_______ 1. The topic of this selection is **(8b)**
   a. learning to speak English.
   b. a Mexican who leaves his country and returns.
   c. playing a guitar.
   d. how to travel over the world.

b
_______ 2. Which sentence from the story best states the main idea? **(8)**
   a. "Pedro was a wonderful person among all the people of the ranch."
   b. "And here he was again, a man who had seen the world but who was happy to be at home."
   c. "But being anxious to see a city, he came to Houston."
   d. "He did not stay in the Sugar Land country long; the dampness was making him have chills."

d
_______ 3. During the time he stays in Houston, Pedro **(9a)**
   a. struts like an only rooster in a small barnyard.
   b. drinks strong coffee and eats beef jerky.
   c. works on the sugar-cane plantations.
   d. sleeps in a room above a garage.

b
_______ 4. Pedro struts about like a rooster because **(9a)**
   a. he owned a chicken farm and studied how roosters walked.
   b. he feels superior to other people.
   c. it amuses the people who give money when he plays the drum with the American women.
   d. he knows how to make strong coffee better than anyone.

c
_______ 5. About the English language, Pedro **(9a)**
   a. never learned how to speak it.
   b. could never learn how to read and write it.
   c. learned it on one of his trips up North.
   d. spoke well enough to sing along with the beautiful Americans.

d ______ 6. Which of these did Pedro miss most from the ranch? **(9a, 9b)**
a. the sound of the guitar
b. strong coffee and beef jerky
c. the lowing of cattle at sundown
d. the odor of the corral

7. Write *major* after each major detail and *minor* after each minor detail about Pedro and the "beautiful American ladies." **(9c)**

a. Pedro left for home at night. minor

b. He played the drum with the ladies. major

c. He grew homesick for the ranch. major

d. He met the women on a Saturday night. minor

e. He learned English in the winter. minor

f. The train was called *el Tren Volador*. minor

g. Pedro wrapped his belongings in a blanket. minor

Interpreting

c ______ 1. We may infer that Pedro ate salt pork three times a day because **(11)**
a. he was homesick for the ranch.
b. it made him strong enough to work on the train.
c. he thought it would help him learn how to speak English.
d. he loved the taste of it and could never get enough.

d ______ 2. *Huisache* and *mesquitales* are probably words that relate to **(1c, 11)**
a. coffee and other hot beverages.
b. cattle.
c. ranches and plantations.
d. plants and flowers.

a ______ 3. We may infer that Pedro passed a plate because **(11)**
a. he was trying to get money.
b. he hoped people would put some beef jerky on it.
c. he had brought the plate from Mexico and was proud to show it to everyone.
d. it was broken and he was trying to have it fixed.

c ______ 4. Probably the train was called *el Tren Volador* — the Flying Train — because **(11)**
a. the conductor was a former airplane pilot.
b. it could travel both on tracks and in the air.
c. it traveled very fast.
d. it was a big black monster.

a ______ 5. We may infer that a "section hand" is **(11)**
a. a helper on part of a job.
b. part of a person's palm.
c. a cook.
d. an auditor.

c ______ 6. We may infer that Pedro left Sugar Land country because **(11)**
a. he could not yet speak English well enough.
b. he found the work there too difficult.
c. he did not like the weather there.
d. he did not like the convicts who worked there.

b ______ 7. The women Pedro met in Houston were **(11)**
a. cooks.
b. street performers.
c. garage mechanics.
d. English teachers.

b ______ 8. We may infer that Pedro thought the convicts **(11)**
a. were well treated.
b. were badly treated.
c. did not travel much.
d. were lucky to have work on the plantation.

a ______ 9. We may infer that if Pedro had the chance to go back to Houston under better working conditions, he **(11)**
a. probably would not go.
b. would be glad to leave the land of his youth.

c. would go if he could take strong coffee and beef jerky with him.
d. would want to learn how to play the guitar.

10. Put a checkmark next to any general statement that you can safely infer from this story. **(11)**

_____ a. Beautiful ladies are friendly to foreigners.

√_____ b. Bad food may drive a person away from an otherwise interesting job.

_____ c. People envy anyone who can play a drum or guitar.

_____ d. Traveling makes people superior.

√_____ e. Traveling is wonderful, but it can make a person homesick.

Vocabulary

Look at the words in italics below. Try to guess each word's meaning from the selection. Then use the words in italics to do the crossword puzzle. Choose the word in italics that best suits each meaning given under *Across* and *Down*. You may have to add an ending to or take one away from each word in order to make the word fit into the space in the puzzle. **(1c)**

anxious to see a city (par 3)
conscious of his superiority (par 1)
convicts (par 1)
dampness was making him have chills (par 2)
homesick for the ranch (par 3)
lowing of the cattle (par 3)
strutted among the vaqueros (par 1)

Across

1. slight wetness
2. wanting to return to a place you lived or were born in
3. aware of
4. walk in a way that shows you think you're very important

Down

1. prisoners
2. mooing
3. eager

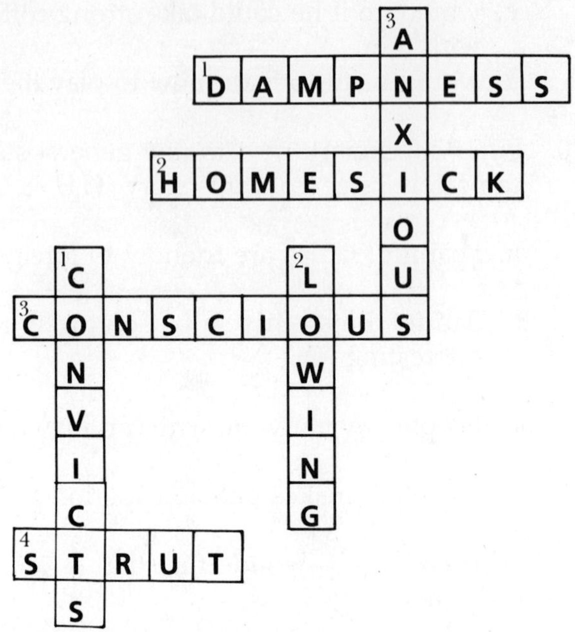

WRITING PRACTICE

1. Write a summary of all the important things that happened to Pedro from the time he got to Houston to the coming of spring. **(12c)**
2. Did you ever get homesick? Write a paragraph in which you tell where you were when you felt homesick and why you felt that way.

4

Greyhound Hopes This Ad Will Never Run Again

This advertisement is from Ebony, *a magazine directed mainly at black Americans. Greyhound Lines, a large bus company, placed the ad. However, the ad is more than just an effort to get us to take more buses. What is the special message of this advertisement?*

Getting Started

Without reading the entire advertisement, preview the ad by following the suggestions below **(4, 5, 6)**. Write your responses on the blank lines. **Student responses will vary.**

1. Read the headline — the first sentence above the photograph. State the meaning of the headline in your own words.

____

____

2. Look at the picture of the child. Describe how he looks.

____

____

3. Read the caption in the lower right corner of the picture. Write a sentence that tells in your own words what the caption says.

____

____

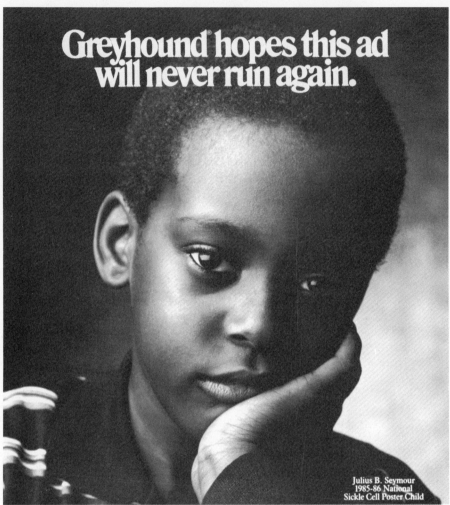

Greyhound® hopes this ad will never run again.

Julius B. Seymour
1985-86 National
Sickle Cell Poster Child

Because if it does, everyone's efforts to wipe out Sickle Cell Anemia have fallen short. About one out of every 500 Black Americans is born with Sickle Cell Anemia. These figures cannot be ignored. And at Greyhound, we're not ignoring them.

Throughout 1986, Greyhound will continue to contribute a portion of every ticket sold to the National Association for Sickle Cell Disease, Inc.

The Association is involved in research, education, screening, counseling, and patient service in the continuing fight against the disease that affects so many Black Americans every day.

So now when you go Greyhound, you get a chance to help in the fight against Sickle Cell Anemia.

And, hopefully, you will never have to see another ad like this again.

GO GREYHOUND
And leave the driving to us.®

© 1986 Greyhound Lines, Inc.

Word Highlights

sickle cell an abnormal body cell shaped like a sickle — that is, like a half circle
anemia blood disease that does not let cells carry enough oxygen
screening identifying groups with special traits
poster a large sign used to advertise something

EXERCISES

Understanding

b 1. The main point of this advertisement is to **(8)**
   a. explain why we should take buses wherever we can.
   b. show how a bus company is trying to help in the fight against a serious disease.
   c. tell how many people are suffering from sickle cell anemia.
   d. ask you to give money to help fight the disease.

b 2. The main idea of the ad is **(8)**
   a. stated in the caption for the picture of the child.
   b. implied throughout the ad.
   c. stated directly in the last paragraph.
   d. implied by the photo of the child and the bus.

c 3. Based on the ad, Julius B. Seymour is **(9a)**
   a. the president of the Greyhound Lines, Inc.
   b. the driver of the bus in the ad.
   c. a child who appears on posters about sickle cell anemia all over the country.
   d. a volunteer worker who is active in the National Association for Sickle Cell Disease, Inc.

d 4. According to the advertisement, sickle cell anemia strikes **(9a)**
   a. Americans of all races and creeds.
   b. members of the National Association for Sickle Cell Disease, Inc.

c. many employees of Greyhound Lines.
d. one out of 500 black people born in America.

a ______ 5. The National Association for Sickle Cell Disease, Inc. **(9a)**
a. is a group that helps fight against the disease.
b. is part of Greyhound Lines, Inc.
c. uses only Greyhound buses for all its local travel.
d. is paying for this advertisement in *Ebony*.

a ______ 6. Greyhound Lines, Inc., is helping to fight sickle cell anemia by **(9a)**
a. giving some money from each ticket sold to the National Association for Sickle Cell Disease, Inc.
b. doing research, screening, counseling, and patient service.
c. providing reduced fares for all people with the disease.
d. hiring people who have the disease.

d ______ 7. Sickle cell anemia is a disease that **(9a)**
a. is often caught from other people on buses.
b. strikes the nervous system.
c. strikes children between the ages of one and fifteen.
d. a person is born with.

Interpreting

d ______ 1. It is opinion that **(10)**
a. one of five hundred blacks get sickle cell anemia.
b. the National Association for Sickle Cell Disease is involved in research and education.
c. Julius Seymour is the poster child.
d. we cannot ignore the high figures that tell how many people get the disease.

b ______ 2. We may infer that about sickle cell anemia, Greyhound Bus Lines **(11)**
a. believes that the disease cannot be cured.
b. believes that having to run this ad again means that we have not succeeded in our efforts to fight the disease.
c. feels that the National Association for Sickle Cell Disease, Inc., is not doing as good a job as they should be doing.
d. is trying to ignore the disease.

a 3. We are expected to infer from the photograph that the child is **(11)**
   a. sad and serious.
   b. playful and energetic.
   c. strange.
   d. tired but happy.

a 4. The word *America* on the top of the bus window is trying to show **(11)**
   a. that Greyhound can take passengers all over the country.
   b. the name of the particular bus in the picture.
   c. the city in which Julius B. Seymour lives.
   d. the place that the National Association for Sickle Cell Disease, Inc., has its main office.

5. Put a checkmark next to any of the following inferences that you can draw from the ad. **(11)**

√ a. The National Association for Sickle Cell Disease provides important services for black Americans.
___ b. Because of help from large businesses, such as Greyhound, Julius Seymour and children like him will be cured of their disease.
√ c. Greyhound Bus Lines hopes that you travel by bus because the more you travel, the more money it can give to the National Association for Sickle Cell Disease.
___ d. Buses offer safe, convenient ways to travel.
___ e. The ad will never again appear in magazines or newspapers.
___ f. Only black people should travel by Greyhound in order to help find a cure for sickle cell anemia.
√ g. Greyhound will earn less profit per ticket in the years that it runs this ad than in years that it doesn't run the ad.

6. In fact, Greyhound Lines no longer runs this ad. Why do you think this is true?

____

____

Vocabulary

Phrases in column *A* below come from the advertisement. Next to each phrase, write the letter of the meaning from column *B* that best matches the word in italics. Column *B* has more items than you will need. **(1)**

A

d 1. this ad will never *run* again

g 2. *have fallen short*

c 3. figures cannot be *ignored*

e 4. continue to *contribute*

f 5. a *portion* of every ticket

B

a. grown smaller
b. go very quickly
c. overlooked
d. appear
e. give money for
f. part of
g. are less than what's needed
h. added up

WRITING PRACTICE

1. Make a list of some actions that you and students in your school could take to help fight sickle cell anemia. **(12b)**
2. Create for your school newspaper an advertisement in which you call attention to a serious problem facing us today. You may want to consider an illness (such as cancer, heart disease or AIDS), a social problem (such as drug addiction), or a political issue (such as low voter turnout on Election Day).

5

Changing Roles Alter Buying Behavior

William M. Pride
O. C. Ferrell

How much influence do children have in spending money as they choose? What effect do children's spending power have on America's economy? Read this selection from a college textbook in marketing for some interesting (and surprising) answers to these questions.

Getting Started

Before you read, do freewriting on this topic: *children spending money.* **(5d)** As you read, use underlining to mark what you think is most important in the selection. **(12a)**

Word Highlights

marketer someone concerned with buying and selling
discretionary for use without any restrictions
peer an equal; someone of the same age or with the same rank, status, or class
apparel clothing
clout power
astute sharp; clever
per se exactly

In some ways they are a marketer's dream. They have billions of dollars in discretionary income — and spend most of it. Although their individual purchases are small, they buy regularly, often in response to peer pressure.

They are heavily influenced by the hours of television advertising they see each week. And, as a result of today's smaller families and the increase in the number of two-income households, they have more to say about family purchase decisions than ever before.

"They" are children, of course, a group whose spending habits are attracting the attention of more and more marketers. One recent study estimates that the thirty million U.S. children 4 to 12 years old receive about $4.7 billion annually from allowances, gifts, and odd jobs. Of that amount, they spend a total of $4.2 billion each year on snacks ($1.4 billion), toys and games ($1.1 billion), movies and sports ($771 million), video games ($766 million), and gifts ($164 million), engaging in some 280 independent purchase transactions annually. Children thirteen to nineteen account for even greater yearly expenditures: $30.5 billion of their own money.

But children's financial muscle does not end there. Researchers estimate that children directly influence more than $40 billion in adult purchases each year. A Nickelodeon/*USA Today*/Yankelovich Youth Monitor study found that children are extremely aware of brands and have considerable input into their parents' selections of apparel, cereal, snacks, cars, videocassette recorders, televisions, and personal computers. Many children are involved in actual household purchasing, especially food; in a recent Teenage Research study, half the teen girls surveyed reported shopping for groceries at least once a week. Recognizing this indirect purchasing power that children have, a growing number of marketers are approaching the youths directly. The National Dairy Board, for example, now airs milk commercials with youth appeal, and Procter & Gamble has developed a Crest for Kids toothpaste.

How did children acquire such buying clout? Researchers point to several factors. As the number of working couples and single-parent households increased, many parents shifted certain household responsibilities onto children's shoulders. Thrust into adult roles, children have ended up with more influence over the family's purchases, and they also tend to spend increased amounts of money themselves. In addition, many older, professional couples have fewer children. These parents can afford to lavish more on their children, including extra spending money for such items as Fisher-Price Toys' $225 children's camcorder and the My First Sony line of electronics gear for children. The bandwagon effect is yet another factor: when one marketer begins to focus on children, competitors follow suit, encouraging even more children's purchases. McDonald's Corp., for example, has aimed advertisements for its hamburgers, meal kits, and parties at children for years; now Hardee's Food Systems, Inc. and Wendy's International Inc. are doing the same.

Astute marketers realize that children actually represent three markets: current consumers, influential consumers, and future buyers. Because children are steadily developing brand awareness and product preferences that someday will translate into purchasing decisions, even companies not selling youth products per se are beginning to pay attention to children. Marketers are overcoming their traditional reluctance to sell directly to children, realizing that, out there somewhere, tomorrow's big-ticket customer is playing video games today. ❑

SOURCES: "Children Come of Age as Consumers," *Marketing News*, Dec. 4, 1987, p. 6; Kim Foltz, "Kids as Consumers: Teaching Our Children Well," *Adweek*, Nov. 30, 1987, p. 40; Ellen Graham, "Children's Hour," *The Wall Street Journal*, Jan. 19, 1988, p. 1; James U. McNeal, *Children as Consumers* (Lexington, Mass.: Lexington Books, 1987); Noreen O'Leary, "Study Portrays Children as Complex, Savvy Media Mavens," *Adweek*, Nov. 30, 1987, p. 42.

EXERCISES

Understanding

b ______ 1. The topic of this selection is **(8b)**
a. marketing products.
b. children's spending patterns.
c. doing surveys of children.
d. the bandwagon effect.

c ______ 2. Which is the main idea of this selection? **(8d)**
a. Children have more to say about family purchase decisions than ever before.
b. Children are important members of the society.
c. Children have a good deal of power as buyers and consumers.
d. Marketers are overcoming lack of interest in selling to children.

a

______ 3. Which is the main point of the fourth paragraph? **(8c)**

a. Children from four to nineteen have lots of money to spend.

b. Thirty million U.S. kids under twelve years old spend over four billion dollars each year.

c. Children engage in about three hundred independent purchase transactions annually.

d. Marketers are paying more and more attention to children's spending habits.

4. On the blank lines, write in your own words the key idea of each sentence. **(8a)**

a. "Researchers estimate that children directly influence more than $40 billion in adult purchases each year."

Children influence what adults buy.

b. "As the number of working couples and single-parent households increased, many parents shifted certain household responsibilities onto children's shoulders."

Children have more responsibilities than before.

c. "Because children are steadily developing brand awareness and product preferences that some day will translate into purchasing decisions, even companies not selling youth products per se are beginning to pay attention to children."

Companies are paying attention to children.

d ______ 5. It is a fact that as a group, children spend most on **(9a)**
a. video games.
b. toys and games.
c. movies and sports.
d. snacks.

6. Write *F* after each statement that is a fact and *O* after each statement that is an opinion. **(10)**

O ______ a. Children are a marketer's dream.

F ______ b. Children between thirteen and nineteen spend over $30 billion of their own money.

F ______ c. Proctor and Gamble has developed a Crest for Kids toothpaste.

F ______ d. Children have major input into parents' selection of several products.

F ______ e. Wendy's International is aiming advertising at children.

Interpreting

d ______ 1. From the statement "They have billions of dollars in discretionary income — and spend most of it," we may infer that **(11)**
a. children have no sense of value regarding money.
b. children should not be given so much money by their parents.
c. children misuse the financial power placed in their hands.
d. children do not save much of their own money.

b ______ 2. About their buying behaviors, we may infer that children are **(11)**
a. not influenced much by advertising.
b. very much influenced by their friends.
c. not influenced by milk commercials with youth appeal.
d. careful about spending on fast foods such as hamburgers.

b 3. As families continue to shrink in size and as more and more parents work, we may safely infer that children will have **(11)**
   a. less influence on family purchase decisions.
   b. more influence on family purchase decisions.
   c. less time to make purchases.
   d. help in making decisions from day care givers other than parents.

c 4. We may infer that marketers believe children who develop "brand awareness" when they are young will **(11)**
   a. reject those brands when they become adults.
   b. purchase video games for their children.
   c. remain loyal to those brands into adulthood.
   d. spend their money wisely and thoughtfully as adults.

5. Put a checkmark next to any general statement that you believe you can safely infer from the selection.

√ a. Some adults value their children's suggestions in making decisions.

√ b. Patterns established when we are children influence our behaviors as adults.

____ c. Children's independence should be encouraged but controlled.

√ d. Children are a very strong force in the U.S. economy.

____ e. Adults are models for children in many areas of life.

Vocabulary

On the blank lines, write your own definition for each word in italics. Whenever possible, use word-part clues from the phrase in which the word appears. **(1c, 1d)** Do not use a dictionary.

1. "One recent study *estimates* that . . ." (paragraph 1)

   guesses based on other information

2. "Children thirteen to nineteen account for even greater yearly *expenditures*: $30.5 billion of their own money."

   spending

3. "Researchers estimate that children directly *influence* more than $40 billion in adult purchases each year."

   affect

4. "Children . . . have considerable *input* into their parents' selections."

   influence; suggestions

5. "Half the teen girls *surveyed* reported shopping for groceries."

   questioned

6. "The National Dairy Board, for example, now *airs* milk commercials with youth appeal."

   broadcasts on television and/or radio

7. "How did children *acquire* such buying clout?"

   get

8. "These parents can afford to *lavish* more on their children, including extra spending money."

   spend generously

9. "The *bandwagon effect* is yet another factor; when one marketer begins to focus on children, competitors follow suit, encouraging even more children's purchases."

   follow-the-leader pattern

10. "Marketers are overcoming their traditional *reluctance* to sell directly to children."

   unwillingness; lack of enthusiasm

WRITING PRACTICE

1. Write a paragraph to summarize this selection. **(12c)**
2. Do you think that children should be given money by parents and relatives and should have the right to spend it freely? Write a paragraph to explain and support your opinion.

6

Young Divers of the Philippines

Howard Hall

In many parts of the world, dangerous work starts at a young age. This selection from a magazine describes what the writer saw when he went on a Philippine fishing boat called the Don Antonio. *He was trying to find out whether the fishermen were ruining the coral reefs. What he found was something far sadder. As you read this selection, try to find out what the writer felt about what he saw.*

Getting Started

1. The kind of fishing described in this selection is not a sport but a business. Think about everything that you know about fishing as a business and draw a word map. Use a separate sheet of paper. **(5b)**
2. The kind of fishing described in this selection uses diving and nets. Make a list describing the different fishing methods that you can think of that use nets and divers. Use a separate sheet of paper. **(5a)**

Word Highlights

Muro Ami a kind of large fishing net, shaped like a bag, eighty feet deep and a half a mile across
scare lines a rope with flags, used to scare the fish into the net
silhouette outline shape
regulator breathing device used by divers

At a depth of 80 feet, I position myself at the corner of the bag net where it is tied to the side panel. Once the fish have been driven in, the net must be pulled up very quickly before the catch turns and rushes out through the scare lines. But first the side panels must be untied and the net untangled from the coral. Soon I see an entire circle of scare lines and the silhouettes of hundreds of swimmers above. There is little evidence of reef destruction. In fact, the swimmers are careful not to strike the coral more than necessary.

I watch a tiny boy start his descent. Slowly, producing maximum glide with each stroke, he reaches the bottom in 40 seconds. He pulls himself across the coral to the side panel of the net which is tied to the bag net with two heavy ropes. I can see his goggles are partially filled with water but this does not bother him nor do the heavy rocks that pass so close to his head.

He grabs one of the ropes and pulls but it fails to come free. If he fails, the fish will swim free, so bracing himself on the rope he pulls with greater effort. The rope is free. He then pulls himself along the bottom to the second rope and repeats the process.

I find myself holding my own breath in empathy for this young man. To dive free and then work so hard at a depth of 80 feet is an absolutely astonishing feat. Yet before he surfaces, a dozen more divers begin their descent. On reaching the bottom, they form a line in front of the bag net and begin lifting it off the coral while others pull from above. As the net lifts, the divers swim beneath, freeing the mesh from the reef. When the last snare is freed, most of the divers head for the surface. But some are too far under the net to make an immediate escape. Suddenly I am convinced that some are about to die.

Then one of the boys pushes himself off the bottom and into the folds of the net. The net wraps around him like a spider's web. He pulls at the nylon mesh in what seems like a desperate effort to tear a hole with his bare hands. I swim towards him. Perhaps I can put my regulator in his mouth and force air into his lungs. But at 80 feet a free diver's lungs are entirely collapsed by the water pressure and inhaling is extremely difficult.

Swimming closer, I see the purpose of his efforts. He actually unties a knot in the net and pulls himself through it and swims for the surface followed by four other divers who have been patiently waiting.

All the divers are soon on the surface and the net containing nearly the entire fish population of the reef below is loaded into the skiffs. Back aboard the *Don Antonio,* the fishermen load the contents into metal tubs, each of which holds about 100 lbs of fish. The drive, in fact, yields 40 full tubs, each containing an amazing variety of reef fish. Nothing is wasted. The Muro Ami fishermen keep everything from baby sharks to the smallest butterfly fish. The fish are later sorted by species and sizes; the most valuable are stored on ice, the rest dried in the sun. Occasionally, a young boy grabs a writhing fish from the living mass and eats it alive.

As I wander to the bridge, I can't stop wondering how many times these divers can repeat such difficult and dangerous dives before a knot fails to come untied, a rock hits someone on the head, someone fails to free himself from the net, or a shark mistakes a beating pair of legs for a tasty morsel.

I ask about shark attacks and the boys say they happen but not often. They say needle fish are just as dangerous, as they can spear swimmers when frightened. When I ask if there is a doctor on board or if injured divers are taken to Manila for medical care, they look at me in amazement. One boy shrugs and says, "No, we don't have a doctor and we don't go to Manila. We just die."

Inside the wheel house, I place my camera bag on the chart table and begin searching for fresh film. I notice a radio message on one of the charts. Each day the 15 Muro Ami boats which work the South China Sea call in to report their positions. At the bottom is the notation: "*Lolita 1:* Returning to station to drop off body for burial."

I ask the captain what happened. He shrugs, squints into the afternoon sun, and says simply, "A boy drowned." ❑

EXERCISES

Understanding

1. Write the main idea of the selection in your own words. **(8d)**

   Boat owners take unfair advantage of the divers.

a
______ 2. The net must be pulled up quickly because **(9a)**
a. the fish might turn and escape through the scare lines.
b. the scare lines might frighten the fish.
c. the needle fish might eat the net.
d. the divers might drown.

b
______ 3. Each drive nets about how many reef fish? **(9a)**
a. too many to count
b. about 4,000 pounds
c. about 100 pounds
d. 15 Muro Ami

b
______ 4. At the ocean bottom, when the net lifts up the divers are supposed to **(9a)**
a. dive free and work hard with the bag net.
b. swim under the net to free it from the reef.
c. prepare for the possibility of death.
d. wait for the dozens of divers still descending.

d
______ 5. How are details ordered in this selection? **(9b)**
a. by time order
b. by space order
c. by order of importance
d. by all of the above

Interpreting

1. Write *F* before each event that actually happens in the story and *O* before each event that is only someone's opinion about what might happen. **(10)**

F ______ a. Needle fish spear swimmers.

F ______ b. A boy gets caught in a net.

O ______ c. Boys under the net drown.

O ______ d. A boy needs medical attention.

F ______ e. A boy on another boat drowns.

F ______ f. A boy eats a live fish.

O g. A knot fails to untie.

O h. A shark attacks the divers.

F i. A rope at first fails to come free.

O j. A rock hits a boy on the head.

O k. The writer shares his regulator with a boy.

a 2. Which inference *cannot* be properly made from the details in the selection? **(11)**
a. The boys are given meals while they work.
b. The boys are not given good equipment.
c. The boys are used to danger.
d. The boy caught in the net has been caught before.

c 3. While underwater, the boys **(11)**
a. use regulators to breathe.
b. have special air lines.
c. hold their breaths.
d. use air stored in their face masks.

d 4. *Lolita 1* is the name of **(11)**
a. the fishing company.
b. the captain.
c. a coast guard boat.
d. a fishing boat like the *Don Antonio.*

b 5. The boy who drowned **(11)**
a. was treated worse than the boys on the *Don Antonio.*
b. was just like the boys on the *Don Antonio.*
c. made the captain of the *Don Antonio* very sad.
d. would not have drowned if a doctor was on board the ship.

c 6. We can infer that the owners of the fishing boat **(11)**
a. do not know how dangerous the boys' work is.
b. are very worried about the boys' welfare.
c. do not care much what happens to the boys.
d. are not responsible for what happens to the boys.

d
_____ 7. We also can infer that the boys **(11)**
   a. expect to be treated better by the owners.
   b. are careless about damaging the reef.
   c. do not work hard because they are angry at the way the owners treat them.
   d. do not expect anybody to be concerned about them.

a
_____ 8. Based on this story, we can infer that in the near future **(11)**
   a. nothing much will change on these boats.
   b. Muro Ami fishing will be outlawed.
   c. the boys will receive better equipment and medical attention.
   d. the owners and captains will be sent to jail.

Vocabulary

Use a word from the following list to fill in each blank in the numbered sentences. **(1c)**

descent	desperate
maximum	writhing
empathy	morsel

1. I could not feel **empathy** with the captain's hard attitude.

2. The fish began **writhing** to try to escape from the shark's jaws.

3. The diver's **descent** took him down into an underwater cave.

4. The butterfly fish would make a tender **morsel** on some table.

5. The ship was filled with the **maximum** load it could handle.

6. The boy was **desperate** to earn enough money to support his family.

WRITING PRACTICE

1. Imagine that you are one of the divers described in this selection. Write a few paragraphs describing what you do, why you do it, and how you feel about it.
2. How do you feel about the activities described in this selection? Write a paragraph describing what aspects of the situation are unfair, who is at fault, and what should be done to improve the situation.

7

Helping Children When a Loved One Dies

Harriet Sarnoff Schiff

How do we help a child who is mourning — feeling sorrow and sadness because of — the loss of a parent? The author of a book called Living Through Mourning *has some ideas. Do you think that her recommendations would help a child whose mother or father has died?*

Getting Started

Do freewriting on the topic of this selection, *the death of a loved one.* **(5d)** Write for at least five minutes, including everything that comes to mind about the topic. Do not stop writing at all until time is up. Use separate sheets of paper.

When you finish, read your freewriting to other people in the class. If your teacher suggests, exchange papers or hand them in.

Word Highlights

platitudes unoriginal, overused remarks or comments
altered changed
impact effect
demise death
abandoned left alone
endured withstood; stood up under
cliché unoriginal, overused remark; platitude
surviving left alive
muster gather up
immersed deep within
bewilderment confusion
condolences words of sympathy to people who have suffered a loss
cope deal with; overcome
void emptiness

Perhaps one of the most difficult tasks any youngster can undergo is that of trying to make some sense out of the death of a parent. So many questions go unexplained. So many feelings are ignored. Frequently children are merely offered platitudes when they deserve the same respect for their pain as any adult deserves and expects.

Without question the child whose parent dies will be altered for all time. That does not mean the child must become an inadequate adult or a nonachieving youngster. Nevertheless, the child's life will always be colored by the death.

One man whose mother died of a heart ailment when he was in his early teens describes the impact of a parent's early demise.

"No matter how I tried to understand and work things through I always came down to the bottom line that she could have lived had she chosen to. The doctors talked with me, my Dad talked with me and it made no real difference. I felt abandoned. Mothers are not supposed to leave their children by up and dying on them! Especially when those kids still play Little League ball and go to Cub Scout meetings where everyone else's mother sits and watches!

"Sometimes I hate her for dying and other times I understand she didn't choose to die. But the bottom line is she died when I still needed a mother."

He was so hurt by this, he said, before he would agree to marry his wife he insisted she have a complete physical examination to make certain his children would never have to face the pain and aloneness he endured.

Ironically, although his experience was painful, he apparently received more help from other adults than most young people get. At least he was in a situation where attempts to answer his questions were made. That is not the general rule.

In most homes when a parent dies virtually no attention is given to the children. Instead they walk around looking for someone with whom to speak. If they are talked to at all, they generally hear clichés or, worse, statements that are simply untrue. "Mommy is away for a while." "Mommy is in the hospital now." In fact, with the best of intentions Mommy is placed anywhere but where she really is and that is dead.

With all the love and care in the world the surviving parent generally simply cannot muster the energy to speak to the children. Instead, immersed in his own pain and bewilderment, he allows them and their needs to be ignored. What most children express when they reach adulthood is that they really lost both parents during that time.

Frequently, these children must deal with a parent who is simply too tired or too uninterested to become involved in their schooling. No one asks whether homework is being done. Unless such youngsters have great inner strength or some friend of the family to whom they can turn, they are like kegs of dynamite waiting for the match. They, too, often turn to negative aspects of their personalities in a bid for attention. Sadly, only then does their parent see or hear them.

Here are some areas in which to act when a child is hurting.

- Call the school the day before your child plans to return and ask the teacher or homeroom counselor to meet the returning student outside the classroom and offer private condolences. Then, if the youngster is willing, the teacher might ask if he would agree to having his classmates offer a moment of silence in memory of the dead person. If this is done in younger grades make certain the time is limited to a few moments as children who feel tension may begin to giggle out of nervousness. Further, the teacher may ask one of the class leaders to help the returning student catch up on his work. This contact with the "popular" student may help the youngster reintegrate with his fellow students more quickly.
- There are support groups for young people whose parents have died. If children are willing to attend it may help immensely to have an arena in which to discuss the problems they are trying to cope with and cope with alone.
- Hire a high school student to come in after school and do homework with your child. If you cannot offer your companionship, try to find someone to help fill the void.
- Force yourself to spend a set amount of time really listening even if that time period is only half an hour after school or before bedtime. You brought these children into the world and you have a responsibility to them.

A woman once asked how she could explain the death of his father to her child when she did not understand it herself. Her therapist gave her a simple rule of thumb: "Don't reply. Hug. When you're ready the replies will come." ❑

EXERCISES

Understanding

c 1. Which statement best tells the main idea of the selection? **(8d)**
a. A child who loses a loved one suffers forever.
b. Death is a terrible reality.
c. Even though death hurts a child terribly, those who love him or her can help soothe some of the pain.
d. There's very little anyone can do to help a child who experiences the death of a loved one.

a 2. What is the main idea of paragraph 1? **(8c)**
a. To make sense of a parent's death, children deserve respect for their pain.
b. Children are offered platitudes when a parent dies.
c. We should ignore children's feelings when death takes one of the child's parents.
d. Adults deserve respect for their pain when a husband or wife dies.

a 3. According to the selection, **(9a)**
a. most relatives find it hard to talk with the child.
b. most relatives find it easy to talk with the child.
c. teachers usually call the child to arrange a discussion.
d. the child can find some comfort in the Cub Scouts and Little League.

d 4. A man whose mother died when he was in his early teens tells the author all these things except which one? **(9a)**
a. He felt abandoned.
b. He felt his mother had died when he still needed her.
c. He felt she could have lived if she had really wanted to.
d. He felt that his father could have made a difference if the two of them had talked about the mother's death.

c 5. When a child's loved one dies, the author believes that we should **(9a)**
a. offer clichés.
b. provide platitudes.
c. answer questions about death honestly.

d. offer soothing statements that are untrue, such as "Mommy is away for a while," because children cannot understand death.

b ______ 6. According to the selection, sometimes a surviving parent cannot talk to a mourning child because the parent **(9a)**
a. has to make funeral arrangements.
b. is immersed in his or her own pain and confusion.
c. has other children to worry about.
d. wants the child to do well in school.

b ______ 7. According to the author, it is a good idea to call the school before the mourning child returns for all the following reasons except which one? **(9a)**
a. A popular student can be asked to help the child catch up.
b. The principal must note the death on all the child's personal records at school.
c. If the child agrees, classmates might offer a moment of silence in memory of the dead person.
d. The teacher or school counselor can offer words of sorrow privately to the child.

c ______ 8. A child who giggles during a moment of silence is probably **(9a)**
a. a troublemaker.
b. not very thoughtful.
c. tense and nervous.
d. not a good friend of the mourning child.

d ______ 9. About a support group, which according to the author is true? **(9a)**
a. Children must be required to attend for their own good.
b. Only those children who need financial support should attend.
c. Only those children who have friends who lost a parent should attend.
d. Only those children who are willing to go should attend.

a ______ 10. According to the selection, to help fill the void after the death of a child's parent we should **(9a)**

a. arrange for someone to come into the house and help the child with homework.
b. have a maid.
c. help the child find a job to take his or her mind off the suffering.
d. take the child out of school for a couple of weeks until the child feels better.

Interpreting

c 1. Which of the following can we infer that the author believes true in most cases after the demise of a child's parent? **(11)**
a. The surviving parent showers the child with love and attention.
b. Adults answer questions carefully and thoughtfully.
c. Attempts to answer the child's questions are not often made.
d. Adults stop loving a mourning child.

b 2. We may infer that for mourning children, statements such as "Mommy is away for a while," and "Mommy is in the hospital now" are **(11)**
a. necessary.
b. lies.
c. stupid.
d. nasty.

d 3. From the statement "What most children express . . . is that they really lost both parents during that time," we may infer that **(11)**
a. often the second parent dies soon after the first.
b. children feel so angry at the surviving parent that they secretly wish the parent would go away.
c. children do not really wish to talk with anyone about the death of a parent.
d. to a mourning child, silence and lack of communication from a surviving parent are like death.

4. Put a checkmark next to each inference you can safely make from this selection. **(11)**

√ a. Schools can play a useful role in helping a child deal with the death of a parent.

______ b. Adults who themselves are mourning should not be expected to help a mourning child.

______ c. Coping with death is easier for teenagers than for younger children.

√ ______ d. Children may feel anger and hate toward parents who die.

a ______ 5. What can you infer from the advice "Don't reply. Hug. When you're ready the replies will come"? **(11)**
 a. that love is more important than words
 b. that silence is always golden
 c. that children should be seen but not heard
 d. that a stitch in time saves nine

Vocabulary

1. *Word part clues.* The first word in italics in each set of words below comes from the selection. All of them contain word part clues such as prefixes and suffixes. **(1d)** Try to figure out the meaning of each word *without* using a dictionary. Write each definition on the blanks provided. Also, try to figure out the meaning of the new word given. When you finish, check your answers in a dictionary.

 a. ". . . any *youngster* . . ." **Student responses will vary.**

 ____

 ____

 What do you think *oldster* means? __________

 ____

 ____

 b. ". . . difficult tasks any youngster can *undergo* . . ."

 ____

 ____

What do you think *underwent* means? ______________

____

____

____

c. ". . . questions go *unexplained*." ______________

____

____

What do you think *explainable* means? ______________

____

____

d. ". . . *inadequate* adult . . ." ______________

____

____

What do you think *adequately* means? ______________

____

____

e. ". . . *nonachieving* youngster . . ." ______________

____

____

What do you think *overachiever* means? ______________

____

____

f. ". . . died of a heart *ailment* . . ." ______________________

____

____

What do you think *ailing* means? ______________________

____

____

g. ". . . *aloneness* he endured." ______________________

____

____

What do you think *lonely* means? ______________________

____

____

h. ". . . children who feel *tension* . . ." ______________________

____

____

What do you think *tensely* means? ______________________

____

____

i. ". . . *reintegrate* with his fellow students . . ." ____________

____

____

What do you think *nonintegration* means? ____________

____

____

j. "*. . . companionship . . .*" ____________

____

____

What do you think *companionable* means? ____________

____

____

2. *Word highlights in your sentences.* Look at the list of word highlights on page 352. Select any five words and write an original sentence for each that shows you understand what the word means.

   Student responses will vary.

   ____

   ____

   ____

   ____

   ____

WRITING PRACTICE

1. Write a summary of the actions that Harriet Sarnoff Schiff believes an adult should take when a child loses a parent. **(12c)**

2. Imagine that a close friend or a relative has just lost a husband or a wife. The person has a ten-year-old child. The friend asks you for advice on how to help the child deal with the death of the parent. Write a letter to the surviving parent. Share your thoughts on how to help the mourning child deal with the death of the parent.

8

Please Straighten Out My Life

Stephanie Winston

Has life ever seemed so confusing that you didn't know what to do or where to begin? Stephanie Winston is an expert in helping getting people organized. Here she gives a few basic rules for starting to put your life in order. As you read, think about whether her ideas will help you.

Getting Started

Do SQ3R as you read this selection. (7) Write your questions here.

Student responses will vary.

Word Highlights

clients customers for a service
principles rules
staples basic supplies that you always need
isolate separate out
inventory supply
fundamental basic
significant important
adjacent next to
articulating identifying
impetus push, force, energy
temperament personality, feelings

It is not uncommon for clients to approach me with the cry, "Please straighten out my life." Their daily life seems overwhelming, and organizing it seems hopeless. Such people cannot see that specific, smaller difficulties must be resolved before the whole becomes manageable. Some clients, on the other hand, feel confronted by so many tiny problems that they are defeated by their very quantity.

The first step toward taking things in hand is to define just what a "problem" is. Never yet, in my experience, has a situation been so complex that it couldn't be unraveled.

To begin, provide yourself with a notebook — either loose-leaf or spiral-bound — small enough to carry around with you. This notebook will become your "master list" — a single continuous list that replaces all the small slips of paper you're probably used to. Use the notebook to keep track of all errands, things to do or buy, and general notes to yourself about anything that will require action. This basic organizing technique is the first in a series of principles that will appear throughout the book highlighting the prime rules of organization.

Principle #1 Use a Single Notebook for Notes to Yourself

Choose a time with no distractions and sit down with your notebook and pencil. List six elements in your life that need to be put in order. Forget about straightening out your life as a whole. Instead, focus on things like these:

I spend so much time looking for kitchen utensils that cooking a meal takes hours. How can I make my kitchen "work" properly?
I want to start woodworking again, but my books and tools are all over the house. What do I do to get them together?
The living room is always a mess because I don't know what to do with all those magazines and newspapers I haven't read.
I'm always running out of soap, toilet paper, and other household staples. How can I plan more effectively?
It takes me forever to get ready in the morning and I'm always late for work. How can I streamline the "up and out" process?
How can I plan enough time for special projects that I like to work on and still leave a comfortable margin for household, family, and other activities?

Substitute your own examples for mine, and you've completed the first step. If your mind tends to blur when you try to isolate problems, the "movie" technique may help. Take a deep breath and relax. Then close your eyes and mentally run through a typical day, letting it unroll like a movie. "I get up, brush my teeth . . ." and so on. When you come to a scene or situation that creates a problem, write it down. While you are screening your day's movie, remember that you may not be consciously aware of some problems but your mind and body are. If your stomach lurches or your muscles tighten or your head aches when you come to a particular scene, then you can be sure you have locked onto a problem.

If, for example, a twinge of tension occurs at the idea of brushing your teeth, perhaps you're always running out of toothpaste — a problem in maintaining an inventory control system for household supplies. Or, the toothpaste might be there, but the medicine chest is so jammed that a dozen other things fall into the sink every time you reach into the cabinet.

Write down each problem as you come to it, then shut your eyes again, relax, and continue. List no more than six problems, otherwise the list itself may overwhelm you!

This procedure of problem definition illustrates a fundamental rule of organizing — every life situation, no matter what it may be, can be divided into its significant parts. Stated as a principle:

Principle #2 Divide Up a Complex Problem into Manageable Segments

Some of the problems on your list will be fairly straightforward. A messy clothes closet, for example, is a small area with one function, and organizing it is a fairly simple procedure. But changing your morning ritual so that you're on time for work is a considerably more complex matter. It may involve changing your habits, revising your time schedule, reorganizing your bathroom or laundry system — or all of these things. Keeping Principle #2 in mind, the next step is to divide the *complex* problems on your list into more manageable units. These more complex situations usually fall into one of two categories:

1. *Physical areas: Rooms.* If an entire room needs reorganizing, you must first isolate its various problem areas. Stand in the doorway of the room and, choosing any corner at random, mentally block out an area about five feet square. Cast a sharp eye over every inch of that area to inspect it for "knots." In the living room, a knot might be a sloppy desk and work area, a disorganized wall unit with books piled in disarray, or an inconvenient and unappealing furniture arrangement. Whatever jars your nerves or sensibilities is a fit subject for reworking. List these specific "knot" areas on your master problem list under the general problem of which they are a part. Block out another five foot square area immediately adjacent to the first and repeat the process. Follow this procedure until you have checked the entire room and have a complete list of individual elements to work on.
2. *Processes or systems.* To break down a process or a system into its manageable parts, use the same movie technique, mentally running through the particular process that's giving you trouble. Each time you feel tension about an action or function, write it down. For instance, the stumbling blocks in the "up-and-out-in-the-morning" process might include some of the following: alarm clock rings too softly; cannot move quickly in the morning; don't have time to decide what clothes or accessories to wear; kitchen always messy so cooking breakfast is a chore.

There is one more very significant step that provides the bridge between defining the problem and finding the solution. On a scale of one to ten, rank each of the six major items on your list according to how much it irritates you. Stated as a principle:

> *Principle #3 After Articulating a Small Group of Projects, Rank Them by Number According to How* Aggravating *They Are*

A problem that creates serious tension is a #1; one that could wait until next year is #10. Write the number next to each item on your list. This is a very important impetus to action. You may end up with two problems which are #1, two #2, one #5 and one #7. Do *not* try to arrange the problems 1, 2, 3, 4, 5, 6 in numerical order of importance. People tend to get so involved in figuring out which problem is fifth and which is sixth or whatever, that they lose sight of what they're trying to accomplish. If any of your six major problems can be subdivided . . . , rank those subdivisions in the same way. . . .

With this step of ranking, the process of establishing order is well and truly begun. The issues have been outlined, priorities have been set, and a foundation for action has been laid. All that remains before actually tackling the problems is to set a specific and regular time for organizing work. If you can't choose a good time, play a little game with yourself. Imagine that for the next several weeks you have a fixed appointment with yourself that you note in your appointment calendar as if it were a regular medical or dental appointment. Your "appointments" could be every day for an hour, or every day for fifteen minutes, or twice a week for two hours each, or an hour a week; whatever is practical in terms of other responsibilities and your own temperament. If you know you'll start getting jittery after half an hour, don't set a two-hour appointment because it will be "good for you" or you "ought" to. Instead, be kind to yourself and give yourself appointments that you know you can keep and handle.

But remember, these are firm appointments and must be kept, except in case of emergency. Making this commitment to yourself will be one of the smartest things you ever did.

Problem-Solving Checklist

Before you begin, review this checklist which summarizes your first steps.

1. Select and list in your notebook no more than six problems at one time.

2. Break the complex problems on the list into manageable units.
3. Rank the problems and their units according to aggravation level.
4. Turn to the appropriate section or sections of this book and solve the first #1 problem on the list; do not omit any units.
5. Go to the next #1 item, then the #2's, and so on until all the problems have been solved.
6. Choose another set of problems and follow the same steps. ❑

EXERCISES

Understanding

d ____ 1. The main idea of this selection is that **(8d)**
   a. the author knows how to straighten out her clients' lives.
   b. you should rank your problems.
   c. complex problems are more difficult to solve than simple ones.
   d. to begin to organize your life, define and rank specific problems.

b ____ 2. To define your problems, you should write down **(9a)**
   a. all your problems on slips of paper.
   b. six problem areas in a single notebook.
   c. your biggest problem on a large sign.
   d. all your problems in a single notebook.

b ____ 3. The "movie technique" is to **(9a)**
   a. go to the movies to forget your problems.
   b. relax and mentally go over your activities, as though they were part of a movie.
   c. take a movie of your activities so that you can watch yourself.
   d. watch a movie on problem solving.

d ____ 4. A complex problem should be **(9a)**
   a. put aside as too hard to handle.
   b. attacked directly as a single unit.
   c. put off for a few days while you think about it.
   d. broken down into smaller parts that you can handle.

c 5. You should rank your problems according to **(9a)**
   a. the order in which you thought of them.
   b. how important they are.
   c. how upsetting they are.
   d. how hard they are to solve.

a 6. Principles 1, 2, and 3 are arranged according to **(9b)**
   a. time order.
   b. space order.
   c. order of importance.
   d. order of difficulty.

7. Write *major* after each important detail and *minor* after each less important detail. **(9c)**
   a. You should keep short appointments with yourself.

      minor

      Making appointments with yourself can help you plan your time. major

   b. Complex situations usually involve either physical areas or processes. major

      You may have problems deciding what to wear.

      minor

   c. Feeling tense about a situation is a sign of a problem area. major

      Feeling tense about brushing your teeth may be a sign that your medicine cabinet is a mess. minor

Interpreting

c 1. It is a fact that **(10)**
   a. complex problems can always be broken down to simple ones.
   b. ranking problems by how much they upset you is better than putting them in numerical order by importance.

c. rooms sometimes have disorganized areas.
d. problems should be written down in a single notebook.

a ______ 2. This selection is mostly based on **(10)**
a. the opinion of someone with a lot of experience.
b. the opinion of someone with no experience.
c. fact.
d. scientific theories.

c ______ 3. We may infer from this selection that **(11)**
a. people need to solve all their problems to feel more organized.
b. you should have no problem remembering your problems.
c. solving just a few problems will give people some sense of relief and control.
d. getting out of the house in the morning is easier than straightening out a messy closet.

4. Put a checkmark next to each statement that is a correct inference you can draw from the selection. **(11)**

√ ______ a. After following the three principles here, a disorganized person will not feel hopeless about getting organized.

______ b. Rules help solve all life's problems.

√ ______ c. Not knowing what to do in complex situations makes people feel overwhelmed.

√ ______ d. Becoming organized requires planning and clear thinking.

______ e. Being organized or disorganized is just a state of mind.

√ ______ f. It is possible to straighten out your life, no matter what the mess.

√ ______ g. If you work on a few clearly defined problems, you will probably have more success than if you work on many problems all at once.

______ h. Your closet will never get organized.

Vocabulary

This selection includes several positive words related to being organized and several negative words related to being disorganized. These positive and negative words are mixed together in list *A*. On the first blank after each word, write the number of the correct definition from list *B*. On the second blank, write *P* if the word is positive or *N* if the word is negative. **(1c, 1d)**

List A		
overwhelming	6	N
manageable	3	P
technique	7	P
tension	4	N
twinge	8	N
disarray	1	N
inconvenient	9	N
unappealing	10	N
appointment	5	P
commitment	2	P

List B

1. confusion
2. promise to do something
3. possible to be controlled
4. state of feeling nervous
5. agreement to do something at a certain time and place
6. too much to handle
7. a method of doing something
8. a small nervous feeling
9. not very easily done
10. not attractive

WRITING PRACTICE

1. Go back to the SQ3R exercise at the beginning of this selection and write the answers to your questions. **(7)**
2. Following the techniques described in this selection, write down six problems that bother you. Then break down the more complex problems into smaller parts. Rank the problems and their parts according to how much they irritate you.
3. Write a paragraph discussing whether you are an organized person or a disorganized one and why you think so.

9

A Close Look at Viruses

Time

Did you ever have mumps or the flu? Those diseases and many others, such as the deadly polio and AIDS, are caused by viruses. This selection from a popular weekly news magazine uses words and illustrations to explain how viruses work.

Getting Started

1. Before you read, think of everything you know about viruses. Warm up by freewriting **(5d)** on the topic *viruses*. Use a separate sheet of paper.
2. Now do SQ3R as you read the selection. **(7)** Use a separate sheet of paper. **Student responses will vary.**

Word Highlights

respiratory related to body organs needed for breathing, such as the lungs, the nose, and the throat
encased enclosed
protective keeping harm or danger away
enveloped surrounded
structure shape; form
site place where something occurs
gene material in cells that is responsible for traits that we are born with
facet flat surface
activated put into action or movement

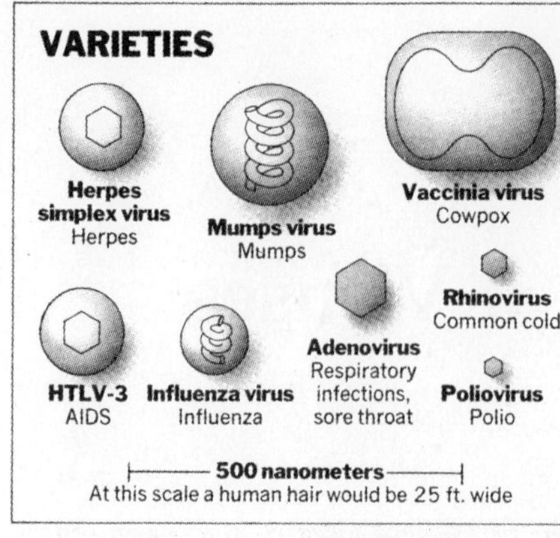

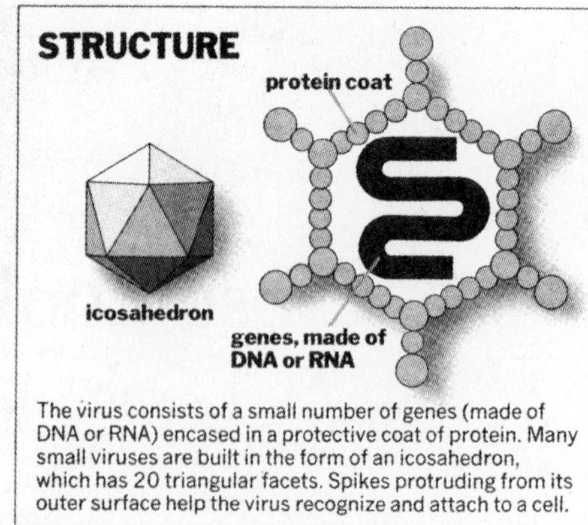

The virus consists of a small number of genes (made of DNA or RNA) encased in a protective coat of protein. Many small viruses are built in the form of an icosahedron, which has 20 triangular facets. Spikes protruding from its outer surface help the virus recognize and attach to a cell.

LIFE CYCLE

attachment

CELL

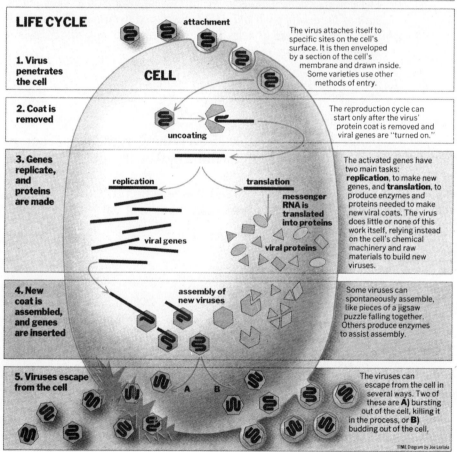

1. Virus penetrates the cell

The virus attaches itself to specific sites on the cell's surface. It is then enveloped by a section of the cell's membrane and drawn inside. Some varieties use other methods of entry.

2. Coat is removed

uncoating

The reproduction cycle can start only after the virus' protein coat is removed and viral genes are "turned on."

3. Genes replicate, and proteins are made

replication

translation

messenger RNA is translated into proteins

viral genes

viral proteins

The activated genes have two main tasks: **replication**, to make new genes, and **translation**, to produce enzymes and proteins needed to make new viral coats. The virus does little or none of this work itself, relying instead on the cell's chemical machinery and raw materials to build new viruses.

4. New coat is assembled, and genes are inserted

assembly of new viruses

Some viruses can spontaneously assemble, like pieces of a jigsaw puzzle falling together. Others produce enzymes to assist assembly.

5. Viruses escape from the cell

A

B

The viruses can escape from the cell in several ways. Two of these are **A)** bursting out of the cell, killing it in the process, or **B)** budding out of the cell.

TIME Diagram by Joe Lertola

EXERCISES

Understanding

d 1. The main idea of this selection is to **(8)**
   a. show how scientists make viruses.
   b. explain how viruses escape from different kinds of cells.
   c. demonstrate how diseases spread in human beings.
   d. illustrate the types of viruses, their makeup, and the way they develop.

2. According to the selection, viruses cause which of the following diseases? Put a checkmark next to each correct answer. **(9a)**

____ a. heart attacks
√ b. AIDS
____ c. hiccoughs
√ d. sore throats
√ e. influenza
____ f. dandruff
√ g. colds
____ h. diabetes
√ i. polio
√ j. herpes
____ k. athlete's foot

c 3. A virus attaches itself to a cell by means of its **(9a)**
   a. genes.
   b. twenty triangular facets.

c. protruding spikes.
d. RNA.

a
4. Of the viruses named below, the smallest is **(6, 9a)**
a. adenovirus.
b. vaccinia virus (cowpox).
c. influenza virus.
d. herpes virus.

a
5. Viruses may break out of a cell by **(6, 9a)**
a. bursting or budding.
b. assembling or translating.
c. replicating or translating.
d. inserting and making protein.

d
6. In order for a virus to reproduce, it must **(9a)**
a. find a neighboring virus of the opposite sex.
b. locate its DNA or RNA.
c. expand to five hundred nanometers.
d. remove its protein coat.

b
7. To make new genes and to produce enzymes and proteins, the virus **(9a)**
a. needs another protein coat.
b. depends on the cell that the virus breaks into.
c. must escape from a cell.
d. must destroy its icosahedral shape.

b
8. Some new viruses can assemble without any outside aid, but others require **(9a)**
a. RNA.
b. enzymes.
c. bursting.
d. icosahedrons.

b
9. In items 1 and 3 of the illustration "Life Cycle," both the bar-shaped and S-shaped objects are showing **(6)**
a. mumps proteins.
b. viral genes.
c. uncoating.
d. viral proteins.

10. Number in correct order the steps in the life cycle of the virus. Use 1 for the first step, 2 for the second step, and so on. **(9b)**

4 a. Viruses assemble new coats.

2 b. Viruses remove coats.

3 c. Genes are made.

5 d. Viruses burst or bud out of the cell.

1 e. Viruses attach themselves to the cells and enter.

Interpreting

a 1. We may infer from this passage that the cell membrane is the **(11)**
   a. outer surface of a cell.
   b. inner coat.
   c. DNA and RNA.
   d. main part of the virus.

c 2. We may infer that a virus unable to carry out replication or translation probably **(11)**
   a. is a rhinovirus (common cold).
   b. will burst out of the cell.
   c. could not remove its coat.
   d. assembled spontaneously.

b 3. We may infer that a nanometer is a **(11)**
   a. viral disease.
   b. unit that is used to measure very small objects.
   c. unit that is used to measure very large objects.
   d. unit that is used to measure only a human hair.

a 4. We may safely infer from the selection that, in general, **(11)**
   a. viruses can take over a cell and make it serve the viruses' own purpose.
   b. all viruses are deadly.
   c. to fight viruses we need to support more serious research in science.
   d. a cure for AIDS will be very hard to find.

Vocabulary

1. *Context clues.* The selection provides context clues (with both words and pictures) for each word below. Go back to figure out the meaning of each word. Do not use a dictionary. Write your definitions on the blanks.

   a. penetrates **breaks or enters into**

   b. icosahedron **shape with twenty facets**

   c. protruding **sticking out**

   d. relying **depending on**

   e. uncoating **removing outer layer**

   f. replication **making new just like the old**

   g. translation **producing substances to make a new viral coat**

   h. assist **help**

   i. bursting **breaking out**

   j. budding **forming an extension**

2. *Sentences for new words.* Look at the *Word Highlights* on page 375. Select any five words and write an original sentence for each. Each sentence should show your understanding of what the word means.

   Student responses will vary.

WRITING PRACTICE

1. Go back to the "Getting Started" activity. Look at your freewriting. Write a brief paragraph about what you didn't know about viruses before you read and what you now know. **(5d)**
2. Go back to the questions you wrote on page 373 for SQ3R at the beginning of this selection. Write the answers to your questions. Use a separate sheet of paper. **(7)**
3. Pretend that you are one of the disease-causing viruses shown in the illustration under "Varieties." Write a paragraph in which you tell other people in the class about your life cycle. In other words, explain all the steps that you take to get into a cell and out again. You might start in this way: "I am a virus, and I break into cells by first . . ."

10

Taking Risks

Lawrence Kutner

How do children react to risk? Dr. Lawrence Kutner, who writes a column called "Parent and Child" for the New York Times, *draws some worrisome conclusions about how young children and teenagers view danger.*

Getting Started

Make a list of ideas and issues that come to your mind when you think of the word *risk.* **(5a)** Include at least three risks that you remember taking when you were a young child or teenager.

Word Highlights

lull soothe; cause to rest
perception insight; knowledge; intuition
incantations ritual reciting of a magic spell
abracadabra word thought to possess magical powers
distorted twisted out of shape
consequences results; outcomes
appraisal an expert evaluation

A few weeks ago 3-year-old Marissa Arnold climbed out of the pool in Minneapolis where her father and two older brothers were playing, took the inflatable floats off her arms, walked over to the ladder and jumped back in the water. When her father, Josh, turned around several seconds later, he saw his daughter completely submerged, holding her breath, and oblivious to the danger that surrounded her.

"That freaked me out," said Mr. Arnold, an investment counselor and a former lifeguard, who immediately pulled his daughter from the water. "Most kids, when they get their head under water for the first time, come up crying and scared. Marissa had this big smile on her face. She wanted to do it again. I thought, what if I hadn't been there?"

Children perceive risks differently than adults. Yet their words and promises can lull parents into believing that their children recognize and avoid danger when in fact they do not. Understanding those different perceptions of risk, and the factors that appear to influence them, can help parents decide at what ages and under what circumstances their children are able to protect themselves from harm.

Preschoolers live in a world filled with magic. Fairy tales, with their stories of mystical spells and incantations, are no less credible to 4-year-olds than the stories their parents tell of their own childhoods. This belief in magical powers strongly influences how children of this age perceive risks.

Automobiles are the largest single cause of children's deaths, the National Center for Health Statistics reports. To help prevent their being hit by a car while crossing the street, most kindergartners and first graders are taught a jingle or poem urging them to look left, then right, then left again before crossing.

When asked, most children this age will dutifully and accurately repeat the instructions for safely crossing a street, thereby reassuring their parents or teachers that they will be safe. There is evidence, however, that such memorized instructions are sometimes of little value to preschoolers because of their belief in magic.

"Some young children will go up to the corner, recite the jingle, move their head back and forth and then walk in front of an oncoming car," said Preston Howard, a former traffic safety researcher at Florida State University who currently works for the Florida Department of Education.

"They use the jingle as if it were a magical incantation that protects them," Mr. Howard continued. "These children also put a lot of faith in crosswalks, but to them it's an abracadabra-type thing. Some children think that the crosswalk magically protects them."

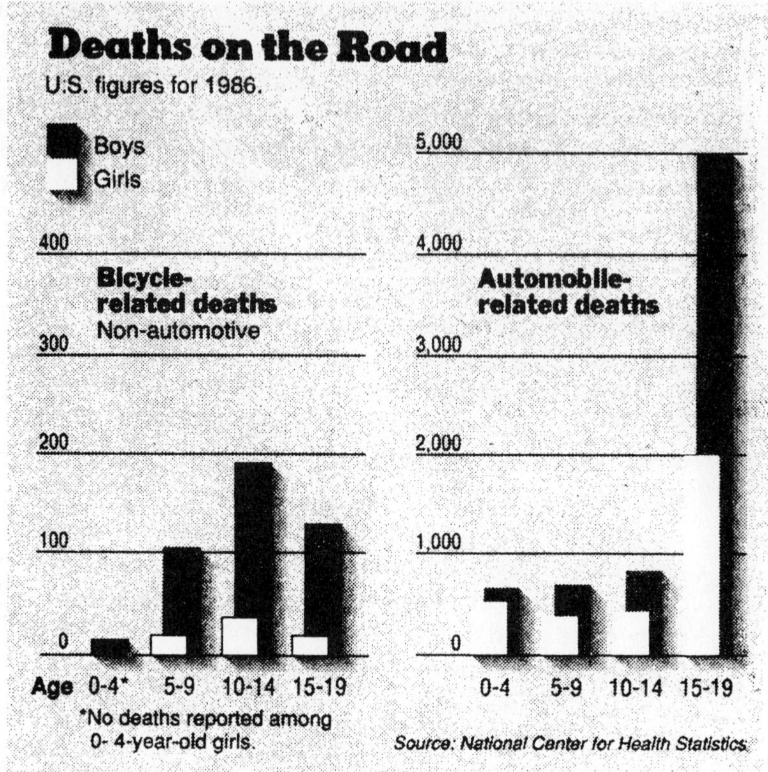

Mr. Howard cited other studies done for the Federal Highway Administration in which young children who were waiting at a stoplight were asked by researchers to say when it was safe to cross the street. Thirty-one percent of the children were wrong — a strikingly high proportion since each had a 50-50 chance of being right simply by guessing.

Not all children who are the same age have an equal chance of being injured or killed in an accident. One of the best predictors of injury is a child's sex. In 1986, nearly four times as many boys as girls between the ages of 5 and 14 were killed in bicycle accidents that did not involve automobiles, the National Center for Health Statistics reported.

Approximately twice as many boys as girls in the same age group were killed in automobile-related incidents, including collisions of cars and bicycles.

Teen-agers' distorted appraisals of risks can be seen in their ratings of the hazards of driving.

"If they're speeding in a car, they're not thinking of the

consequences of an accident," said Andrew Halper, the associate director of youth health promotion at the University of Minnesota School of Public Health. He is directing the Massachusetts Saving Lives Program, which is trying to curtail drunken driving among high-school students.

"Instead, they're more concerned about getting a ticket or getting home too late," Mr. Halper said. "These are different concerns than adults have."

The recent findings about how teen-agers perceive risks are challenging the previous educational approach taken by high-school drunken-driving prevention programs, which emphasized the dangers of accidents. Instead, they are focusing on issues that already worry teen-agers, like losing their license, while all their friends are still allowed to drive. ❑

EXERCISES

Understanding

d ____ 1. The topic of this selection is **(8b)**
   a. drowning deaths among young children.
   b. taking risks.
   c. bicycle- and automobile-related deaths among young people.
   d. dangerous behavior in children.

b ____ 2. Which sentence from the selection best states the main idea? **(8d)**
   a. "Preschoolers live in a world filled with magic."
   b. "Children perceive risks differently than adults."
   c. "Automobiles are the largest single cause of children's death. . . . "
   d. "Not all children who are the same age have an equal chance of being injured or killed in an accident."

3. Write the main point of the first paragraph in your own words. **(8c)**

   A three-year-old girl jumped into a pool without being aware of the danger.

a
_____ 4. Which statement is true regarding magical powers? **(9a)**
  a. Preschoolers believe in them.
  b. Most children do not believe in them.
  c. Parents try to help their children avoid such powers.
  d. They help children crossing the street.

b
_____ 5. When they cross the street, most kindergartners **(9a)**
  a. know how to cross safely.
  b. say a little jingle about how to cross but ignore danger anyhow.
  c. wait for the light to change to green.
  d. go into an intersection as quickly as they can with their eyes closed.

6. Write *major* after each major detail from the selection and *minor* after each minor detail. **(9c)**

  a. Marissa Arnold lives in Minneapolis. minor

  b. Preschoolers believe that magic will protect them. major

  c. Children do not see dangers in the same way adults see dangers. major

  d. Preston Howard used to be a traffic safety worker at Florida State University. minor

  e. Andrew Halper is an associate youth director. minor

a
_____ 7. In 1986, approximately sixty bicycle deaths were reported for girls between five and fourteen. How many boys could you estimate were killed? **(9a)**
  a. 240
  b. 1,240
  c. thirty
  d. no deaths reported

b
_____ 8. The graphs on page 382 try to show **(6, 8)**
  a. road deaths for all U.S. citizens since 1986.

b. 1986 road deaths for U.S. boys and girls up to nineteen years of age.
c. bicycle-related deaths for young children and teenagers.
d. that boys and girls can avoid accidents if they try.

9. Use the graphs to answer each question. **(6)**
   a. Where does the information in the graphs come from?

   National Center for Health Statistics

   b. What does "bicycle-related deaths non-automotive" mean? **deaths from accidents involving bicycles but not cars**

   c. In bicycle-related accidents, which sex and age group had the highest death rate? **boys aged ten to fourteen**

   d. In automobile-related deaths, which sex and age group had the highest rate? **boys aged fifteen to nineteen**

   e. When you look at rates for both bicycle-related deaths and automobile-related deaths, which group by age and sex has the greatest chance of getting killed? **boys aged fifteen to nineteen**

Interpreting

a 1. We may infer that Marissa Arnold **(11)**
   a. cannot swim.
   b. swims very well for her age.
   c. can swim only in a pool.
   d. is being taught to swim by her brothers.

d
_____ 2. Marissa had a smile on her face probably because **(11)**
   a. her father accidentally tickled her as he pulled her from the water.
   b. she was embarrassed.
   c. her brothers were telling jokes.
   d. she enjoyed being submerged under the water even though it was very dangerous.

b
_____ 3. We may infer that for street safety, a jingle such as "Cross at the green, not in between" is **(11)**
   a. a very good way of teaching children about traffic safety.
   b. not always a good way of teaching children about traffic safety.
   c. hard for most children to memorize and, therefore, not too effective.
   d. would have more meaning if the magic word *abracadabra* were added to the jingle.

d
_____ 4. About a young child's crossing the street at a stoplight, in general, a parent should **(11)**
   a. trust his or her child to cross safely alone.
   b. call the Federal Highway Administration for the latest children's safe-crossing data.
   c. trust his or her child to cross safely only if the child is a girl.
   d. not trust his or her child to cross safely.

b
_____ 5. You may infer from the selection that an effective educational approach to teenage drunk driving would **(11)**
   a. stress adult concerns.
   b. not stress adult concerns.
   c. stress driver education programs.
   d. involve police and teachers working together.

c
_____ 6. You may safely infer that to help a teenager cut down on his speeding in a car, the teenager should think about **(11)**
   a. the danger of possible accidents.
   b. how his parents would feel if he were arrested.
   c. losing his license and not being able to drive.
   d. cutting down on excess drinking.

Vocabulary

1. Several words in the selection are either compound words or words that contain prefixes, suffixes, or roots that you can recognize. Ten such words appear in the list below. Using the clues provided, write each word in the crossword puzzle.

credible	oncoming
crosswalk	preschoolers
dutifully	reassuring
inflatable	stoplight
lifeguard	submerged

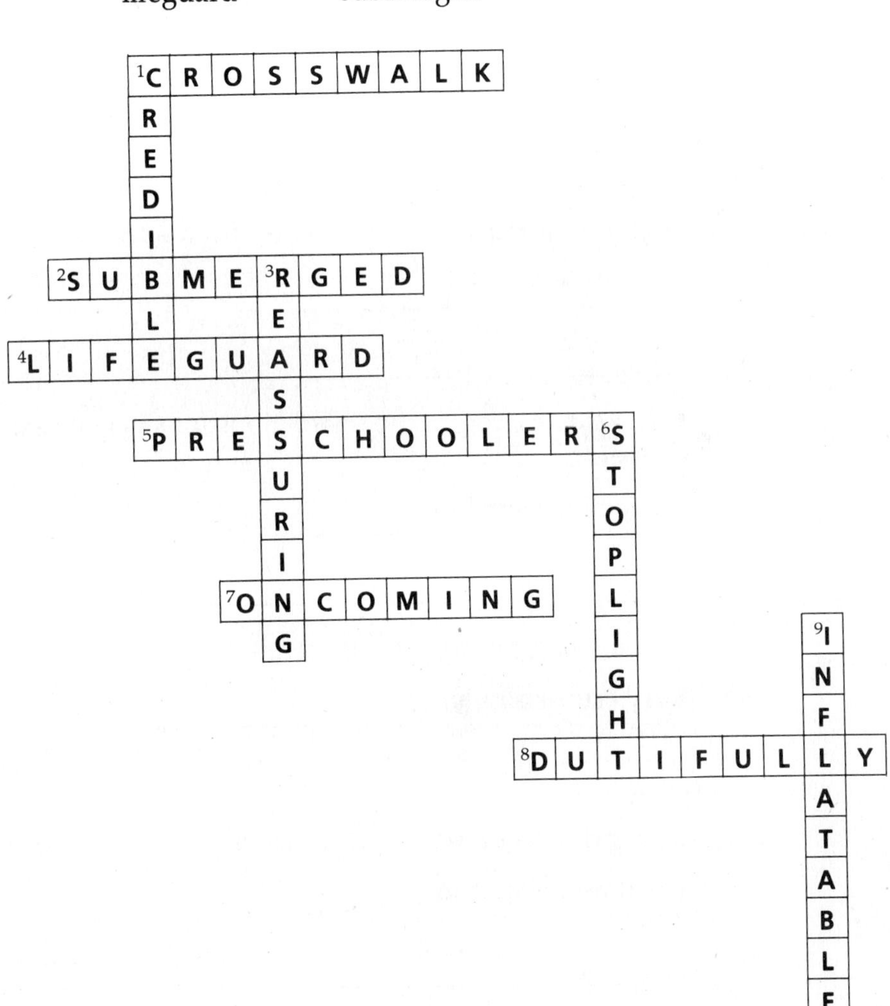

Across

1. area to cross street more safely
2. kept under, as in water
4. person who oversees safety at water area
5. group not yet ready for classroom instruction
7. heading directly toward
8. in an obeying manner

Down

1. believable
3. making to feel confident again
6. device for signaling traffic to halt
9. what can be expanded by the introduction of air

2. From context clues in the selection, write in your own words the definition for each word in italics. **(1c)**

   a. ". . . *oblivious* to the danger surrounding her."

   not paying attention

   b. "Children *perceive* risks differently from adults."

   see; think about

   c. ". . . *accurately* repeat the instructions for safely crossing a street."

   correctly; exactly

   d. ". . . a *strikingly* high proportion."

   very; surprisingly

   e. ". . . trying to *curtail* drunken driving."

   cut down on; stop

WRITING PRACTICE

1. Why do young children not avoid danger? Write your response in a paragraph. Include specific details drawn from the selection.
2. Explain how you would teach a young child to cross a street safely.

11

Toughlove

Dann Denny

What should parents do when their teenage children get out of control? Should they be understanding and forgiving? Or should they be strict and demanding? This article from a Bloomington, Indiana, newspaper describes some parents' solution to problem teenagers. This group of parents follows the philosophy of Toughlove. As you read this selection, think about what Toughlove means and how well the Toughlove method might work with people you know.

Getting Started

Freewrite on the subject of problem teenagers and their parents. **(5d)** Use a separate sheet of paper.

Word Highlights

adolescent teenager
licensed officially approved
therapist a person who helps with social and psychological problems
propagating making known, spreading
modify change
tenets strong beliefs
ostracized shut out of a group, shunned
misconceptions wrong ideas
invariably always

■ John, a 14-year-old boy, is a gifted artist. But he also has a violent temper, having kicked a hole through his bedroom wall, physically assailed his parents and threatened his school teacher with bodily harm. His No. 1 goal? To get expelled from school.

"He's on a course toward self-destruction," says his mother, kneading her brow with the tips of her fingers. "And he doesn't seem to care."

- Angie, a 15-year-old girl, has been expelled from a private school for lying and truancy. Her mother, a single parent, is desperately searching for a school that will take her.

John and Angie are just two of the many adolescents who have caused their parents enough grief to drive them to Bloomington's Parents in Crisis, one of the more than 800 support groups across the United States and Canada patterned after the Toughlove philosophy of David and Phyllis York. The Yorks (each a licensed family therapist) founded Toughlove in Doylestown, Pa., in 1978, formulating their principles while dealing with their own wayward daughter.

"Toughlove is a loving solution for families that are being torn apart by unacceptable adolescent behavior," writes York in the *Toughlove* manual. "It's the same kind of loving approach we used when our little children had to take their medicine. We knew they did not like it but we insisted on their taking it anyway."

York feels many of today's parents have been duped by books, movies and magazines propagating the notion that understanding, active listening and tender loving care will invariably produce well-behaved children.

"With some children these approaches seem to work," admits York. "Toughlove is for those many parents whose teenagers will not accept tender loving care — not from their parents, teachers, guidance counselors or other concerned adults."

"Some of these kids are as big and as strong as their parents," says Dick Sanders, whose wife (Carole) co-founded Parents in Crisis in 1982. "They can be abusive, both physically and verbally. And with many of them, no amount of persuasion will get them to change their behavior."

The Yorks say what these out-of-control kids need is Toughlove — a firm-but-loving attempt to modify the behavior of an insubordinate child. Unfortunately, the word often conjures up a bushel of misconceptions.

"When some people think of Toughlove they think, 'Oh,

yah, those are the parents who throw their kids out of the house,'" says Carole. "That's not it at all. We love our kids enough to be tough on them rather than bail them out of jail or make excuses for their irresponsible behavior."

One of the Toughlove tenets is to "take a stand," or, as York puts it, "make real demands with real consequences." This often takes the form of a contract drawn up by parents (and signed by the adolescent) in which unacceptable behavior is clearly defined and its consequences outlined.

If the child violates one of the contract's stipulations, he may lose a privilege (such as talking to his friends on the telephone), or forfeit the use of something (such as his stereo or the family car).

"My husband recently cleaned everything out of my son's room," says one mother. "All that was left was his mattress. By improving his behavior, he can get his things back."

If an adolescent's contract violation involves vandalism, he may have to get a job and earn enough money to pay for the damage.

"We are trying to show them that they can do anything they want to, but that there are consequences for socially repulsive behavior," says Dick. "That's a fact of life. If an adult behaves irresponsibly, he may be ostracized, arrested or fired. Our ultimate goal is to help our children become responsible citizens."

"And we try to never surprise a kid with a consequence," says Carole. "By explaining ahead of time what the consequences will be, it's really up to the child whether he suffers them or not."

In every case, banishing one's child from the house is the last resort, done only after every other option has been exhausted.

"It's hard," admits Carole. "But sometimes when a child comes home he finds a note on the front door with a quarter and list of phone numbers of Toughlove parents he can call. Each of the parents has agreed to put him up for the night." ❑

EXERCISES

Understanding

c ______ 1. The main idea of this selection is that **(8d)**
a. John and Angie are out of control.

b. some parents are too soft with their children.
c. a group of parents is trying to help their problem teenagers through the Toughlove philosophy.
d. the Toughlove philosophy was developed by David and Phyllis York.

b ______ 2. How many parent-support groups based on the Toughlove philosophy are there? **(9a)**
a. six hundred
b. eight hundred
c. fifty
d. one hundred

d ______ 3. The Bloomington support group is called **(9a)**
a. Toughlove Parents.
b. Bloomington Parents' Support Group.
c. Toughlove.
d. Parents in Crisis.

c ______ 4. The Toughlove philosophy says that insubordinate children most need **(9a)**
a. tenderness and understanding.
b. rules and punishment.
c. firmness and love.
d. being thrown out of the house.

a ______ 5. Parents and adolescents following the Toughlove method **(9a)**
a. sign a contract.
b. talk over their disagreements.
c. forgive each other.
d. rely on outsiders to enforce discipline.

d ______ 6. According to Toughlove, children should be **(9a)**
a. surprised by the consequences of their actions.
b. punished whenever the parents decide.
c. always well behaved.
d. aware of the consequences of bad behavior ahead of time.

a ______ 7. Punishments mentioned in the article include all the following except **(9a)**
a. not allowing the child out of the house.

b. taking away the child's belongings.
c. making the child pay for damages.
d. throwing the child out of the house.

Interpreting

1. Write *F* if the statement is a fact or *O* if the statement is an opinion. **(10)**

F ______ a. Angie has been expelled from a private school.

F ______ b. Her mother is searching for a school.

O ______ c. Her mother is desperate.

F ______ d. John is fourteen years old and Angie is fifteen.

O ______ e. John is a gifted artist.

F ______ f. He kicked a hole through his bedroom wall.

O ______ g. His goal is to get expelled from school.

O ______ h. He is on a course toward self-destruction.

d ______ 2. "Tender loving care will invariably produce well-behaved children" is **(10)**
a. a fact.
b. the opinion of the Yorks.
c. the opinion of many parents.
d. the opinion that the Yorks believe that many parents hold.

c ______ 3. You can infer that John and Angie **(11)**
a. cannot be helped.
b. will be in trouble with the police.
c. may be helped by the Toughlove method.
d. will definitely become better behaved through Toughlove.

b ______ 4. You can infer that the parents described here **(11)**
a. are disgusted with their children.
b. are worried about their children.

c. enjoy punishing their children.
d. are mean and cruel.

d ______ 5. You can infer that the parents described here believe that **(11)**
a. you can force children to obey.
b. love will solve all problems.
c. teenagers will get into trouble no matter what you do.
d. teenagers sometimes behave better if they know the rules ahead of time.

c ______ 6. If a teenager damages school property, you can predict that a Toughlove parent will probably **(11)**
a. get angry with the teenager.
b. pay for the damage.
c. make the teenager pay for the damage.
d. banish the child from the house.

a ______ 7. You can infer that the Toughlove method **(11)**
a. has helped some families cope with problem children.
b. is the best method for dealing with problem children.
c. cannot work because the teenagers will become angrier.
d. is approved by all family therapists.

c ______ 8. From this article, you can infer that **(11)**
a. all children need strict rules.
b. parents should not try to understand and listen to their children.
c. parents should not be afraid to be strict with their children.
d. children should do what their parents tell them to do.

Vocabulary

1. The words in list *A* describe problems of teenagers mentioned in the article. On each blank, write the number of the correct definition from list *B*. **(1)**

List A

5 ______ a. truancy

7 ______ b. wayward

2 c. vandalism

6 d. abusive

4 e. repulsive

1 f. insubordinate

3 g. irresponsible

List B

1. not obeying parents or teachers
2. the willful destruction of property
3. not to be trusted
4. disgusting
5. skipping school
6. insulting
7. wanting one's own way

2. The words in list *A* have to do with agreements about rewards and punishments used to help change the teenagers' behavior. On each blank, write the number of the correct definition from list *B*. **(1)**

List A

3 a. consequences

2 b. stipulations

5 c. privilege

1 d. forfeit

6 e. contract

4 f. violation

List B

1. give up
2. specific terms of an agreement
3. results

4. the breaking of a rule
5. a special thing one is allowed to do
6. a legal agreement

WRITING PRACTICE

1. In a paragraph summarize the Toughlove philosophy and method. **(12c)**
2. Describe in a paragraph what your parents did when you misbehaved as a teenager and whether that method worked. Then in another paragraph discuss this question: When you are a parent of teenagers, will you treat them in the same way that your parents treated you?

12

How Do Computers Work?

Betty J. Brown
John E. Clow

It's hard to imagine a world without computers. Banks, supermarkets, colleges, and many other modern organizations would be lost without the speed and convenience of these efficient yet complicated machines. Did you ever wonder how the complex technology works? This selection from a business and economics textbook points out the basic features that underlie all computers.

Getting Started

Do SQ3R as you read this selection. **(7)** Write your questions on the blanks.

____

____

____

____

____

____

____

____

____

____

Word Highlights

data information
assembly line line of workers putting together a product one step at a time
capacity ability to hold or contain
graphics the making of drawings; visual representations
detector something that recognizes and registers a signal
wafer a small, thin, flat disk
miniaturization state of making something smaller
delicate very fine; easily broken
intricate complex
synthesis something formed by combining several elements; artificial

A computer is a machine that runs on electricity. It is also a machine that processes data faster than you can blink an eye. Another name for a computer is hardware. *Hardware* refers not only to the computer, but also to any equipment attached to the computer. Hardware includes equipment such as a printer or a display terminal.

You have probably also heard the term software. *Software* is the computer program, or set of instructions, that tells the computer what to do. There are two basic types of software: system software and application software. Some system software is stored permanently in the computer. Such software tells the computer what to do when you first turn it on. Other system software, such as a disk operating system (or DOS for short), may be stored on a diskette. A disk operating system tells the computer how to use the information that is entered into the computer.

System software tells the computer how to run. On the other hand, application software tells the computer how to do a certain job, or application. There are many different kinds of application software. Some of the more common applications are computer games, such as sports or adventure games. Other application software will allow you to write and edit papers or to set up and keep a budget. Businesses use many application programs. These include doing payrolls for their employees and operating robots on an assembly line.

The computer stores the information you give it in its memory.

The types of applications that can be done on a computer depend, in part, on how much memory a computer has. *Memory* is the computer's ability to store information in an electronic form. If you've ever looked at an ad for a computer in a magazine or newspaper, you may have noticed a description such as 256K. The term 256K refers to an amount of memory. The memory capacity of a computer is measured in bytes. A *byte* equals one character. A character can be a letter, a number, or a space. Although computer memory is measured in bytes, it is usually expressed in kilobytes. One kilobyte is equal to 1,024 bytes. Kilobyte is what the K stands for in 256K.

It sounds like 256 kilobytes is a lot of memory, but it is roughly equal to 128 double-spaced, typewritten pages. Many computers today have very large memories. They are measured in megabytes, which are millions of bytes!

Using a Computer

There are three basic steps in using a computer. These steps are input, processing, and output. Input is the data you put into the computer. It includes any instructions you give to the computer. One of the most common ways of data input is through a keyboard. But there are other ways to put data into the computer.

One input device you're familiar with if you've played computer games is the joystick. A *joystick* lets you move a picture, line, word, or cursor from one point to another on a display screen. Another input device is a mouse. A *mouse* is not a small, gray, furry creature, but a small box with one or more buttons. You use a mouse by moving it around to move the cursor to an item on the screen. When the cursor is at the item you want, you press a button on the mouse. The computer performs the action you have chosen.

With touch-sensitive keyboards and display screens, even your hands can be input devices. Other input devices are the graphics tablet and the light pen. A *graphics tablet* lets you use a pen or your finger to draw a design on a flat surface. This is much like the etching toys that you may have played with as a child. Your drawing appears on the computer screen as you complete it. A *light pen* has a light-sensitive detector in its tip. You can use the light pen to draw and write by touching the tip of the pen to the screen. The computer reads the light and makes your drawing on the screen.

Still another input device is the *optical character reader* (OCR). An OCR scans a typed or printed page. The OCR changes the characters into electronic signals. These signals can then be recorded on magnetic tape or on a disk that the computer can read.

One of the newest input methods is *voice recognition*. A voice-recognition device allows you to talk to a computer. It will follow your spoken instructions. Most voice devices recognize only a few words, but they are being improved all the time.

Processing

You've probably heard that the processor is the "brain" of the computer. The processor is the central processing unit, or CPU. The CPU uses instructions and data input to find an answer to do a specific activity. The CPU then sends the results of the activity to the user or to the computer's memory, or to both.

The CPU has two parts: an arithmetic/logic unit and a control unit. The arithmetic/logic unit does math calculations. It also makes decisions such as whether one number is greater than another. The control unit directs the work of the arithmetic/logic unit. For example, the control unit tells the arithmetic/logic unit whether to add, subtract, or compare the numbers it has been given.

In early computers, the CPU required a lot of space. The size of the CPU today varies with the size of the computer. In a microcomputer the CPU can be as small as a single silicon chip. A *silicon chip* is a thin wafer, about ¼-inch square, that plugs into a computer.

The CPU in a microcomputer is called a *microprocessor*. Microprocessors are really miniature computers. The process of miniaturization is a wonder of modern technology. The miniaturization process starts with the design of an integrated circuit. An integrated circuit is made up of thousands of tiny, connected electric circuits. An electric circuit is simply a path through which electricity flows. Once the integrated circuit is designed, it is printed in very large scale on a piece of paper. This paper print is then reduced photographically to the size of a silicon chip.

Imagine this miniature photo in its negative form. If you hold a negative up to light, you can see images through the light. Other parts of the negative are dark. Likewise, when you put the negative over a silicon chip and expose it to light, the light will go through the clear spots in the negative. No light goes through the dark spots. The parts of the chip exposed to the light (through the negative) become hard. The other parts (not exposed to the light) are scraped off. This process is called "etching the chip." The chip is etched to create a pattern for wiring the chip. Thousands of very fine metal wires fit on the chip to create an integrated circuit. Can you imagine how hard it is to place thousands of tiny wires on a surface smaller than the tip of your finger! Businesses use robots to do this very delicate work.

Output

Just as there are many ways to get data into a computer, so are there many ways to get data out of a computer. Such data is called *output* — the result of the computer's work. The most common output devices are the display screen and the printer.

A display screen is commonly called a CRT, or cathode ray tube. The CRT provides the same type of picture as a home television set. Indeed, many home computers use the TV as a display screen. Another type of display screen is called a moni-

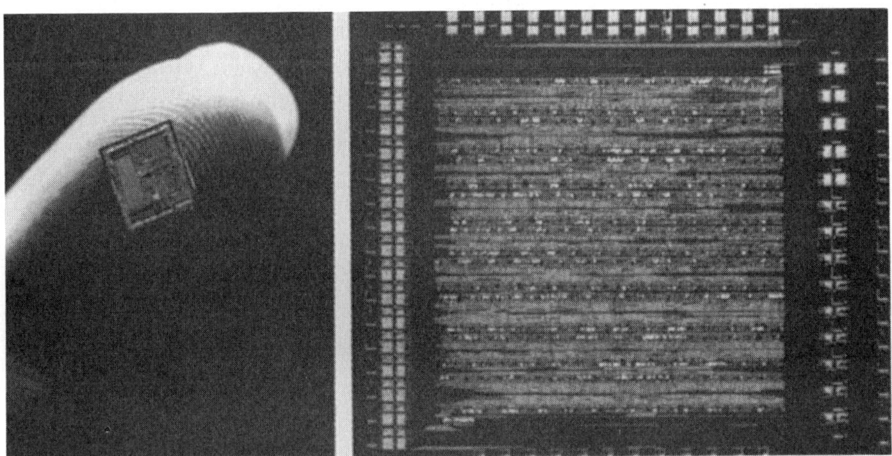

A silicon chip is smaller than your fingertip, but covered with thousands of electrical circuits (*right*).

tor. Monitors serve only as output devices for computers. Monitors come in one color, called monochrome, or in full color.

With special computer programs display screens can provide output for both text and graphics. Text output is made up of letters and/or numbers. Graphics output gives pictures or images like charts or the design for a new car. Many engineers and architects work at computers to make new designs or building plans.

A printer is another output device. A printer creates a copy of the data shown on the screen. Such copy is often called a *printout*. A special type of printer that creates a copy of graphic images is a plotter. A plotter controls the movement of a pen, or several pens, to make highly intricate drawings for engineers, architects, or doctors.

Voice synthesis is also another form of output. It is used in cars to remind drivers to fasten their seat belts. ❑

EXERCISES

Understanding

c___ 1. The main idea of this selection is to **(8d)**
   a. explain the difference between hardware and software.
   b. point out the uses of the computer.

c. explain how computers work.
d. define key terms, such as *microprocessor* and *output*.

b ______ 2. The main point of the second paragraph in the selection is to **(8c)**
a. explain what DOS is.
b. define *software* and give some examples of it.
c. show how to store system software on a diskette.
d. tell the computer how to use the information entered into the computer.

b ______ 3. Which three steps are basic in using a computer? **(9a)**
a. memory, bytes, and kilobytes
b. input, processing, and output
c. joystick, mouse, and graphics tablet
d. monochrome, printout, and plotter

c ______ 4. A joystick, mouse, and graphics tablet are all examples of **(9a)**
a. computer toys.
b. output devices.
c. input devices.
d. printout devices.

a ______ 5. The process of ''etching the chip'' **(9a)**
a. helps create CPUs in microcomputers.
b. is used to develop photograph negatives.
c. allows computers to avoid integrated circuits.
d. is a way of creating cathode ray tubes (CRT).

a ______ 6. Compared with a kilobyte, a byte is **(9a)**
a. smaller.
b. larger.
c. just about equal in size.
d. either larger or smaller depending on the computer.

7. Number in correct order from 1 to 5 the steps taken in etching a chip. **(9b)**

2 ______ a. The integrated circuit is printed in large scale.

1 ______ b. The integrated circuit is designed.

4 ____ c. The part of the chip exposed to the light becomes hard.

3 ____ d. The paper print is reduced photographically to the size of a silicon chip.

5 ____ e. Parts of the chip not exposed to the light are scraped off.

Interpreting

d ____ 1. We may infer that without a control unit in the CPU, the computer would **(11)**
   a. direct the work of the arithmetic/logic unit.
   b. draw on the power in its silicon chips.
   c. rely on its memory to carry out basic functions.
   d. be unable to make the arithmetic/logic unit work.

d ____ 2. We may infer from the cartoon that the child **(11)**
   a. does not know how to use a computer correctly.
   b. will speak to the computer.
   c. is very puzzled by what the computer is saying.
   d. has asked the computer a very simple question in arithmetic.

a ____ 3. You can infer from this selection that if a synthetic voice tells you to put on your seatbelt in your car, **(11)**
   a. it is a result of a computer's calculations.
   b. your automobile is relying on DOS software.
   c. your automobile is using a voice recognition device.
   d. you are in danger of an accident.

c ____ 4. You can infer from this selection that if a computer cannot add or subtract numbers, there may be something wrong with its **(11)**
   a. mouse.
   b. optical character reader.
   c. arithmetic/logic unit.
   d. integrated circuit design.

d ____ 5. You can infer that to store a manuscript of about 150 pages in a computer, you would need a computer with **(11)**
   a. memory measured in megabytes.
   b. at least one kilobyte of memory.

c. 256 kilobytes of memory.
d. more than 256 kilobytes of memory.

b 6. In general, which inference can we safely make from the selection? **(11)**
a. In today's society every child should become computer literate, and schools should teach children how to use computers early in their school careers.
b. Complex technology can be explained and understood by nonexperts.
c. Modern technology can accomplish whatever scientists set their minds to achieve.
d. More and more, computers will take over jobs in our society.

Vocabulary

Each word in italics is defined through context clues. Write a definition for each word in your own language. Do not use a dictionary. **(1c)**

1. "Software is the *computer program,* or set of instructions, that tells the computer what to do."

   Computer program means **a set of instructions that tells a computer what to do**.

2. "The types of applications that can be done on a computer depend, in part, on how much memory a computer has. *Memory* is the computer's ability to store information in an electronic form."

   Memory means **the computer's ability to store information electronically**.

3. "A *mouse* is not a small, gray, furry creature but a small box with one or more buttons."

   Mouse means **a small device used to put data into the computer**.

4. "The size of the CPU today varies with the size of the computer. In a *microcomputer* the CPU can be as small as a single silicon chip. A *silicon chip* is a thin wafer, about ¼-inch square, that plugs into a computer."

   Microcomputer means **a small-sized computer**
   ______.

   Silicon chip means **a small, thin wafer used in a computer**.

5. "Just as there are many ways to get data into a computer, so are there many ways to get data out of a computer. Such data is called *output* — the result of the computer's work."

   Output means **data taken out of a computer; the result of the computer's work**.

6. "Another type of display screen is called a *monitor*. Monitors are made to be used only as output devices for computers. Monitors come in one color, called *monochrome*, or in full color."

   Monitor means **a display screen**
   ______.

   Monochrome means **having only one color**
   ______.

7. "A printer creates a copy of the data shown on the screen. Such copy is often called a *printout*."

   Printout means **a printed copy of the data**
   ______.

WRITING PRACTICE

1. Write a summary of the section of the article "Using a Computer." **(12c)**
2. Write a paragraph in which you describe an experience, either good or bad, that you had with a computer.

13

Moon on a Silver Spoon

Eudora Welty

What is the role of reading in the life of a young child? Eudora Welty, one of America's best fiction writers, gives some fresh views on learning in this passage from her autobiography One Writer's Beginnings.

Getting Started

Do a word map **(5b)** or a list **(5a)** on the topic *childhood reading*. Let your map or list reflect your own memories of books from your childhood and the experience of reading or being read to. Use a separate sheet of paper.

Word Highlights

Dickens Charles Dickens (1812–70), famous English novelist who wrote *Great Expectations* and *Oliver Twist* among many other books
enchanted-looking magical in appearance
wizardry magic
acute serious
participation act of taking part in something
enlightenment state or quality of giving knowledge and understanding to
opulence grand wealth
radiance the giving off of light or heat
reposing living
insatiability not able to be satisfied
cadences flows of rhythm and movement

n a visit to my grandmother's in West Virginia, I stood inside the house where my mother had been born and where she grew up.

"Here's where I first began to read my Dickens," Mother said, pointing. "Under that very bed. Hiding my candle. To keep them from knowing I was up all night."

"But where did it all *come* from?" I asked her at last. "All that Dickens?"

"Why, Papa gave me that set of Dickens for agreeing to let them cut off my hair," she said. "In those days, they thought very long, thick hair like mine would sap a child's strength. I said *No!* I wanted my hair left the very way it was. They offered me gold earrings first. I said *No!* I'd rather keep my hair. Then Papa said, 'What about books? I'll have them send a whole set of Charles Dickens to you, right up the river from Baltimore, in a barrel.' I agreed."

My mother had brought that set of Dickens to our house in Jackson, Miss.; those books had been through fire and water before I was born, she told me, and there they were, lined up — as I later realized, waiting for *me*.

I learned from the age of two or three that any room in our house, at any time of day, was there to read in, or to be read to. My mother read to me. She'd read to me in the big bedroom in the mornings, when we were in her rocker together, which ticked in rhythm as we rocked, as though we had a cricket accompanying the story. She'd read to me in the dining room on winter afternoons in front of the coal fire, with our cuckoo clock ending the story with "Cuckoo," and at night when I'd get in my own bed. I must have given her no peace.

It had been startling and disappointing to me to find out that storybooks had been written by *people*, that books were not natural wonders, coming up of themselves like grass. Yet regardless of where they came from, I cannot remember a time when I was not in love with them — with the books themselves, cover and binding and the paper they were printed on, with their smell and their weight and with their possession in my arms, captured and carried off to myself.

Neither of my parents had come from homes that could afford to buy many books, but though it must have been something of a strain on his salary, my father was all the while carefully selecting and ordering away for what he and Mother thought we children should grow up with.

Besides the bookcase in the living room, which was always called the library, there were the encyclopedia tables and dictionary stand under windows in our dining room. There was a full set of Mark Twain and a short set of Ring Lardner in our bookcase, and those were the volumes that in time united us as parents and children.

I live in gratitude to my parents for initiating me — and as early as I begged for it, without keeping me waiting — into knowledge of the word, into reading and spelling, by way of the alphabet. They taught it to me at home in time for me to begin to read before starting school. I believe the alphabet is no longer considered an essential piece of equipment for traveling through life. In my day it was the keystone to knowledge. You learned the alphabet as you learned "Now I lay me" and the Lord's Prayer, and your father's and mother's name and address and telephone number, all in case you were lost.

My love for the alphabet, which endures, grew out of reciting it, but before that, out of seeing the letters on the page. In my own storybooks, before I could read them for myself, I fell in love with various winding, enchanted-looking initials at the heads of fairy tales. In "Once upon a time," an "O" had a rabbit running it as a treadmill, his feet upon flowers. When the day came, years later, for me to see the Book of Kells, Gospels from the ninth century, all the wizardry of letter, initial and word swept over me, a thousand times over, and the illumination, the gold, seemed a part of the word's beauty and holiness that had been there from the start.

In my sensory education I include my physical awareness of the word. Of a certain word, that is; the connection it has with what it stands for. Around age six, perhaps, I was standing by myself in our front yard waiting for supper, just at that hour in a late summer day when the sun is already below the horizon and the risen full moon in the visible sky stops being chalky and begins to take on light. There comes the moment, and I saw it then, when the moon goes from flat to round. For the first time it met my eyes as a globe. The word "moon" came into my mouth as though fed to me out of a silver spoon. Held in my mouth the moon became a word. It had the roundness of a Concord grape that Grandpa took off his vine and gave me to suck out of its skin and swallow whole, in Ohio.

Long before I wrote stories, I listened for stories. Listening *for* them is something more acute than listening *to* them. I suppose it's an early form of participation in what goes on.

Listening children know stories are *there*. When their elders sit and begin, children are just waiting and hoping for one to come out, like a mouse from its hole.

When I was six or seven, I was taken out of school and put to bed for several months for an ailment the doctor described as "fast-beating heart." I never dreamed I could learn away from the schoolroom, and that bits of enlightenment far-reaching in my life went on as ever in their own good time.

An opulence of storybooks covered my bed. As I read away, I was Rapunzel, or the Goose Girl, or the princess in one of the *Thousand and One Nights* who mounted the roof of her palace every night and of her own radiance faithfully lighted the whole city just by reposing there.

My mother was very sharing of this feeling of insatiability. Now, I think of her as reading so much of the time while doing something else. In my mind's eye *The Origin of Species* is lying on the shelf in the pantry under a light dusting of flour — my mother was a bread maker; she'd pick it up, sit by the kitchen window and find her place, with one eye on the oven.

I'm grateful, too, that from my mother's example, I found the base for worship — that I found a love of sitting and reading the Bible for myself and looking up things in it.

How many of us, the Southern writers-to-be of my generation, were blessed in one way or another, if not blessed alike, in not having gone deprived of the King James Version of the Bible. Its cadence entered into our ears and our memories for good. The evidence, or the ghost of it, lingers in all our books.

"In the beginning was the Word." ❑

EXERCISES

Understanding

b ______ 1. The main idea of this passage is that **(8d)**
   a. the writer is forever grateful to her parents for reading to her.
   b. letters, words, and books played a major part in the writer's childhood life.
   c. the writer never could understand why people paid so much attention to books when television and movies interested her so much more.

d. the writer liked to read the *Thousand and One Nights* when she was sick.

d ______ 2. The main point of paragraph 4 (beginning with "Why, Papa gave me that set of Dickens . . . ") is to show **(8c)**
   a. how silly little girls can be.
   b. the value of jewelry over books.
   c. how hard it was to ship books from one place to another.
   d. that the writer's mother liked books more than long hair or jewelry.

a ______ 3. The writer's mother read Dickens under the bed at night because **(9a)**
   a. she didn't want her parents to know that she was awake and reading late at night.
   b. it was the only comfortable place to read in their crowded house.
   c. Dickens was considered to be too grown up for a young child and she didn't want to get caught reading his books.
   d. she was looking for the mouse and the silver spoon.

c ______ 4. According to the selection, the writer's mother read to her every place except which one? **(9a)**
   a. the child's bedroom at night
   b. near the cuckoo clock
   c. the front yard
   d. on the rocking chair in the big bedroom

d ______ 5. A big disappointment for the writer was the time she **(9a)**
   a. received the set of Dickens.
   b. read the enchanted-looking initials from fairy tales.
   c. found that she had to listen for stories.
   d. learned that people wrote stories.

a ______ 6. Buying books was **(9a)**
   a. a strain on the writer's father's salary.
   b. impossible because of the poverty into which the writer was born.
   c. unnecessary because of the books shipped up from Baltimore.

d. something the writer learned to do after reading *The Origin of Species.*

b ______ 7. The writer learned to love the alphabet from **(9a)**
a. the alphabet song her grandmother always sang to her.
b. both seeing it and saying it.
c. *Sesame Street.*
d. the Book of Kells.

c ______ 8. Why does the writer tell us about the late summer day that she was watching the moon? **(9a)**
a. to explain how she first learned what a concord grape tastes like
b. to help us see how a young child can learn the alphabet from the great outdoors
c. to show us how she learned to connect a word with what it stands for
d. to paint a picture of how the moon goes from flat to round

a ______ 9. What do "listening children" wait for to have come out "like a mouse from its hole"? **(9a)**
a. stories
b. the alphabet
c. their elders
d. the moon

d ______ 10. The writer feels that the South's writers-to-be of her generation were blessed by **(9a)**
a. the warm, mild weather in their part of the country.
b. learning the alphabet together.
c. having Charles Dickens, Ring Lardner, and Mark Twain to read.
d. not having missed reading the King James Version of the Bible.

Interpreting

a ______ 1. From the statement "those books had been through fire and water before I was born," we may infer that the collection of Dickens **(11)**
a. had survived rough times.
b. had been blown up during the Civil War.

c. was flooded on the trip from Baltimore to Jackson, Mississippi.
d. had been set fire to but then saved by someone who poured water over the books.

b ______ 2. We may infer that in regard to finances, the writer's parents were **(11)**
a. quite wealthy.
b. middle class.
c. poor.
d. poor, rich, and then poor again.

d ______ 3. The book *The Origin of Species* was dusted with flour probably because the writer's mother **(11)**
a. was a poor housekeeper.
b. needed it as a cookbook for her bread recipes.
c. was hiding it from her husband.
d. would go from baking bread to reading, with flour on her hands.

b ______ 4. We may assume that, if the writer Eudora Welty wanted to read late at night, her parents would **(11)**
a. be very angry.
b. understand.
c. be very puzzled.
d. let her read only Dickens.

b ______ 5. In the writer's mother's childhood, people thought that a girl with short hair was **(11)**
a. weak.
b. strong.
c. pretty.
d. foolish.

6. Put *F* next to each statement that is a fact and *O* next to each statement that is an opinion. **(10)**

F ______ a. A set of Charles Dickens was sent in a barrel up the river from Baltimore.

O ______ b. It's disappointing to know that books are written and are not natural wonders, such as grass.

O ______ c. The alphabet is no longer considered an essential piece of equipment for traveling through life.

F ______ d. The writer's parents gave her the knowledge of words before she went to school.

O ______ e. Southern writers benefited from knowing the Bible.

7. Put a checkmark next to each statement that you think the writer should agree with. **(11)**

√ ______ a. Learning to read at home before going to school is something that a child can be grateful for.

______ b. Children should agree to cut their hair in exchange for a collection of Dickens.

√ ______ c. People today are wrong not to view the alphabet as an important part of life.

√ ______ d. Reading books is a great joy for a young child.

______ e. Parents should allow their children to read as late into the night as the children wish.

√ ______ f. Even without schooling, a child can learn as long as he or she has books.

Vocabulary

1. Each action word in list *A* appears in the selection, although sometimes in a different form. On each blank, write the number of the correct definition from list *B*. Each word in parentheses shows the form of the word as it is found in the selection. **(1d)**

List A

5 ______ a. sap

6 ______ b. startle (startling)

3 ______ c. endures

2 ______ d. initiate (initiating)

4 ______ e. unite (united)

1 ______ f. accompany (accompanying)

List B

1. come along
2. start; get something going
3. survives; lasts
4. join together as one
5. drain strength from
6. surprise

2. Look at list *A*. It contains words taken from the passage. Use context clues to figure out each word's meaning. **(1c)** Then fill in the numbered blanks in the puzzle with the words from list *A* that best fit the definitions given in list *B*.

   When you finish, the letters in the boxes will form two words that are very important in the story "Moon on a Silver Spoon."

List A

binding	keystone	sensory
captured	reciting	ailment
gratitude	treadmill	deprived
essential	holiness	lingers

List B

1. thanks
2. illness
3. took control of
4. taken away from
5. machine used by walking on the moving steps of a wheel or an endless sloping belt
6. saying aloud
7. remains as though not wanting to leave
8. the fastening and cover of a book
9. relating to sight, sound, smell, taste, and touch
10. quality of religion and divine power
11. a central piece that locks all the other pieces together
12. of the greatest importance

1. G [R] A T I T U D E
2. A I L M [E] N T
3. C [A] P T U R E D
4. [D] E P R I V E D
5. T R E A D M [I] L L
6. R E C I T I [N] G
7. L I N [G] E R S
8. [B] I N D I N G
9. S E N S [O] R Y
10. H [O] L I N E S S
11. [K] E Y S T O N E
12. E [S] S E N T I A L

WRITING PRACTICE

1. Write a short paragraph that explains how you know that Eudora Welty loved books as a child.
2. Write a brief paragraph that explains how you felt about books when you were a child.

14

The Invention of Writing and the First Schools

John P. McKay
Bennett D. Hill
John Buckler

How did writing begin? What were the first schools for teaching it like? This selection from a college history textbook traces the early development of one of humanity's basic skills.

Getting Started

1. Before you read, brainstorm on the following idea: *the beginnings of written language.* **(5c)**
2. As you read, use underlining to mark what you think is most important in the selection. **(12a)**

Word Highlights

Mesopotamian related to the ancient land and people between the Tigris and Euphrates rivers
evolution gradual process of change
Sumerians people of the ancient land of Sumer in south Mesopotamia
millennium a thousand years
abstract opposite of concrete; not easily understood; theoretical
conventionalized agreed on by the same group
symbolized stood for; represented
lore collected facts, knowledge, or beliefs on a particular subject
scribe public clerk or secretary; a copier of manuscripts
caned beaten with a stick or cane

Mesopotamian culture spread quickly, largely because of the invention and evolution of writing. Until recently, scholars thought that the Sumerians invented writing. Sumerian writing was called *cuneiform.* This word comes from the Latin term for "wedge-shaped." Using a stylus (a pointed writing tool), writers made wedge-shaped strokes.

Recent work, however, suggests that *cuneiform* may have come in a late stage in the growth of writing. The origins of writing probably go back thousands of years earlier than people thought. In about the ninth millennium B.C., Near Eastern peoples used clay tokens to keep their records. By the fourth millennium B.C., people had learned that drawing pictures of the tokens on clay was simpler than making the tokens. This breakthrough in turn suggested that adding pictures of still other objects could give even more information. The result was a complex system of *pictographs.* In pictographs, each sign pictured an object. Pictographs were the forerunners of cuneiform writing.

How did pictographs work? How did they lead to cuneiform writing? At first, if a scribe wanted to show a star, he simply drew a picture of it on a wet clay tablet. (See line A of Figure 1.1.) The tablet became rock-hard when baked. Anyone

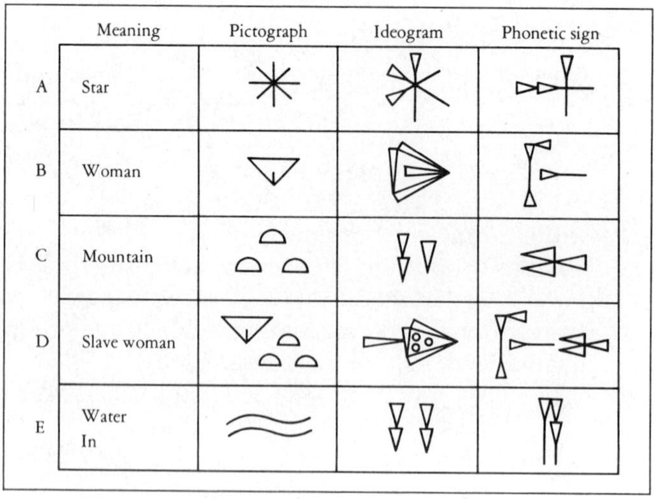

	Meaning	Pictograph	Ideogram	Phonetic sign
A	Star			
B	Woman			
C	Mountain			
D	Slave woman			
E	Water In			

FIGURE 1.1 Sumerian Writing (Excerpted from S. N. Kramer, *The Sumerians: Their History, Culture and Character,* University of Chicago Press, Chicago, 1963, pp. 302–306)

looking at the picture would know what it meant and would think of the word for star. But this complex and difficult system was very limited because it could not show abstract ideas or combinations of ideas. For instance, how could it show a slave woman?

But a scribe soon discovered that he could combine signs to express meaning. To refer to a slave woman, he used the sign for woman (line B) and the sign for mountain (line C). The signs together meant "mountain woman" (line D). Since the Sumerians regularly took slave women from the mountains, people understood this mix of signs easily.

The next step was to make the system easy. Instead of drawing pictures, the scribe made conventionalized signs. Thus, the signs became *ideograms,* which symbolized ideas. The sign for star could also be used to indicate heaven, sky, or even god. (See the ideograms in Figure 1.1.)

The real breakthrough came when the scribe learned to use signs to mean sounds. For instance, the scribe drew two parallel wavy lines for the word *a,* meaning *"water"* (line E). Besides *water,* the word *a* in Sumerian also meant "in." The word *in* names an idea that is very hard to show with a picture. Instead of trying to make up a sign to mean *in,* some clever scribe used the sign for water. The two words (*water* and *in*) sounded alike. This phonetic use of signs made it possible to combine signs to name abstract ideas.

The use of writing let merchants keep business records. More important, the learning, lore, and history of a culture could be recorded and kept for unborn generations.

The Sumerian system of writing was so complicated that only scribes mastered it. Even they had to study it for many years. By 2500 B.C., schools for scribes flourished throughout Sumer. Most students came from wealthy families and were male. Each school had a master, teachers, and monitors. Discipline was strict, and students were caned for sloppy work and misbehavior. One graduate of a scribal school had few good memories of the joy of learning:

> *My headmaster read my tablet, said: "There is something missing." caned me.*
>
> . . . .
>
> *The fellow in charge of silence said: "Why did you talk without permission," caned me*
> *The fellow in charge of the assembly said: "Why did you stand at ease without permission," caned me.*

The Sumerian system of schooling set the educational standards for Mesopotamian culture. Other cultures used its techniques. Students began by learning how to prepare clay tablets and make signs. They studied grammar and word lists and solved simple math problems. Mesopotamian education always had a practical side because scribes were important in the economy. Most scribes took administrative positions in the temple or palace. They kept records of business dealings, accounts, and inventories. But schools for scribes did not limit their study to business only; they were also centers of culture and learning. Topics of study included math, botany, and language. Advanced students copied and studied the classics of literature, and some students and scribes wrote works of their own. As a result, many literary, mathematical, and religious texts survive today. Through them we see a full picture of Mesopotamian life of the mind and spirit. ❑

EXERCISES

Understanding

d ______ 1. The topic of this selection is **(8b)**
   a. how to write in the Sumerian manner.
   b. how writing developed.
   c. education in ancient Mesopotamia.
   d. how writing was invented and how ancient schools trained writers.

a ______ 2. Which is the main idea of this selection? **(8d)**
   a. Writing evolved from a system of pictures and signs, and the writing system was so complicated that schools in Sumer had to train scribes over many years.
   b. Mesopotamian education always had a practical side, and business transactions connected to slave owning more than anything else led to the development of writing.
   c. Scribes were required to study for many years under generally unpleasant learning conditions.
   d. Writing was invented when ancient scribes in Sumeria learned to use signs to mean sounds.

3. Write the main idea of the first paragraph in your own words. **(8c)**

Writing began with pictures first drawn on clay tokens.

____

____

c 4. In their record keeping, Near Eastern people counted things by using **(9a)**
a. slave women.
b. wedge-shaped styluses.
c. clay tokens.
d. Sumerians.

a 5. The correct sequence in the development of writing is **(9b)**
a. record keeping, pictograph, cuneiform, and phonetic sign.
b. pictograph, ideogram, phonetic sign, and cuneiform.
c. phonetic sign, pictograph, ideogram, and business transaction.
d. phonetic sign, cuneiform, and pictograph.

a 6. By putting together different pictures in the pictograph system, scribes could **(9a)**
a. show abstract ideas and combinations of ideas.
b. finally show signs for the stars and the heavens.
c. obtain their women slaves from the mountains.
d. bake their writing on wet clay tablets.

c 7. In the development of writing, the importance of ideograms was that this system **(9a)**
a. finally used pens like the ones we now know.
b. used stars to indicate heaven, sky, or god.
c. used agreed-on signs that represented ideas.
d. was very simple.

d 8. The development of phonetic signs was an important breakthrough in writing development because **(9a)**
a. pictures represented words.
b. words represented pictures.
c. sounds represented signs.
d. signs represented sounds.

d ______ 9. To write the words *slave woman,* scribes combined signs for **(6, 9a)**
   a. *slave* and *woman.*
   b. *star* and *slave.*
   c. *star* and *mountain.*
   d. *mountain* and *woman.*

b ______ 10. In Sumerian, the word for *water* and the word for *in* are **(9a)**
   a. hard to represent in pictures.
   b. the same.
   c. cannot be used in the same sentence.
   d. unrelated.

11. Write the purpose of Figure 1.1 in your own words. **(6)**

   to show the different stages in the development of

   Sumerian writing

   ____

d ______ 12. The education in scribal schools concentrated on **(9a)**
   a. making clay tablets.
   b. business affairs.
   c. Akkadian and Babylonian history.
   d. practical as well as academic learning.

Interpreting

a ______ 1. We may infer that the phonetic sign for *mountain* is different from the pictograph for *mountain* in that the sign **(6, 11)**
   a. stands for the sounds in the word instead of giving a picture of it.
   b. is a conventionalized form of the word.
   c. is much harder to read than other forms of writing.
   d. stands for the visual elements in Sumerian and Mesopotamian cultures.

b ______ 2. About writing, we may infer that the Sumerians **(11)**
   a. invented it.
   b. helped advance it.

c. helped move it to clay tablets.
d. learned it from the Akkadians.

d ______ 3. We may infer that in the early pictograph system, if a scribe wanted to represent ideas such as *love* and *fear of dying*, the scribe would **(11)**
a. simply combine words.
b. start with the picture of a star on a wet clay tablet.
c. use a special stylus.
d. find it very difficult.

c ______ 4. If an advanced Sumerian scribe were writing the English words *through* (meaning "into" or "between") and *threw* (meaning "let go with a swift motion of the arm"), we can predict that he would probably **(11)**
a. show an arm between two objects.
b. have to check a complicated dictionary of sound-alike words.
c. use the same sign for both words.
d. use completely different signs for both words.

a ______ 5. From the poem by the scribal school graduate, we may infer that Sumerian education was **(11)**
a. strict and painful.
b. friendly but silent.
c. foreign and expensive.
d. sloppy and complicated.

Vocabulary

1. Use word-part clues to determine the meaning of each word from the selection. First, break the word down into its parts and write the parts on the blank in the appropriate column. Then write each definition in your own words on the blank in the appropriate column.

Word	*Word Broken Down into Parts*	*Definition*
a. breakthrough	break through	a new, revolutionary step

Word	Word Broken Down into Parts	Definition
b. forerunners	**fore runners**	**those who came before**
c. combinations	**combine tions**	**the results of combining**
d. unborn	**un born**	**not yet born**
e. rock-hard	**rock hard**	**hard as a rock**
f. scribal	**scribe al**	**relating to scribes**

2. Several important words in the selection are defined by sentence clues. Write the definitions of each word. Do not use a dictionary. **(1c)**

   a. cuneiform **wedge-shaped writing**

   b. pictographs **writing by means of pictures**

   c. ideograms **pictures that represent ideas**

3. Use sentence clues to find the meaning of each word in italics. Then write the letter of the best definition. **(1c)**

c 1. "Using a *stylus* . . ."
   a. bat
   b. hand
   c. writing implement
   d. wedge shape

b ______ 2. ". . . combine signs to *express* meaning."
a. draw
b. make known
c. question
d. memorize

a ______ 3. ". . . *recorded* and kept for unborn generations."
a. written down
b. reserved
c. kept
d. prevented

d ______ 4. ". . . schools for scribes *flourished* . . ."
a. disappeared
b. wrote
c. went bankrupt
d. grew well

c ______ 5. ". . . education always had a *practical* side . . ."
a. written
b. unfortunate
c. useful
d. practiced

WRITING PRACTICE

1. Write a paragraph in which you explain Figure 1.1. What does the illustration show? What visual details support the main point?
2. Write a brief paper in which you tell about one of your own early experiences in learning how to write.

PRONUNCIATION KEY

Spelling	*Symbol*	*Spelling*	*Symbol*
p***a***t	ă	c***augh***t, p***aw***, f***o***r	ô
p***ay***	ā	n***oi***se	oi
c***ar***e	âr	t***oo***k	o͝o
f***a***ther	ä	b***oo***t	o͞o
bi***b***	b	***ou***t	ou
chur***ch***	ch	***p***o***p***	p
dee***d***, mill***ed***	d	***r***oa***r***	r
p***e***t	ĕ	***s***au***c***e	s
b***ee***	ē	***sh***ip, di***sh***	sh
fi***f***e, ***ph***ase, rou***gh***	f	***t***igh***t***, stopp***ed***	t
ga***g***	g	***th***in	th
hat	h	***th***is	*th*
which	hw	c***u***t	ŭ
p***i***t	ĭ	***ur***ge, t***er***m, f***ir***m, w***or***d, h***ear***d	ûr
p***ie***, b***y***	ī	***v***al***v***e	v
p***ier***	îr	***w***ith	w
ju***dg***e	j	***y***es	y
ki***ck***, ***c***at, pi***que***	k	***z***ebra, ***x***ylem	z
lid, need***le***	l (nēd′l)	vi***s***ion, plea***s***ure, gara***g***e	zh
mu***m***	m	***a***bout, it***e***m, ed***i***ble, gall***o***p, circ***u***s	ə
no, sudd***en***	n (sŭd′n)	butt***er***	ər
thi***ng***	ng		
p***o***t, h***o***rrid	ŏ		
t***oe***, h***oa***rse	ō		

Vocabulary List with Pronunciation Key

This vocabulary list includes, in alphabetical order, all the words that are highlighted in the *Reading Selections* part of the book. The groups of letters that follow the main entry tell you how to say the word. The letters stand for special sounds. To find out what sounds the letters make, refer to the pronunciation key on the opposite page. The pronunciation key is adapted from *The American Heritage Student's Dictionary*. The definition given for each word is the contextual meaning of the word as it is used on the page indicated.

abandoned (ə-băn'dənd) *adj.* left alone, pp. 352, 353.
abracadabra (ăb'rə-kə-dăb'rə) *n.* word thought to possess magical powers, pp. 380, 381.
absorb (ăb-sôrb', -zôrb') *v.* soak up, pp. 307, 310.
abstract (ăb'străkt', ăb-străkt') *adj.* opposite of concrete; not easily understood; theoretical, pp. 419, 420.
activated, past tense of **activate** (ăk'tə-vāt') *v.* put into action or movement, pp. 374, 375.
acute (ə-kyo͞ot') *adj.* serious, pp. 409, 411.
adjacent (ə-jā'sənt) *adj.* next to, pp. 364, 366.
adolescent (ăd'l-ĕs'ənt) *adj.* teenager, pp. 390, 391.
align (ə-līn') *v.* put in a straight line, pp. 317, 319.
altered, past tense of **alter** (ôl'tər) *v.* changed, pp. 352, 353.
anemia (ə-nē'mē-ə) *n.* blood disease that does not let cells carry enough oxygen, pp. 332, 333.
apparel (ə-păr'əl) *n.* clothing, pp. 337, 338.
appraisal (ə-prā'zəl) *n.* an expert evaluation, pp. 380, 383.
articulating, present participle of **articulate** (är-tĭk'yə-lāt') *v.* identifying, pp. 364, 367.
assembly line *n.* line of workers putting together a product one step at a time, p. 399.
astute (ə-sto͞ot', ə-styo͞ot') *adj.* sharp; clever, pp. 337, 339.

auditors, plural of **auditor** (ô'də-tər) *n.* here, the word means "listeners," pp. 324, 325.

bewilderment (bĭ-wĭl'dər-mənt) *n.* confusion, pp. 352, 353.

cadences, plural of **cadence** (kād'ns) *n.* flows of rhythm and movement, pp. 409, 412.

calculating, present participle of **calculate** (kăl'kyə-lāt') *v.* figuring out mathematically, p. 399.

caned, past tense of **cane** (kān) *v.* beaten with a stick or cane, pp. 419, 421.

capacity (kə-păs'ĭ-tē) *n.* ability to hold or contain, pp. 399, 400.

cliché (klē-shā') *n.* unoriginal, overused remark; platitude, pp. 352, 353.

clients, plural of **client** (klī'ənt) *n.* customers for a service, p. 364.

clout (klout) *n.* power, pp. 337, 338.

condolences, plural of **condolence** (kən-dō'ləns) *n.* words of sympathy to people who have suffered a loss, pp. 352, 353.

consequences, plural of **consequence** (kŏn'sĭ-kwĕns', -kwəns) *n.* results; outcomes, pp. 380, 383.

conventionalized, past tense of **conventionalize** (kən-vĕn'shə-nə-līz') *v.* agreed on by the same group, pp. 419, 420.

cope (kōp) *intr.v.* deal with; overcome, pp. 352, 354.

corral (kə-răl') *n.* a pen for cows and horses, pp. 324, 325.

data (dā'tə, dăt'ə, dä'tə) *n.* information, p. 399.

deceive (dĭ-sēv') *v.* mislead on purpose, pp. 307, 309.

delicate (dĕl'ĭ-kĭt) *adj.* very fine; easily broken, pp. 399, 402.

demise (dĭ-mīz') *n.* death, p. 352.

detector (dĭ-tĕk'tər) *n.* something that recognizes and registers a signal, pp. 399, 401.

Dickens (dĭk'ĭnz) *n.* Charles Dickens (1812–1870), famous English novelist who wrote *Great Expectations* and *Oliver Twist* among many other books, pp. 409, 410.

discretionary (dĭ-skrĕsh-ə-nĕr'ē) *adj.* for use without any restrictions, p. 337.

distorted (dĭ-stôr'tĭd) *adj.* twisted out of shape, pp. 380, 382.

el Tren Volador Spanish for "the Flying Train," pp. 324, 325.

encased, past tense of **encase** (ĕn-kās') *tr.v.* enclosed, pp. 374, 375.

enchanted, past tense of **enchant** (ĕn-chănt') *tr.v.* looking magical in appearance, pp. 409, 411.

endured, past tense of **endure** (ĕn-door') *v.* withstood; stood up under, pp. 352, 353.

enlightenment (ĕn-līt'n-mənt) *n.* state or quality of giving knowledge and understanding to, pp. 409, 412.

enveloped, past tense of **envelop** (ĕn-vĕl'əp) *tr.v.* surrounded, pp. 374, 375.

envy (ĕn'vē) *n.* wanting to have what someone else has; jealousy, pp. 324, 325.
evolution (ĕv'ə-lo͞o'shən) *n.* gradual process of change, pp. 419, 420.
exhilaration (ĭg-zĭl'ə-rā'shən) *n.* excitement, pp. 307, 310.
facet (făs'ĭt) *n.* flat surface, pp. 374, 375.
fundamental (fŭn'də-mĕn'tl) *adj.* basic, pp. 364, 365.
gene (jēn) *n.* material in cells that is responsible for traits that we are born with, pp. 374, 375.
graphics (grăf'ĭks) *n.* the making of drawings; visual representations, pp. 399, 401.
immersed, past tense of **immerse** (ĭ-mûrs') *tr.v.* deep within, pp. 352, 353.
impact (ĭm'păkt') *n.* effect, pp. 352, 353; collision, pp. 307, 310.
impetus (ĭm'pĭ-təs) *n.* push, force, energy, pp. 364, 367.
incantations, plural of **incantation** (ĭn'kăn-tā'shən) *n.* ritual reciting of a magical spell, pp. 380, 381.
inconspicuous (ĭn'kən-spĭk'yo͞o-əs) *adj.* hard to find, pp. 317, 319.
insatiability, noun form of **insatiable** (ĭn-sā'shə-bəl) *n.* not able to be satisfied, pp. 409, 412.
interference (ĭn'tər-fîr'əns) *n.* something that gets in the way of something else, pp. 307, 309.
intermediate (ĭn'tər-mē'dē-ĭt) *adj.* going between two extremes, pp. 307, 310.
intricate (ĭn'trĭ-kĭt) *adj.* complex, pp. 399, 403.
invariably, adverbial form of **invariable** (ĭn-vâr'ē-ə-bəl) *adv.* always, pp. 390, 392.
inventory (ĭn'vən-tôr'ē) *n.* supply, pp. 364, 365.
isolate (ī'sə-lāt') *tr.v.* separate out, pp. 364, 365.
jerky (jûr'kē) *n.* beef prepared by smoking or drying in the sun, pp. 324, 325.
licensed, past tense of **license** (lī'səns) *tr.v.* officially approved, pp. 390, 391.
lore (lôr, lōr) *n.* collected facts, knowledge, or beliefs on a particular subject, pp. 419, 420.
lull (lŭl) *v.* soothe; cause to rest, pp. 380, 381.
marketer (mär'kĭt-tər) *n.* someone concerned with buying and selling, p. 337.
mellow (mĕl'ō) *adj.* soft and full, pp. 324, 325.
Mesopotamian (mĕs'ə-pə-tā'mē-ən) *adj.* related to the ancient land and people between the Tigris and Euphrates rivers, pp. 419, 420.
millennium (mĭ-lĕn'ē-əm) *n.* a thousand years, pp. 419, 420.
miniaturization (mĭn'ē-ə-chər-ĭ-zā'shən, mĭn'ə-) *n.* state of making something smaller, pp. 399, 402.

misconceptions, plural of **misconception** (mĭs'kən-sĕp'shən) *n.* wrong ideas, pp. 390, 392.
modify (mŏd'ə-fī') *v.* change, pp. 390, 391.
Muro Ami (pronunciation not given) *n.* a kind of large fishing net, shaped like a bag, eighty feet deep and a half mile across, pp. 345, 347.
muster (mŭs'tər) *v.* gather up, pp. 352, 353.
nonchalant (nŏn'shə-länt') *adj.* seeming relaxed, pp. 317, 319.
opulence, noun form of **opulent** (ŏp'yə-lənt) *adj.* grand wealth, pp. 409, 412.
ostracized, past tense of **ostracize** (ŏs'trə-sīz') *tr.v.* shut out of a group, shunned, pp. 390, 392.
participation (pär-tĭs'ə-pā'shən) *n.* act of taking part in something, pp. 409, 411.
peer (pîr) *n.* an equal; someone of the same age or with the same rank, status, or class, p. 337.
perception (pər-sĕp'shən) *n.* insight; knowledge; intuition, pp. 380, 381.
per se (pər sā', sē') *adv.* exactly, pp. 337, 339.
platitudes, plural of **platitude** (plât'ĭ-to͞od') *n.* unoriginal, overused remarks or comments, pp. 352, 353.
poster (pō'stər) *n.* a large sign used to advertise something, pp. 332, 333.
principle (prĭn'sə-pəl) *n.* rule, p. 364.
propagating, present participle of **propagate** (prŏp'ə-gāt') *v.* making known, spreading, pp. 390, 391.
protective (prə-tĕk'tĭv) *adj.* keeping harm or danger away, pp. 374, 375.
radiance (rā'dē-əns) *n.* the giving off of light or heat, pp. 409, 412.
rank (răngk) *adj.* strong in odor, pp. 324, 325.
rationalize (răsh'ə-nə-līz') *v.* to develop self-satisfying but not really correct reasons to do something, pp. 307, 308.
regulator (rĕg'yə-lā'tər) *n.* breathing device used by divers, pp. 345, 347.
renowned (rĭ-nound') *adj.* well known everywhere, p. 324.
reposing, present participle of **repose** (rĭ-pōz') *n.* living, pp. 409, 412.
respiratory (rĕs'pər-ə-tôr'ē) *adj.* related to body organs needed for breathing, such as the lungs, the nose, and the throat, pp. 374, 375.
scare lines, plural of **scare line** (skâr līn) *n.* a rope with flags, used to scare the fish into the net, pp. 345, 347.
screening (skrē'nĭng) *n.* identifying groups with special traits, pp. 332, 333.
scribe (skrīb) *n.* public clerk or secretary; a copier of manuscripts, pp. 419, 420.

scrimmage (skrĭm'ĭj) *n.* practice game between teams, pp. 307, 308.
sickle cell (sîk'əl sĕl) *n.* an abnormal body cell shaped like a sickle—that is, like a half circle, pp. 332, 333.
significant (sĭg-nĭf'ĭ-kənt) *adj.* important, pp. 364, 365.
silhouette (sĭl'o͞o-ĕt') *n.* outline shape, pp. 345, 347.
site (sīt) *n.* place where something occurs, pp. 374, 375.
staples, plural of **staple** (stā'pəl) *n.* basic supplies that you always need, pp. 364, 365.
structure (strŭk'chər) *n.* shape, form, pp. 374, 375.
Sumerians, plural of **Sumerian** (so͞o-mîr'ē-ən, -mər'-) *n.* people of the ancient land of Sumer in south Mesopotamia, pp. 419, 420.
superiority, noun form of **superior** (sə-pîr'ē-ər) *n.* being better than others, p. 324.
surviving, present participle of **survive** (sər-vīv') *v.* left alive, pp. 352, 353.
symbolized, past tense of **symbolize** (sĭm'bə-līz') *v.* stood for; represented, pp. 419, 420.
synthesis (sĭn'thĭ-sĭs) *n.* something formed by combining several elements; artificial, pp. 399, 403.
transgression (trăns-grĕsh'ən, trănz-) *n.* bad deed; lie, pp. 307, 309.
temperament (tĕm'prə-mənt) *n.* personality, feelings, pp. 364, 367.
tenets, plural of **tenet** (tĕn'ĭt) *n.* strong beliefs, pp. 390, 392.
therapist (thĕr'ə-pĭst) *n.* a person who helps with social and psychological problems, pp. 390, 391.
vaquero (vä-kâr'ō) *n.* cowboy, p. 324.
varsity (vär'sə-tē) *n.* the principal team representing a school in sports competition, pp. 307, 309.
void (void) *adj.* emptiness, pp. 352, 354.
wafer (wā'fər) *n.* a small, thin, flat disk, pp. 399, 402.
wizardry (wĭz'ər-drē) *n.* magic, pp. 409, 411.

Acknowledgments

Text Credits

American Geological Institute, INVESTIGATING THE EARTH. Reprinted by permission of Houghton Mifflin Company. *Pages 291–292.*

Robert F. Biehler and Lynne Hudson, DEVELOPMENTAL PSYCHOLOGY, Third Edition. Reprinted by permission of Houghton Mifflin Company. *Pages 282–285.*

Betty J. Brown and John E. Clow, OUR BUSINESS AND ECONOMIC WORLD. Reprinted by permission of Houghton Mifflin Company. *Pages 209–210, 234, 398–403.*

Dann Denny, "Toughlove—Parents in Crisis," copyright 1986, SUNDAY HERALD-TIMES. Used by permission. *Pages 390–392.*

Delia Ephron from HOW TO EAT LIKE A CHILD AND OTHER LESSONS IN NOT BEING A GROWN-UP by Delia Ephron. Copyright © 1977, 1978 by Delia Ephron. All Rights Reserved. Reprinted by permission of Viking Penguin, a division of Penguin Books USA Inc. *Pages 303, 317–319.*

From Ira Epstein and Ernest B. Nieratka, THE PROFICIENT READER. Reprinted with permission of Houghton Mifflin Company. *Pages 144–149.*

From N. L. Gage and David C. Berliner, EDUCATIONAL PSYCHOLOGY, 4th Edition. Reprinted with permission of Houghton Mifflin Company. *Pages 201–202.*

Merwyn S. Garbarino and Rachel R. Sady, PEOPLE AND CULTURES, copyright © 1975, Rand McNally. Reprinted by permission of Houghton Mifflin Company. *Pages 239, 274.*

Getchell, HOUGHTON MIFFLIN HEALTH. Reprinted by permission of Houghton Mifflin Company. *Pages 95–100, 135, 207–208, 241–243.*

Getis and Getis, GEOGRAPHY. Reprinted by permission of Houghton Mifflin Company. *Pages 185, 212–213.*

Gitelson, Alan R., Dudley, Robert L., and Dubnick, Melvin L., AMERICAN GOVERNMENT. Reprinted with permission of Houghton Mifflin Company. *Page 211.*

Jovita Gonzalez, "Pedro the Hunter" from TONE THE BELL EASY (J. Frank Dobie, Editor), copyright 1932, Texas Folklore Society. Reprinted by permission. *Pages 324–325.*

Henry F. Graff, AMERICA: THE GLORIOUS REPUBLIC, copyright © 1985, Houghton Mifflin Company. Reprinted by permission. *Pages 171, 176, 252–253.*

Howard Hall, "Sea Urchins" from ASIA MAGAZINE, 1 June 1986, pp. 25–26. Reprinted by permission. *Pages 345–347.*

Richard J. Hardy, GOVERNMENT IN AMERICA (including Figure 33). Reprinted by permission of Houghton Mifflin Company. *Pages 134, 185, 190, 202.*

Duane R. Johnson and Donn W. Maryott, "Predriving Checks" from TOMORROW'S DRIVERS, copyright © 1986, Houghton Mifflin Company. Reprinted by permission. *Pages 281–282.*

Lawrence Kutner, "Children Don't See Risks as Adults Do," THE NEW YORK TIMES, July 13, 1989. Copyright © 1989 by The New York Times Company. Reprinted by permission. *Pages 380–383.*

Richard Marius and Harvey S. Wiener, "Appendix A" from THE McGRAW-HILL COLLEGE HANDBOOK, Second Edition (1988). Reprinted by permission of McGraw-Hill Publishing Company. *Pages 106–111.*

Marilyn Marshall excerpts from "Texas TV Pioneer: Clara McLaughlin" are reprinted by permission of EBONY MAGAZINE, © 1987 Johnson Publishing Company, Inc. *Page 295.*

McKay, John P., Hill, Bennett D., and Buckler, John. A HISTORY OF WESTERN SOCIETY, 3rd Edition. Reprinted with permission of Houghton Mifflin Company. *Pages 419–422.*

McLaren, Stasik, and Levering: SPACESHIP EARTH: LIFE SCIENCE. Copyright © 1981, Houghton Mifflin Company. Reprinted by permission. *Pages 49–50, 111–118, 198, 213–214, 287–289.*

Gary Mihoces, "Those Refs Don't Always Whistle While They Work." Copyright 1986, USA WEEKEND. Reprinted with permission. *Pages 269–270.*

New Mexico Tourism and Travel Division material is reprinted by permission. *Pages 221–222.*

From Mary Beth Norton et al., A PEOPLE AND A NATION: A HISTORY OF THE UNITED STATES, 3rd Edition. Reprinted with permission of Houghton Mifflin Company. *Page 201.*

Perry, A HISTORY OF THE WORLD. Reprinted with permission of Houghton Mifflin Company. *Pages 296–299.*

Pride, William M. and Ferrell, O. C., MARKETING: BASIC CONCEPTS AND STRATEGIES, 6th Edition. Reprinted with permission of Houghton Mifflin Company. *Pages 85–94, 337–339.*

Mrs. Elliot Richardson, THE RIF (READING IS FUNDAMENTAL) GUIDE TO ENCOURAGING YOUNG READERS, ed. Ruth Graves, 1987. Reprinted by permission of Doubleday, a division of Bantam, Doubleday, Dell Publishing Group, Inc. *Page 75.*

Elmo Sabo, "Magic Mineral's Hazards Known Before Legal, Health Issues Known," copyright 1986, SUNDAY HERALD-TIMES. Reprinted by permission. *Pages 219–220.*

Michael Satchell, "Paul Newman: It's an Epidemic," copyright © 1985, Parade Publications, Inc., used by permission of the author and publisher. *Pages 250–251.*

Richard T. Schaefer excerpts from SOCIOLOGY, First Edition (1983) are reprinted by permission of McGraw-Hill, Inc. *Pages 169, 172, 188, 191.*

Harriet Sarnoff Schiff from LIVING THROUGH MOURNING: FINDING COMFORT AND HOPE WHEN A LOVED ONE HAS DIED by Harriet Sarnoff Schiff. Copyright © 1986 by Harriet Sarnoff Schiff. All Rights Reserved. Reprinted by permission of Viking Penguin, a division of Penguin Books USA Inc. *Pages 352–354.*

Sherman, A., Sherman, S. J., and Russikoff, L., BASIC CONCEPTS OF CHEMISTRY, 4th Edition. Reprinted with permission from Houghton Mifflin Company. *Pages 203, 210.*

Bruce Shertzer from CAREER PLANNING. Reprinted with permission of Houghton Mifflin Company. *Pages 175, 185–186, 191.*

J. M. Stanchfield and Thomas G. Gunning, VOYAGERS. Reprinted by permission of Houghton Mifflin Company. *Page 212.*

J. M. Stanchfield and Thomas G. Gunning, PASSAGES, New Directions in Reading Series, Copyright © 1986, Houghton Mifflin Company. Reprinted by permission. *Pages 153–159.*

John Stossel excerpts are reprinted by permission of The Putnam Publishing Group from SHOPPING SMART by John Stossel. Copyright © 1980 by John Stossel. *Pages 177, 178, 186.*

Caroline Sutton excerpts from HOW DID THEY DO THAT? by Caroline Sutton. Copyright © 1984 Hilltown Press. By permission of William Morrow Inc. *Pages 224, 237–238, 267–268, 271–272.*

Irving Wallace and David Wallechinsky excerpts from THE PEOPLE'S ALMANAC #2. Copyright © 1978 by Irving Wallace and David Wallechinsky. By permission of William Morrow & Co. Inc. *Pages 217, 260–261.*

Eudora Welty, "Moon on a Silver Spoon" reprinted by permission of the publishers from ONE WRITER'S BEGINNINGS by Eudora Welty, Cambridge, Mass.: Harvard University Press, Copyright © 1983, 1984 by Eudora Welty. *Pages 409–412.*

Stephanie Winston. Reprinted from GETTING ORGANIZED by Stephanie Winston, by permission of W. W. Norton & Company, Inc. Copyright © 1978 by Stephanie Winston. *Pages 363–368.*

David O. Woodbury: THE FRIGID WORLD OF CRYOGENICS. Copyright © 1966. Dodd, Mead & Co. Reprinted by permission. *Pages 195, 226.*

Jim Yoshida, "Two Worlds" reprinted by permission of John Hawkins & Associates, Inc. *Pages 307–311.*

Art Credits

"Avestan to Axiom" copyright © 1985 by Houghton Mifflin Company. Adapted and reprinted by permission from THE AMERICAN HERITAGE DICTIONARY, SECOND COLLEGE EDITION. *Page 53.*

"Pronunciation Key," copyright © 1986 by Houghton Mifflin Company. Adapted and reprinted by permission from THE AMERICAN HERITAGE STUDENT'S DICTIONARY. *Page 430.*

Jack Ballard. *Page 281.*

Courtesy Beef Industry Council. *Page 264.*

Reprinted with special permission of King Features Syndicate, Inc. *Page 259.*

Betty J. Brown and John E. Clow, OUR BUSINESS AND ECONOMIC WORLD. Reprinted by permission of Houghton Mifflin Company. *Pages 133, 400.*

Figure 18.1, Culver Pictures, Inc. *Page 242.*

Courtesy of Field Museum of Natural History, Chicago, IL. *Page 131.*

Courtesy of Ford Motor Company. *Page 93.*

"Step by Step/Cutting a Chicken" by Pierre Franey, artwork by Doug Taylor, THE NEW YORK TIMES, October 8, 1986. Copyright © 1986 by The New York Times Company. Reprinted by permission. *Pages 126–127.*

Figures 1.1, 1.2, and 13.4, Getchell, HOUGHTON MIFFLIN HEALTH. Reprinted by permission of Houghton Mifflin Company. *Pages 97, 98, 135.*

"Index" from Graff: AMERICA: THE GLORIOUS REPUBLIC, copyright © 1985, Houghton Mifflin Company. Reprinted by permission. *Page 73.*

© 1986 Greyhound Lines, Inc. *Page 332.*

Hoppes/Rothco cartoon. © Hoppes/Rothco. Reprinted by permission of Rothco Cartoons, Brooklyn, NY. *Page 145.*

"Table of Contents" from Jackson/Evans: SPACESHIP EARTH: EARTH SCIENCE, copyright © 1980, Houghton Mifflin Company. Reprinted by permission. *Pages 69–72.*

Paul E. Johnson. *Page 157.*

Lejeune/Stock Boston. *Page 257.*

Figure 1.4, Mary E. Messenger. *Page 98.*

"Deaths on the Road," THE NEW YORK TIMES, July 13, 1989. Copyright © 1989 by The New York Times Company. Reprinted by permission. *Page 382.*

Pilot Pen/ABP Adv. *Page 253.*

Pride, William M. and Ferrell, O. C., MARKETING: BASIC CONCEPTS AND STRATEGIES, 6th edition. Reprinted with permission of Houghton Mifflin Company. *Page 91.*

"Table of Contents" from Reece/O'Grady: BUSINESS, copyright © 1987 Houghton Mifflin Company. Reprinted by permission. *Page 66.*

Courtesy of Residence Inns. *Page 21.*

Figure 1.1, "Sumerian Writing" from THE SUMERIANS: THEIR HISTORY, CULTURE AND CHARACTER by S. N. Kramer, University of Chicago Press, Chicago, 1963, pp. 302–306. Copyright © 1963 by The University of Chicago. Reprinted by permission. *Page 420.*

Stouffer Food Corporation. *Page 86.*

"Diagram on Viruses," from TIME Magazine November 2, 1986. Copyright 1986 Time Inc. Reprinted by permission. *Page 374.*

"Sneezes, Sniffles Strike Youth," USA TODAY, November 3, 1986. Copyright 1986, USA TODAY. Reprinted with permission. *Page 133.*

"Estimated Number of Aliens," USA TODAY, October 17, 1986. Copyright 1986, USA TODAY. Reprinted with permission. *Page 121.*

Subject Index

Author Index

To the Student:

We hope that you will take a few minutes to fill out this questionnaire. The comments you make will help us plan future editions of BASIC READING SKILLS HANDBOOK. After you have completed the following questions, please mail this sheet to:

College Marketing
Houghton Mifflin Company
One Beacon Street
Boston, MA 02108

1. Name of college or university ______________________
2. Did you find the discussion of the specific reading skills easy to understand? ______________________

   Were any sections especially difficult? ______________________

   ____
3. Which chapters in the *Handbook* did you find most helpful?

   ____

   Why? ______________________
4. Which chapters did you find least helpful? ______________________

   Why? ______________________
5. Were the exercises in the *Handbook* useful? ______________________

   Were there enough exercises? ______________________
6. Did you find the reading passages used for the examples and in the exercises interesting? ______________________

   Which did you enjoy most? ______________________

   Which did you enjoy least? ______________________
7. Were the exercises that accompanied the *Reading Selections* useful to you? ______________________
8. Did you find the cross-referencing system that keys each question in the *Reading Selections* to the appropriate section in the *Handbook* easy to use?

   ____
9. Did your reading improve after using this text? ______________________

   ____

10. Please rate the *Reading Selections*.

	Excel-lent	*Good*	*Fair*	*Poor*	*Didn't Read*
1. Two Worlds	____	____	____	____	____
2. How to Behave at School	____	____	____	____	____
3. Pedro	____	____	____	____	____
4. Greyhound Hopes This Ad Will Never Run Again	____	____	____	____	____
5. Changing Roles Alter Buying Behavior	____	____	____	____	____
6. Young Divers of the Philippines	____	____	____	____	____
7. Helping Children When a Loved One Dies	____	____	____	____	____
8. Please Straighten Out My Life	____	____	____	____	____
9. A Close Look at Viruses	____	____	____	____	____
10. Taking Risks	____	____	____	____	____
11. Toughlove	____	____	____	____	____
12. How Do Computers Work?	____	____	____	____	____
13. Moon on a Silver Spoon	____	____	____	____	____
14. The Invention of Writing and the First Schools	____	____	____	____	____

11. Please make any additional comments that you think might be useful.

____

Thank you very much.

Your name (optional) ______________________________